Modern Critical Views

Modern Critical Views

Katherine Mansfield
Christopher Marlowe
Andrew Marvell
Herman Melville
George Meredith
James Merrill
John Stuart Mill
Arthur Miller
Henry Miller
John Milton
Yukio Mishima
Molière
Michel de Montaigne
Eugenio Montale
Marianne Moore
Alberto Moravia
Toni Morrison
Alice Munro
Iris Murdoch
Robert Musil
Vladimir Nabokov
V. S. Naipaul
R. K. Narayan
Pablo Neruda
John Henry Newman
Friedrich Nietzsche
Frank Norris
Joyce Carol Oates
Sean O'Casey
Flannery O'Connor
Christopher Okigbo
Charles Olson
Eugene O'Neill
José Ortega y Gasset
Joe Orton
George Orwell
Ovid
Wilfred Owen
Amos Oz
Cynthia Ozick
Grace Paley
Blaise Pascal
Walter Pater
Octavio Paz
Walker Percy
Petrarch
Pindar
Harold Pinter
Luigi Pirandello
Sylvia Plath
Plato

Plautus
Edgar Allan Poe
Poets of Sensibility & the
    Sublime
Poets of the Nineties
Alexander Pope
Katherine Anne Porter
Ezra Pound
Anthony Powell
Pre-Raphaelite Poets
Marcel Proust
Manuel Puig
Alexander Pushkin
Thomas Pynchon
Francisco de Quevedo
François Rabelais
Jean Racine
Ishmael Reed
Adrienne Rich
Samuel Richardson
Mordecai Richler
Rainer Maria Rilke
Arthur Rimbaud
Edwin Arlington Robinson
Theodore Roethke
Philip Roth
Jean-Jacques Rousseau
John Ruskin
J. D. Salinger
Jean-Paul Sartre
Gershom Scholem
Sir Walter Scott
William Shakespeare
    Histories & Poems
    Comedies & Romances
    Tragedies
George Bernard Shaw
Mary Wollstonecraft
    Shelley
Percy Bysshe Shelley
Sam Shepard
Richard Brinsley Sheridan
Sir Philip Sidney
Isaac Bashevis Singer
Tobias Smollett
Alexander Solzhenitsyn
Sophocles
Wole Soyinka
Edmund Spenser
Gertrude Stein
John Steinbeck

Stendhal
Laurence Sterne
Wallace Stevens
Robert Louis Stevenson
Tom Stoppard
August Strindberg
Jonathan Swift
John Millington Synge
Alfred, Lord Tennyson
William Makepeace Thackeray
Dylan Thomas
Henry David Thoreau
James Thurber and S. J.
    Perelman
J. R. R. Tolkien
Leo Tolstoy
Jean Toomer
Lionel Trilling
Anthony Trollope
Ivan Turgenev
Mark Twain
Miguel de Unamuno
John Updike
Paul Valéry
Cesar Vallejo
Lope de Vega
Gore Vidal
Virgil
Voltaire
Kurt Vonnegut
Derek Walcott
Alice Walker
Robert Penn Warren
Evelyn Waugh
H. G. Wells
Eudora Welty
Nathanael West
Edith Wharton
Patrick White
Walt Whitman
Oscar Wilde
Tennessee Williams
William Carlos Williams
Thomas Wolfe
Virginia Woolf
William Wordsworth
Jay Wright
Richard Wright
William Butler Yeats
A. B. Yehoshua
Emile Zola

Modern Critical Views

ELIZABETHAN DRAMATISTS

Edited and with an introduction by
Harold Bloom
Sterling Professor of the Humanities
Yale University

CHELSEA HOUSE PUBLISHERS
NEW YORK ◊ PHILADELPHIA

© 1986 by Chelsea House Publishers, a division of
Main Line Book Co.

Introduction copyright © 1986 by Harold Bloom

Printed and bound in the United States of America

10   9   8   7   6   5   4   3

∞ The paper used in this publication meets the minimum
requirements of the American National Standard for Permanence
of Paper for Printed Library Materials, Z39.48–1984.

Library of Congress Cataloging-in-Publication Data
Main entry under title;
Elizabethan dramatists.
   (Modern critical views)
   Bibliography:p.
   Includes index.
   Summary: A collection of critical essays on
major sixteenth and seventeenth-century English
dramatists and their works.
   1. English drama—Early modern and Elizabethan,
1500–1600—History and criticism—Addresses, essays,
lectures. 2. English drama—17th century—History
and criticism—Addresses, essays, lectures.
[1. English drama—Early modern and Elizabethan,
1500–1600—History and criticism—Addresses, essays,
lectures. 2. English drama—17th century—History
and criticism—Addresses, essays, lectures]
1. Bloom, Harold. II. Series.
PR653.E645 1986   822'.3'09   85-29102
ISBN 0-87754-675-4

Contents

Editor's Note

This volume gathers together what its editor considers to be the best criticism available on the most significant Elizabethan dramatists, excluding Shakespeare, Marlowe, and Jonson, to whom other books in this series are devoted. The editor is grateful to Douglas Smith for bringing to his attention some of these essays. They are arranged here in the chronological order of their publication.

The editor's introduction centers upon the Jacobean hero-villain, from Marlowe's Barabas through Shakespeare on to Marston, Tourneur, and Webster, with an excursus upon crucial later developments of this figure in Milton, Wordsworth, Shelley, and Browning. It can be argued that the metamorphoses of such a figure are the principal legacy of Elizabethan drama for later English poetry, aside from the overwhelming influence of Shakespeare himself.

Jocelyn Powell's essay upon John Lyly defends the most "artificial" of the Elizabethan playwrights from judgments that he wearies the reader with elaborate ingenuities and rhetorical excesses. In Powell's view, Lyly plays elaborate symbolic games, and his multiple allusions work to manifest the mind's power over matter, and to illuminate the forces at play in our lives. In Scott McMillin's reading of Kyd's *The Spanish Tragedy*, the virtually silent Old Man, who appears in just one scene of Act III, is taken as the trope or figure for Hieronimo's situation and fate. Related to this reading, but stressing even more the violence of Hieronimo's despairing assault upon language, is the analysis of Peter Sacks, who sees Hieronimo the avenger as a tragic Orpheus, both suffering and inflicting a *sparagmos*.

A very different Elizabethan triumph, Dekker's comedy *The Shoemaker's Holiday*, receives a careful exegesis by Harold E. Toliver, who finds in the play a craftsman's vision of a festive blessing "on the borderline between innocence and irresponsibility." We move back to the dark world of revenge tragedy, with Alvin B. Kernan's classical analyses of "tragical satire" in Marston and Webster, and with G. Wilson Knight's Shakespearean description of *The Duchess of Malfi*. Darkness in the Jacobean mode elaborates with two complementary readings of the stoic tragedian George Chapman. Jackson I. Cope reads the tragicomedy *The Gentleman Usher* as a metaphysical and quasi-theological parable, while the Scottish poet Edwin Muir centers upon Chapman's heroes, Bussy D'Ambois and Byron, "unfallen men among the fallen," who yet lack Adamic virtues and possess, instead, the spirit and dignity of the stoic humanism of the Renaissance.

The darkest of all Jacobeans, Cyril Tourneur, is examined here in two contrasting essays upon *The Revenger's Tragedy*. L. G. Salingar, in relating the play to the Morality tradition, seeks to find a link with medieval conventions in the apparently wild and lawless Tourneur. This emphasis upon Tourneur's deliberate artistry is reinforced by B. J. Layman's remarks upon the design of the play, a design that seems to demonstrate an authentic nihilist's despair of human life and its possibilities.

Tragicomedy, the mode of much Shakespeare and some Chapman, is always associated with the plays of Beaumont and Fletcher, whose characteristic rhetoric receives its classical treatment by Eugene Waith. Middleton, another darker eminence, wrote one masterpiece, the enigmatic *The Changeling*, which is read by Muriel Bradbrook as possessing an almost Shakespearean control of action and characterization, as well as an admirable verbal "simplicity" wholly other than the ferocious rhetoric of Marston and Tourneur, and the elliptical sufferings of Webster.

Michael Neill's tracing of the social vision of Massinger's *A New Way to Pay Old Debts* suggests ambiguities in Massinger's supposed cultural conservatism, which may be a mask for concealing the forms of impending change. In R. J. Kaufmann's bold summary of what is taken to be John Ford's "tragic perspective," the playwright's heroes are judged to be free of illusions about their own motives, and so Ford ceases to be "the purposeless and soulless opportunist of T. S. Eliot's caricature."

The final discussion, by the noted textual scholar Fredson Bowers, centers upon the "decadence of revenge tragedy" in James Shirley, the last stand of the Jacobean drama in an age dominated by John Dryden's more tempered Muse. Shirley's insistence upon having his characters do their thinking off stage is rightly seen as a retreat from much of what we value most greatly in Shakespeare and his contemporaries. With the plangent suggestion of a great tradition's dying fall, this volume reaches its appropriate end.

Introduction

Why, I, in this weak piping time of peace,
Have no delight to pass away the time,
Unless to see my shadow in the sun
And descant on mine own deformity.
And therefore, since I cannot prove a lover
To entertain these fair well-spoken days,
I am determined to prove a villain
And hate the idle pleasures of these days.

The opening ferocity of Richard, still Duke of Gloucester, in *The Tragedy of Richard the Third*, is hardly more than a fresh starting-point for the development of the Elizabethan and Jacobean hero-villain after Marlowe, and yet it seems to transform Tamburlaine and Barabas utterly. Richard's peculiarly self-conscious pleasure in his own audacity is crossed by the sense of what it means to see one's own deformed shadow in the sun. We are closer already not only to Edmund and Iago than to Barabas, but especially closer to Webster's Lodovico who so sublimely says: "I limn'd this nightpiece and it was my best." Except for Iago, nothing seems farther advanced in this desperate mode than Webster's Bosola:

O direful misprision!
I will not imitate things glorious,
No more than base: I'll be mine own example.—
On, on, and look thou represent, for silence,
The thing thou bear'st.

1

Iago is beyond even this denial of representation, because he does will
silence:

> Demand me nothing; what you know, you know;
> From this time forth I never will speak word.

Iago is no hero-villain, and no shift of perspective will make him into
one. Pragmatically, the authentic hero-villain in Shakespeare might be
judged to be Hamlet, but no audience would agree. Macbeth could justify
the description, except that the cosmos of his drama is too estranged from
any normative representation for the term hero-villain to have its oxymoronic
coherence. Richard and Edmund would appear to be the models, beyond
Marlowe, that could have inspired Webster and his fellows, but Edmund is
too uncanny and superb a representation to provoke emulation. That returns
us to Richard:

> Was ever woman in this humor woo'd?
> Was ever woman in this humor won?
> I'll have her, but I will not keep her long.
> What? I, that kill'd her husband and his father,
> To take her in her heart's extremest hate,
> With curses in her mouth, tears in her eyes,
> The bleeding witness of my hatred by,
> Having God, her conscience, and these bars against me,
> And I no friends to back my suit [at all]
> And the plain devil and dissembling looks?
> And yet to win her! All the world to nothing!
> Hah!
> Hath she forgot already that brave prince,
> Edward, her lord, whom I, some three months since,
> Stabb'd in my angry mood at Tewksbury?
> A sweeter and a lovelier gentleman,
> Fram'd in the prodigality of nature—
> Young, valiant, wise, and (no doubt) right royal—
> The spacious world cannot again afford.
> And will she yet abase her eyes on me,
> That cropp'd the golden prime of this sweet prince
> And made her widow to a woeful bed?
> On me, whose all not equals Edward's moi'ty?
> On me, that halts and am misshapen thus?
> My dukedom to a beggarly denier,

I do mistake my person all this while!
Upon my life, she finds (although I cannot)
Myself to be a marv'llous proper man.
I'll be at charges for a looking-glass,
And entertain a score or two of tailors
To study fashions to adorn my body:
Since I am crept in favor with myself,
I will maintain it with some little cost.
But first I'll turn yon fellow in his grave,
And then return lamenting to my love.
Shine out, fair sun, till I have bought a glass,
That I may see my shadow as I pass.

Richard's only earlier delight was "to see my shadow in the sun /And descant on mine own deformity." His savage delight in the success of his own manipulative rhetoric now transforms his earlier trope into the exultant command: "Shine out, fair sun, till I have bought a glass, / That I may see my shadow as I pass." That transformation is the formula for interpreting the Jacobean hero-villain and his varied progeny: Milton's Satan, the Poet in Shelley's *Alastor*, Wordsworth's Oswald in *The Borderers*, Byron's Manfred and Cain, Browning's Childe Roland, Tennyson's Ulysses, Melville's Captain Ahab, Hawthorne's Chillingworth, down to Nathanael West's Shrike in *Miss Lonelyhearts*, who perhaps ends the tradition. The manipulative, highly self-conscious, obsessed hero-villain, whether Machiavellian plotter or later, idealistic quester, ruined or not, moves himself from being the passive sufferer of his own moral and/or physical deformity to becoming a highly active melodramatist. Instead of standing in the light of nature to observe his own shadow, and then have to take his own deformity as subject, he rather commands nature to throw its light upon his own glass of representation, so that his own shadow will be visible only for an instant as he passes on to the triumph of his will over others.

II

No figure in this tradition delights me personally more than Barabas, Marlowe's Jew of Malta, who so fittingly is introduced by Machiavel himself:

Albeit the world think Machiavel is dead,
Yet was his soul but flown beyond the Alps,
And now the Guise is dead, is come from France,
To view this land, and frolic with his friends.

To some perhaps my name is odious,
But such as love me guard me from their tongues;
And let them know that I am Machiavel,
And weigh not men, and therefore not men's words.
Admired I am of those that hate me most.
Though some speak openly against my books,
Yet will they read me, and thereby attain
To Peter's chair: and when they cast me off,
Are poisoned by my climbing followers.
I count religion but a childish toy,
And hold there is no sin but ignorance.
Birds of the air will tell murders past!
I am ashamed to hear such fooleries.
Many will talk of title to a crown:
What right had Caesar to the empire?
Might first made kings, and laws were then most sure
When, like the Draco's they were writ in blood.
Hence comes it that a strong-built citadel
Commands much more than letters can import;
Which maxim had but Phalaris observed,
H'had never bellowed, in a brazen bull,
Of great ones' envy. Of the poor petty wights
Let me be envied and not pitied!
But whither am I bound? I come not, I,
To read a lecture here in Britain,
But to present the tragedy of a Jew,
Who smiles to see how full his bags are crammed,
Which money was not got without my means.
I crave but this—grace him as he deserves,
And let him not be entertained the worse
Because he favors me.

From Shakespeare's Richard III and Macbeth through Webster's Bosola
and Flamineo on to Melville's Ahab and, finally, to West's Shrike, the
descendants of Marlowe's Machiavel have held there is no sin but ignorance,
and have become involuntary parodies of what ancient heresy called *gnosis*,
a knowing in which the knower seeks the knowledge of the abyss. Nihilism,
uncanny even to Nietzsche, is the atmosphere breathed cannily by the Jacobean hero-villain, who invariably domesticates the abyss. Barabas, Mach-

iavel's favorite, wins our zestful regard because of the Groucho Marxian
vitalism of his deliciously evil self-knowings:

> As for myself, I walk abroad a'nights
> And kill sick people groaning under walls:
> Sometimes I go about and poison wells;
> And now and then, to cherish Christian thieves,
> I am content to lose some of my crowns,
> That I may, walking in my gallery,
> See 'em go pinioned along by my door.
> Being young, I studied physic, and began
> To practice first upon the Italian;
> There I enriched the priests with burials,
> And always kept the sexton's arms in ure
> With digging graves and ringing dead men's knells:
> And after that was I an engineer,
> And in the wars 'twixt France and Germany,
> Under pretense of helping Charles the Fifth,
> Slew friends and enemy with my strategems.
> Then after that was I an usurer,
> And with extorting, cozening, forfeiting,
> And tricks belonging unto brokery,
> I filled the jails with bankrupts in a year,
> And with young orphans planted hospitals,
> And every moon made some or other mad,
> And now and then one hang himself for grief,
> Pinning upon his breast a long great scroll
> How I with interest tormented him.
> But mark how I am blessed for plaguing them;
> I have as much coin as will buy the town.
> But tell me now, how hast thou spent thy time?

The hyperboles here are so outrageous that Marlowe's insouciant identification with Barabas becomes palpable, and we begin to feel that this is
how Tamburlaine the Great would sound and act if he had to adjust his
overreachings to the limits of being a Jew in Christian Malta. Barabas is too
splendidly grotesque a mockery to set a pattern for dramatic poets like
Webster, Tourneur, Ford, and Middleton. They found their model for revenge tragedy in Kyd rather than Shakespeare, for many of the same reasons
that they based their dark knowers upon Marston's Malevole in *The Malcontent*
rather than upon Barabas. We begin to hear in Malevole what will culminate

in Tourneur's *The Revenger's Tragedy* and in Webster's *The White Devil* and *The Duchess of Malfi*. Disdaining to take revenge upon his craven enemy, Mendoza, Malevole expresses a contempt so intense and so universal as to open up the abyss of nihilism:

> O I have seene strange accidents of state,
> The flatterer like the Ivy clip the Oke,
> And wast it to the hart: lust so confirm'd
> That the black act of sinne it selfe not shamd
> To be termde Courtship.
> O they that are as great as be their sinnes,
> Let them remember that th'inconstant people,
> Love many Princes meerely for their faces,
> And outward shewes: and they do covet more
> To have a sight of these then of their vertues,
> Yet thus much let the great ones still conceale,
> When they observe not Heavens imposd conditions,
> They are no Kings, but forfeit their commissions.

That, for a Jacobean, leaves not much, and is the prelude to the hysterical eloquence of Tourneur's Vindice the revenger:

> And now methinks I could e'en chide myself
> For doting on her beauty, though her death
> Shall be revenged after no common action.
> Does the silkworm expend her yellow labors
> For thee? For thee does she undo herself?
> Are lordships sold to maintain ladyships
> For the poor benefit of a bewitching minute?
> Why does yon fellow falsify highways
> And put his life between the judge's lips
> To refine such a thing, keeps horse and men
> To beat their valors for her?
> Surely we're all mad people and they,
> Whom we think are, are not: we mistake those.
> 'Tis we are mad in sense, they but in clothes.
>
> Does every proud and self-affecting dame
> Camphor her face for this, and grieve her maker
> In sinful baths of milk, when many an infant starves
> For her superfluous outside—all for this?

Who now bids twenty pound a night, prepares
Music, perfumes and sweetmeats? All are hushed,
Thou may'st lie chaste now! It were fine, methinks,
To have thee seen at revels, forgetful feasts
And unclean brothels; sure 'twould fright the sinner
And make him a good coward, put a reveler
Out of his antic amble,
And cloy an epicure with empty dishes.
Here might a scornful and ambitious woman
Look through and through herself; see, ladies, with false forms
You deceive men but cannot deceive worms.
Now to my tragic business. Look you, brother,
I have not fashioned this only for show
And useless property, no—it shall bear a part
E'en in its own revenge. This very skull,
Whose mistress the duke poisoned with this drug,
The mortal curse of the earth, shall be revenged
In the like strain and kiss his lips to death.
As much as the dumb thing can, he shall feel;
What fails in poison we'll supply in steel.

It takes some considerable effort to recall that Vindice is addressing
the skull of his martyred mistress, and that he considers her, or any woman
whatsoever, worth revenging. These remarkable lines were much admired
by T. S. Eliot, and one sees why; they are close to his ideal for dramatic
poetry, and their intense aversion to female sexuality suited his own difficult
marital circumstances during one bad phase of his life. What the passage
clearly evidences is that Vindice is a true Jacobean hero-villain; he is more
than skeptical as to the value of his own motivations, or of anyone else's as
well. But this is hardly the historical skepticism that scholars delight in
tracing; it has little to do with the pragmatism of Machiavelli, the naturalism
of Montaigne, or the Hermeticism of Bruno. The horror of nature involved,
whatever Tourneur's personal pathology, amounts to a kind of Gnostic asceticism, akin to the difficult stance of Macbeth and Lady Macbeth. Perhaps
the hero-villain, like Milton's Satan, is truly in rebellion against the God
of the Jews and the Christians, the God of this world.

III

Though the central tradition of the hero-villain goes directly from
Shakespeare through Milton on to the High Romantics and their heirs, we

might be puzzled at certain strains in Browning, Tennyson, Hawthorne, and Melville, if we had not read John Webster's two astonishing plays, *The White Devil* and *The Duchess of Malfi*. Russell Fraser memorably caught Webster's curious link to Marlowe, whom he otherwise scarcely resembles:

> His violent protagonists are memorable as they are endowed with the same amoral energy with which Barabas and Tamburlaine and Mortimer are endowed. Unlike these Marlovian heroes or hero-villains, they do not speak to us—quoting from Michael Drayton's tribute to Marlowe—of "brave translunary things," rather of the charnel house and the grisly business appurtenant to it.

Here is the death scene of Flamineo, and of his sister, Vittoria Corombona, in *The White Devil*:

> VIT. COR. Oh, my greatest sin lay in my blood!
> Now my blood pays for't.
> FLAM.   Thou'rt a noble sister!
> I love thee now. If woman do breed man,
> She ought to teach him manhood. Fare thee well.
> Know, many glorious women that are famed
> For masculine virtue have been vicious,
> Only a happier silence did betide them.
> She hath no faults who hath the art to hide them.
> VIT. COR. My soul, like to a ship in a black storm,
> Is driven I know not whither.
> FLAM.   Then cast anchor.
> Prosperity doth bewitch men, seeming clear,
> But seas do laugh, show white, when rocks are near.
> We cease to grieve, cease to be fortune's slaves,
> Nay, cease to die, by dying. Art thou gone?
> And thou so near the bottom? False report,
> Which says that women vie with the nine Muses
> For nine tough durable lives! I do not look
> Who went before, nor who shall follow me;
> No, at myself I will begin and end.
> While we look up to heaven, we confound
> Knowledge with knowledge. Oh, I am in a mist!
> VIT. COR. Oh, happy they that never saw the court,

Nor ever knew great men but by report!
VITTORIA *dies*.

FLAM. I recover like a spent taper, for a flash,
And instantly go out.

> Let all that belong to great men remember the
> old wives' tradition, to be like the lions i' the
> Tower on Candlemas-day: to mourn if the sun
> shine, for fear of the pitiful remainder of
> winter to come.

'Tis well yet there's some goodness in my death;
My life was a black charnel. I have caught
An everlasting cold; I have lost my voice
Most irrecoverably. Farewell, glorious villains!
This busy trade of life appears most vain,
Since rest breeds rest where all seek pain by pain.
Let no harsh flattering bells resound my knell;
Strike, thunder, and strike loud, to my farewell!
Dies.

Vittoria Corombona rides her black ship to Hell without final knowledge, but Flamineo is a knower, a Machiavel in the high Marlovian sense, which has its Gnostic aspect. By beginning and ending "at myself," Flaminio seeks to avoid a final agon between his self-knowledge and a rival Christian knowledge: "While we look up to heaven, we confound / Knowledge with knowledge." And yet, Flamineo cries out: "Oh, I am in a mist!", which is what it is to the confounded, and perhaps leads to the self-epitaph: "My life was a black charnel." The mist appears also in the death speech of a greater hero-villain than Flamineo, Bosola in *The Duchess of Malfi*:

> In a mist; I know not how;
> Such a mistake as I have often seen
> In a play. Oh, I am gone.
> We are only like dead walls, or vaulted graves
> That ruined, yields no echo. Fare you well;
> It may be pain, but no harm to me to die
> In so good a quarrel. Oh, this gloomy world,
> In what shadow, or deep pit of darkness
> Doth womanish and fearful mankind live?

> Let worthy minds ne'er stagger in distrust
> To suffer death or shame for what is just.
> Mine is another voyage.
>
> *Dies.*

Bosola's final vision is of the cosmic emptiness, what the Gnostics called the *kenoma*, into which we have been thrown: "a shadow, or deep pit of darkness." When Bosola dies, saying: "Mine is another voyage," he may mean simply that he is not suffering death for what is just, unlike those who have "worthy minds." But this is Bosola, master of direful misprision, whose motto is: "I will not imitate things glorious, / No more than base; I'll be mine own example." This repudiation of any just representation of essential nature is also a Gnostic repudiation of nature, in favor of an antithetical quest: "On, on: and look thou represent, for silence, / The thing thou bearest." What Bosola both carries and endures, and so represents, by a kind of super-mimesis, is that dark quest, whose admonition, "on, on" summons one to the final phrase: "Mine is another voyage." As antithetical quester, Bosola prophesies Milton's Satan voyaging through Chaos towards the New World of Eden, and all those destructive intensities of wandering self-consciousness from Wordsworth's Solitary through the Poet of *Alastor* on to their culmination in the hero-villain who recites the great dramatic monologue, "Childe Roland to the Dark Tower Came":

> Burningly it came on me all at once,
>   This was the place! those two hills on the right,
>   Crouched like two bulls locked horn in horn in fight;
> While to the left, a tall scalped mountain . . . Dunce,
> Dotard, a-dozing at the very nonce,
>   After a life spent training for the sight!
>
> What in the midst lay but the Tower itself?
>   The round squat turret, blind as the fool's heart,
>   Built of brown stone, without a counterpart
> In the whole world. The tempest's mocking elf
> Points to the shipman thus the unseen shelf
>   He strikes on, only when the timbers start.
>
> Not see? because of night perhaps?—why, day
>   Came back again for that! before it left,
>   The dying sunset kindled through a cleft:

The hills, like giants at a hunting, lay,
Chin upon hand, to see the game at bay,—
    'Now stab and end the creature—to the heft!'

The Machiavel spends a life training for the sight, and yet is self-betrayed, because he is self-condemned to be "blind as the fool's heart." He will see, at the last, and he will know, and yet all that he will see and know are the lost adventurers his peers, who like him have come upon the Dark Tower unaware. The Jacobean hero-villain, at the end, touches the limit of manipulative self-knowledge, and in touching that limit gives birth to the High Romantic self-consciousness which we cannot evade, and which remains the affliction of our Post-modernism, so-called, as it was of every Modernism, from Milton to our present moment.

JOCELYN POWELL

John Lyly and the Language of Play

It's not the marbles matter, but the game.
—Dutch Proverb

A modern reader, approaching the works of Lyly for the first time, could be pardoned for wondering if they were not irredeemably precious. He could be pardoned; but he would be wrong. It is easy to find a sentence like the following jejune:

> Well, well, seeing the wound that bleedeth inwards is most dangerous, that the fire kept close burneth most furious, that the oven damned up baketh soonest, that sores having no vent fester inwardly, it is high time to unfold my secret love to my secret friend.
>
> (*Euphues,* i. 21)

High time, indeed. The pile of unremarkable proverbs, the punning parallelism of "secret love" and "secret friend," and the liberal spattering of alliteration seem to occupy considerably more of the author's attention than the matter to be expressed. Also, considerably more space. One might agree with David Daiches that "with these excessive efforts he [Lyly] wearies the reader and demonstrates clearly that Elizabethan prose had not grown up"; or with the two eminent French professors, Legouis and Cazamian, that Euphuism is "a disease of language."

From *Elizabethan Theatre*, Stratford-Upon-Avon Studies no. 9 (1966). © 1966 by Edward Arnold (Publishers) Ltd.

But isn't this to miss the point? The criticism is based on a presupposition: that prose is better the more direct the relationship is between the
words and the ideas. This is a presupposition that needs to be questioned—
that must be questioned if an understanding of Lyly is to be achieved (and
surely the endeavour to understand and enjoy the unfamiliar is one of the
chief purposes of criticism). Why should one suppose that the only, or even
the main, interest of words lies in the meaning behind them? C. S. Lewis
took a contrary view when he wrote of *Euphues*: "The book can now only be
read, as it was chiefly read by his contemporaries, for the style. It is worse
where it is least euphuistic."

The style may be absurd, self-indulgent, and sensational, heaped with
similitude, word-play, proverb lore, and unnatural natural history, but it
is almost always sustained by a magnificent sense of extravagance and fun.

> He that always singeth one note without descant breedeth no
> delight, he that always playeth one part bringeth loathsomeness
> to the ear. It is variety that moveth the mind of all men.
>
> (*Euphues*, i. 272)

Euphuism is essentially a game, and games are not merely childish.

It is only relatively recently that play has come to be regarded as
important in its own right—a phenomenon with particular properties vital
to the history of civilisation. History shows a need for organised forms of
play in all societies, and Huizinga, in his book *Homo Ludens*, demonstrated
the importance of play forms in the shaping of Law, and the rules of war,
as well as philosophy, art, and literature.

That function of play of particular interest to aesthetic criticism is its
apparent uselessness. Play "interpolates itself as a temporary activity, satisfying in itself and ending there." It "begins and ends in itself and the
outcome does not contribute to the necessary life processes of the group."
"It is an activity connected with no material interest, and no profit can be
gained by it." Play, in fact, is an apparently essential human activity which
seems to lack any immediately obvious practical purpose; and Lyly, likewise,
is a prime example of those authors who have to be approached from without
the pale of utilitarianism which bounds so much literary criticism. His work
may from time to time give evidence of moral sensibility, provide some
relevant "criticism of life," but even when it does so that is not what is
important in it. What is important is its recreative function. . . .

One of the essential conditions of play, Huizinga tells us, is that it is
"different from ordinary life." The recreative spirit turns the mind away
from life so that it may return to it refreshed. It re-creates the mind in a

world created for recreation which is without the inescapable consequences that otherwise attend a human act, so that the mind is refitted for human action. Such, in utilitarian terms, is the purpose of play. The manner by which the mind is refitted—and it is not a simple matter of escape—the manner of which Lyly is a master, can be ascertained by a further discussion of Elizabethan play forms. . . .

The plays of Lyly give these impulses we have been discussing dramatic expression. They organise into an elaborate aesthetic game the exploratory, recreational activities of the court for which they were written. They reflect and absorb the multitudinous excitement of life in the royal presence, and give this excitement concrete expression:

> Oh, the gallant life of the Court, where so many are the choices of contentment, as if on earth it were the paradise of the world: the majesty of the sovereign, the wisdom of the Counsel, the honour of the lords, the beauty of the ladies, the care of the officers, the courtesy of the gentlemen, the divine service of morning and evening, the witty, learned, noble and pleasant discourses all day, the variety of wits with the depths of judgments, the dainty fare—sweetly dressed and neatly served,—the delicate wines and rare fruits, with excellent music and admirable voices, masks and plays, dancing and riding; diversity of games, delightful to the gamesters purposes; and riddles, questions and answers; poems, histories, and strange inventions of wit, to startle the brains of a good understanding; rich apparel, precious jewels, fine proportions and high spirits, princely coaches, stately horses, royal buildings and rare architecture, sweet creatures and civil behaviour: and in course of love such carriage of content as sets the spirit in a lap of pleasure.

In its magnificently random fashion this extravaganza by Nicholas Breton summarises those aspects of court recreation discussed above. There are the recreations of the spirit—worship, majesty, wisdom; of the mind—wit, discourse, art; of the body—riding, dancing; of the senses—sights, sounds, and tastes. Lyly seizes upon all these. His plays address themselves to the courtier to replenish his faculties by use, exercising his reason by play of logic, his fancy by play of image, his memory by display of learning, and his senses, over all, with word, spectacle, and music. This practice has an important aesthetic consequence. The experience that results in seizure in this kind of play is not the experience to which the words of the play directly refer; it is rather the experience of thinking, fancying, remembering. The plays are not about the ideas expressed; they are about the faculties employed.

Lyly's plays are games for the sense, and games for the mind. They are aimed at a difficult audience that was at least as interested in itself and its sovereign as in the play (Ben Jonson was later to complain of its behaviour). He attempted therefore to amuse easily and gracefully, drawing the attention to the play imperceptibly by catching at the senses, and holding it there by an elegant employment of matters close to a courtier's heart. He allowed the drama to play on every level, and further arranged that each separate part should lightly reflect the whole so that the attention could be detached almost at will without encountering any difficulty when it returned.

The settings for the plays are without exception fanciful and curious. *Campaspe* brings together a painter's studio, full of half-finished and finished pictures, the palace of Alexander the Great, the tub of Diogenes; *Sapho and Phao*, a river, the sybyl's cave, the forge of vulcan, as well as Sapho's palace; *Gallathea* gives us the nymphs of Diana on the Humber estuary; *Love's Metamorphoses* includes a tree which speaks with the voice of a nymph. The movement from scene to scene in the plays clearly demands some form of continuous staging, and so it seems certain that all, or almost all, of the scenic elements required would be present throughout, deployed about the playing space.

Against his spectacular background Lyly carefully orchestrates his action in order to create a continually changing visual pattern upon the stage. The first Act of *Sapho and Phao* is a good example. The play opens with a monologue for Phao, then a dialogue between Venus and Cupid and their encounter with Phao, then the appearance of a scholar and a courtier with their servants, followed by dialogue and a song for the servants, and then an extended conversation among the ladies of Sapho's court, six in all. This sequence illustrates two points: first the play of sight, solo, ensemble, dialogue; and second a consequent play of rhythm. This latter is emphasised by Lyly. He handles the different dramatic groups in a different dramatic manner, so that the play of movement is accompanied by a complementary play of mood. It is as well to note here that this mood is not dependent upon situation so much as upon character.

There are four main moods in the first Act of *Sapho and Phao*: the lyrical, represented in Phao's monologue, and the dialogue with Venus; the didactic, in the scene with the scholar and courtier; the farcical, in the parody of the pages; and the mannered, in the conversation of the ladies. Beneath all these lies a streak of mockery. The interest of the Act lies in our being aware of variety of pattern and difference of mood. One is fascinated by the interplay of mood and movement, and one's sense of the difference of several distinct modes of being is explored and sharpened.

> For as the spring time doth marvellously delight the eyes with
> sundry sorts of flowers which it bringeth forth, so these some, by
> the diversity and variety of their discourse, give wonderful re-
> freshment to our minds.
>
> (*Guazzo*, i. 188)

The delight of Lyly's plays is the delight of the courtier's conversation. One
is playing with one's experience.

This effect is basic to the structure of the plays. In his organisation of
plot and sub-plot Lyly juxtaposes, in almost every play (in *The Woman in
the Moon* and *Love's Metamorphoses* mood is rather differently employed) contrasted dramatic moods and manners. Different groups of figures—Gods,
courtiers, pages (the distinction is not always so obviously one of class)—
have their particular rhythm of talk and life. Individual differences within
the group are not strongly marked. Nor are differences attendant upon
situation. The particular manner is important and persistent, and is sometimes heightened by excursion into song and dance—the love-songs of Sapho
and Appelles, the dance of the fairies at the Lunar Bank, the grotesque
routine of the Cyclops forging Venus' arrows, and the boisterous songs of
the pages.

Curiously enough the effect of this variety of movement is one of stasis.
This is Lyly's great dramatic discovery, for which, perhaps, Shakespeare is
most indebted to him; it is the secret of the conversation piece. Narrative
drama moves from each new situation on to the next, each development is
in its turn a starting point, and the interest is held by curiosity as to what
new possibility will obtain from each new situation. Such form is almost
useless for the contemplation of ideas. It can develop, but it cannot discuss.
The conversation piece is essentially discursive, and the problem inherent
in this is the concentration of the attention upon a static concept and the
possibilities inherent in it, when the form employed moves relentlessly
forward. The conversation piece depends upon an extended stillness in which
interest is centred wholly in the present, and not in movement from the
present to the future. This stillness Lyly provides. The rhythmic contrasts
assuage the desire for movement, while the short contrasted episodes, through
which the rhythm is deployed, arrest in combination not in sequence. In
this way the horizontal, melodic energy of drama is transformed into a
harmonic energy. Melody extends, where harmony explores. Stillness
achieved, the scene is set for the play of mind.

Most of Lyly's plays revolve around some sort of debate. Debate was
in its own right an important entertainment form in the courts of the

sixteenth century. Many occasional entertainments are couched in the form
of argument between two sides on the relative merits of two opposed ideas
or ways of life. The form is found in many moralities and interludes and
owes its provenance to seasonal festivity, the flyting match, and the battles
of summer and winter. Lyly uses the debate form as a base for plot, subplot, and conversation.

The plots of *Endimion* are united in their discussion of merits of fleshly
and spiritual love; *Midas* opens with three courtiers counselling Midas as to
which gift he should require from Bacchus, one counselling for Love ("I
would wish to possess my mistress"), one for War ("I would wish to be
monarch of the world"), and one for wealth ("I would wish that everything
I touched might turn to gold"); in *Sapho and Phao* we find the age-old dispute
between love and chastity argued in the contention between Venus and Sapho.
Hunter defines the debate theme of *Campaspe* as: "wherein lies true kingliness?
Is it in the power to command others or in the power to command ourselves?",
a theme which dominates the main plot and occurs again and again throughout the play. In a central scene Alexander argues the matter with his friend
Hephaestion, who states the theme at length in a monologue:

> I cannot tell, Alexander, whether the report be more shameful
> to be heard or the cause sorrowful to be believed. What! Is the
> son of Philip, King of Macedon, become the subject of Campaspe,
> the captive of Thebes? Is that mind whose greatness the world
> could not contain drawn within the compass of an idle, alluring
> eye? . . . O Alexander, that soft and yielding mind should not be
> in him whose hard, unconquered heart hath made so many yield.
> . . . It is thought wonderful, among the seamen that the mugil,
> of all fishes the swiftest, is found in the belly of the bret, of all
> the slowest, and shall it not seem monstrous to wise men that
> the heart of the greatest conqueror of the world should be found
> in the hands of the weakest creature of nature—of a woman, of
> a captive?
>
> (*Campaspe*, II. ii. 29)

In *Sapho and Phao* such dialectic has a whole strand of the play to itself in
the scenes between Trachinius and Pandion, the courtier and scholar, and
in their dialogue with the court ladies. There is a similar level in the
discussions in *Campaspe* between Clitus and Parmenio. Often the farcical
characters are allowed to parody this type of formal argument. In *Midas* the
discussion of the merits of singing, dancing, and telling tales is placed as a
complement to the earlier dispute on Wealth, Love, and War. Debate is

used to hold scenes together, to form a structure for conversation, and to set one episode off against another.

Debate and the techniques of debate are fundamental to the dialogue throughout the plays. Lyly has often been admired as the first writer to present conversation on the stage, and the closeness of his rhetorical style of discussion to the conventional manner of his day should by now be clear. The renaissance rhetoricians, following Cicero, divided talk into two types— the discourse, and the repartee. The discourse was the personal amplification of the matter of the conversation; repartee was the neat turning of the arguments of another, the retort courteous. The rhythm of the plays is intimately dependent on the organisation of these two forms of discussion. One moves constantly from the light repartee of the pages, or the courtiers in the palaces of Cynthia and Sapho, to the more formal arguments of Geron and Eumenides in *Endimion*, or the Lords in *Midas*, and on to the discourses of Hephaestion or the Sibil, whose tone is taken up, more particularly, in the internal disputes of Sapho or Endimion.

"Judgment," wrote Hobbes, "begets the strength and structure, and fancy begets the ornaments of the poem." We have seen how the rational exercise of debate is the foundation of Lyly's plays; they are adorned through-out by the imaginative exercise of fancy. The exercise of fancy permeates the imagery of both plot and language.

It is in the lyrical episodes of the plot that fancy is naturally most apparent. Lyly adorns his themes with fables, and his fables with elaborate and artificial symbolism. This symbolism, like the themes themselves, is drawn from the current fancy of the court—notably Italian Neo-Platonism. As a result one feels continually, when reading, that one has happened upon the incarnation of one of the allegories of Botticelli. In *Gallathea* Neptune appears in his proper rôle as the demon-king of Passion, demanding the sacrifice of a virgin to Agar the sea-monster. Gallathea and Phillida, hidden from such a fate by their doting fathers, none the less fall in love. Cupid invades Diana's nymphs, and for his pains Diana captures him and clips his wings. The plot is resolved when both Venus and Diana appeal to the raging Neptune. After a debate it is decided that Neptune will forgo the sacrifice if Diana will restore Cupid, so the virgins are saved for, in Spenser's words, "married chastity."

Endimion is probably Lyly's most elaborate symbolic game. A description might run as follows: Endimion loves Cynthia but cannot posses her; he is loved by Tellus, the earth, whom he once encouraged. Tellus enchants him by the aid of Dipsas, a witch, who signifies "desire" (her name is that of a serpent whose bite causes raging thirst). He is cast into a deep sleep in which he grows old, and is finally awakened to chaste and humble love by the kiss of Cynthia. The predicament of Endimion is the predicament of the courtly lover whose unfulfilled love of his unobtainable mistress leads him up the ladder from earth to heaven. Entangled by his lust he is cast into a sleep, just as the soul, attracted by its reflection in matter takes on the earthly and impure form of man; but he is finally enabled to triumph by the grace of his goddess, and is redeemed to the love of the spirit.

This conflict between spirituality and sensuality is echoed on all levels of the plot. Corsites breaks his word to Cynthia and tries to obtain his love by trial of physical strength; the fairies pinch him for his pains, the prescribed punishment for the sensual, and leave him like a spotted conscience. Eumenides leaves his beloved to rescue his friend, comes to a fountain, a love image as old as, and older than, the *Romance of the Rose*, clears the waters with the tears of true love, and is confronted with the need to choose whether to obtain his desire or release his friend. He chooses Endimion, thus preferring the spiritual over the fleshly love. The episode at the fountain echoes another platonic image of the soul's descent to earth: that of Narcissus who fell in love with his reflection in the water, the element of passion. In his choice Eumenides is advised by Geron, a morality figure of Good Counsel. But he is more than this—he was once the husband of Dipsas, who procured him to live in a desert, doubtless to expiate in a waste land the sin of lust. Even the comic Sir Tophas falls in love with the witch Bagoa, puts away his arms, such as they are, and falls asleep.

The important thing about this symbolism is its lack of intensity. It forms an important part of the structural pattern of the play, but is quite without the mysticism many of the same images acquire—in Spenser, for instance. It is essentially an ornament. Lyly does not think with it. He does not use it to reconstruct experience. He uses it simply to amuse. It is here we come to the play of memory. He could expect his audience to be familiar with the patterns, so he employs them as a form of wit. His art, like the art of a courtier's conversation, is the art of the commonplace. The pleasure it gives is the pleasure of recognition. He does not aim to startle with something new, but to play with conceptions that were already common property. Lyly handles conventional material and adds little to its significance. The interest is held, not be revelation, but by the delight of seeing old concepts in new contexts. What matters is its exuberance and its inventiveness.

To the rhetoricians invention meant not the discovery of new images, but the accurate recalling of suitable authorities. The authorities, similitudes, and well-worn proverbs would be used to "amplify" the matter. It is a game that has both authority and novelty: it guarantees truth without foregoing surprise. Lyly plays it with expertise on every level of drama. In *Endimion* the matter is amplified in the plot by parallelism (Corsites), by contrary (Eumenides), by similitude (the fable) and enriched by pleasant jest (Tophas). In such a way is the fancy of his audience exercised. The matter is also amplified in two further ways: by allusion, and by words.

One of the chief devices for amplifying matter was by instance. There is not room here for much discussion of Lyly's historical allegory, but it must be mentioned for its place in the play pattern. Wilson Knight remarks that throughout the plays we get the feeling of allusions lost. There is a shimmer of references whose meaning has disappeared. They can probably never be recovered; buy one may imagine their effect. They are a necessary extension of the poet's wit.

Wit is that faculty which "sees similitudes in things apparently different," and topical reference is a particularly entertaining form of similitude. The allusion from idea to contemporary fact always sets up a shower of imaginative sparks. The greed of Midas touches off thoughts about Philip of Spain; Cynthia and Sapho liken the true course of living to the life of the Queen. Many characters, by a word or phrase, suddenly recall a friend or enemy. As with the ideas and images, so are known facts of life suddenly given a new context. In this way allusion goes to satisfy the fancy, the memory, and the reason.

The language of the plays operates on the same basis. Fancy and learning are deployed around a firm frame of logic. Lyly is particularly fond of figures of thought, those tropes that appeal to the mind rather than to the emotion, whose purpose is to explore and define, rather than re-create experience. Exploration and definition are, after all, important exercises of the mind. His use of language incorporates on this level two important elements of play—play of sound, and play of meaning. A return to the speech of Hephaestion already quoted can demonstrate both these points.

The speech is mainly constructed upon the figure of antithesis, balancing the right action against the wrong fact. The antithesis is drawn into the form of a paradox by the image developed from the plot, of Alexander and Campaspe in a master-servant-mistress relationship. The figures of thought, here employed to embody the logic of the argument, are augmented by figures of sound. The main propositions in the argument are connected by alliteration: Son-subject, King-Campaspe-captive. Sometimes the alliteration modulates: swiftest-slowest, shameful-sorrowful. The latter pair are further linked by repeated endings. Sometimes the progress of thought is illustrated in a kind of onomatopoeia by vowel modulation and assonance as in the following: "Is that mind whose greatness the world could not contain, drawn within the compass of an idle, alluring eye?" The dance of words and the dance of thought accompany one another. Finally the whole is set off by an excursion into pure fantasy with the intrusion of the fish mugil, where reason dissolves into fancy. This curious blend of the rational and the absurd is one of the chief charms of Lyly's work.

Just as the patterns of thought and fancy in the plot are set off by allusion so are they in the language; the handling of commonplace here also is an important part of the game. Much of the dialogue is a treasure house of reference, more or less obscure. Take for instance Alexander's first encounter with Diogenes, where all the cynic's most famous utterances are woven into a dialogue of twenty or so brisk lines; or Appelles' countering of Campaspe's comment that Phidias only used five colours with a reference to the demands of contemporary fashion. The delight in the former lies in finding the comments you know so neatly ordered, of the latter in an abrupt collision between learning and fact. Again it is old knowledge in a new context. One of the wittiest examples of this exercise of ingenuity is probably Endimion's long discourse on the constancy of the moon. The whole pleasure of this speech lies in the knowledge that in using the moon in a love story the poet has got himself in a quandary:

> O swear not by the moon, th'inconstant moon,
> That nightly changeth in her circled orb.

Lyly accepts the challenge, laid out by the story, that Cynthia is not merely Diana and chaste, but also the moon and changing, and in a charming exercise in rhetoric proves the constancy of the moon. The speech is long and there is no room to quote it here. Also it is exquisite, and it would be a shame to summarise it. Suffice to say that Lyly takes each accepted disparagement of the moon in turn and overturns it. To an audience versed in wit the speech could never lack tension, long as it is. It is a magnificent *agon* between man and myth.

Through all the plays, then, the emphasis in plot, character and language is on figures of thought, on definition and exploration, thinking not feeling. This is curious in a dramatic writer, for it is just these elements of plot and character that carry in most plays the burden of emotional effect. It is not so here. Not that the emotions are disregarded. They are not. But they are exercised not by plot or character but by mood. It is as we have seen, the rhythm, the involvement in different modes of being, that provides the emotional experience of the play. The body of the play is a game for the mind.

One aspect of the plays that particularly emphasises this element of play has yet to be discussed—the performance. The plays were all written with their would-be performers, the Children of Paul's, very firmly in mind, and the effect of children on the stage is highly individual. This has nothing to do with the goodness or badness of their performance. Many children are naturally highly skilled actors, and can provide well observed and technically excellent performances of a large range of rôles, including those of women and old people. The point about boys acting women and old men is not that physically they are unable to represent convincingly the tricks and manners of the characters they are playing—in this they often acquit themselves well—it is that they do not suppress themselves to do so. One never loses the awareness of a dual personality. This gives a child performance in an adult rôle a peculiar quality not often observed in adult actors. The quality of self-awareness.

It was this quality that Bertolt Brecht particularly wanted to develop in the company he formed in Berlin—and he found it very difficult. He wanted to do so for two main reasons. He wanted his audience to be aware of what was involved in the actions on the stage, rather than be absorbed in them; and he wanted this so that they would be surprised by the actions and not take them for granted. Brecht's aims in desiring these results were obviously very different from Lyly's, but one can easily perceive how acting of this nature would complete the dramatic texture I have been describing. The self-awareness of the performance, Brecht tells us, does not entirely reject the spectators' sympathy: "The audience identifies itself with the actor as being an observer, and accordingly develops the attitude of looking on." One is therefore constantly aware of the characters of the drama as part of the intellectual pattern, and this in turn produces another type of similitude, or playful cross reference: of idea to fact. The characters themselves, and the human characteristics of their rôles, become instances and metaphors—figures of action.

A sense of surprise, too, is automatically involved in making such connections, as it was involved in the recognition of commonplaces of plot and language; and this sense of surprise, at thought, word and deed, finally creates and completes the play world essential to recreation. All play, Huizinga says; "is a free activity standing quite consciously outside 'ordinary' life as being 'not serious', but at the same time absorbing the player intensely and utterly." And we can see now the reason for the creation of this extraordinary world; it is not only to exercise the faculties of the soul, but also to liberate them from the limitations of fact. The power of the games of the mind is that they give mind the power over matter. Aesthetic organisation, by releasing physical objects (words, shapes, colours), from the pressures of existence, can reorganise them with freedom. Language allows man:

> to distinguish, to establish, to state things: in short to name them and by naming them to raise them into the domain of spirit. In the making of speech and language the spirit is continually "sparking" between matter and mind, as it were, playing with this wondrous nominative faculty. Behind every abstract expression there lie the boldest of metaphors, and every metaphor is a play upon words. Thus in giving expression to life man creates a second, poetic, world along side his own.

The play world, the poetic world, is needed so that a man can explore himself fully, more thoroughly than the limitations of life allow. The pleasure of play comes from the sense of extension, the freedom that comes from passing the boundaries of reality.

> The use of this *feigned history* hath been to give some shadow of satisfaction to the mind of man in those points wherein the nature of things doth deny it, the world being in proportion inferior to the soul; by reason whereof, there is agreeable to the spirit of man, a more ample greatness, a more exact goodness, and a more absolute variety than can be found in the nature of things.
>
> (Bacon, *Adv. of Learning*, Bk. II)

Lyly's most poetic virtue is his sense of fantasy. His play world is made welcoming by its extravagance. He reaches to the limits of mind and fancy:

> So much for prophecy, that nothing can prevent: and this for counsel, which thou maist follow. Keep not company with ants that have wings, nor talk with any near the hill of a mole; where thou smellest the sweetness of serpent's breath, beware thou touch no part of the body. Be not merry among those that put bugloss in their wine, and sugar in thine. If any talk of the eclipse of the sun, say thou never sawest it. Nourish no conies in thy vaults, nor swallows in thine eaves. Sow next thy vine *Mandrage*, and ever keep thine ears open, and thy mouth shut, thine eyes upward and thy fingers down: so shalt thou do better than otherwise, but never so well as I wish.
>
> (*Sapho and Phao*, II. i. 128)

I doubt if any scholar now could ever gloss that passage fully. I doubt if any of the original audience would have been capable of it. Or would even

have tried to. The exact meaning scarcely matters; what does is the imaginative ability to bring so much so close. One simply gasps at the acrobatics
of the mind. Lyly's proverbs, allusions, unnatural natural-history, are all
part of that "more absolute variety than can be found in the nature of things."
They are a demonstration of the cornucopia of the mind:

> Art thou the sacrifice to appease Neptune, and satisfy the custom,
> the bloody custom, ordained for the safety of thy country? Ah,
> Haebe, poor Haebe, men will have it so, whose forces command
> our weak natures; nay the Gods will have it so, whose powers
> dally with our purposes. The Egyptians never cut their dates from
> the tree, because they are so fresh and green. It is thought wicked-
> ness to pull roses from the stalks in the garden of Palestine, for
> that they have so lively a red: and whoso cutteth the incense from
> the tree in Arabia before it fall, committeth sacrilege.
>
> (*Gallathea*, V. ii. 11.)

The race of ideas and images is breath-taking. It exploits to the full the
great power of the imagination—suggestion. It seems niggardly to stickle
for fact.

The effect of Lyly's plays is in the best sense *dilettante*; they exercise
the faculties to no other end but their delight. As C. S. Lewis remarked,
"The lightness of Lyly's touch, the delicacy, the blessed unreality, were real
advances in civilisation." And yet his comedies are "like life" not in the
simple, imitative sense, but in the sense that the forces at play in them,
intellectual, sensual, and imaginative, are the forces at play in life. His
writing is a stimulant. It sets the mind playing with possibilities; it activates
it; and, like all other good games, gives the players a simple choice: sleep,
or work. After all, when the imagination is at white heat the line between
work and play becomes indefinable. It is submerged in excitement.

SCOTT McMILLIN

The Figure of Silence
in The Spanish Tragedy

One of many unexpected events in *The Spanish Tragedy* is the appearance
in Act III of a character called the Senex or Old Man, who plays no other
part in this intrigue of revenge, and whose one scene interrupts a plot that
has just seemed to turn toward a conclusion. After long delay, Hieronimo
has shown his determination to take revenge upon the murderers of his son.
Precisely then, instead of laying his plan and carrying it out, he must confront
an unexpected and unknown Old Man, and for more than 100 lines the hero
of vengeful purpose gives over to such business as running in and out of the
stage doors and uttering some incomprehensible lines about how the raging
sea tosses its upper billows while lesser waters labor in the deep. It is an
exasperating scene to those who like straightforward plots—exactly the kind
of scene in which it is part of Kyd's erratic brilliance to supply meanings.

To some extent this encounter with the Old Man participates in an
easily observed design. Like Hieronimo, he has had a son murdered, and
this duplication of experience is typical of Elizabethan revenge plays. By the
end of the action four fathers have lost their sons; the play concerns the
experience of men becoming "old men," fathers made childless. What is
distracting to observers of easily observed designs, however, is that this Old
Man, whose plight seems expressly like Hieronimo's, cannot say what is on
his mind. His son has been murdered, but the language to tell of his grief,
the words to rehearse this outrage of the past, cannot be made into present
speech. His language can only be written in a legal document, which the
audience never hears, and which can be torn apart (as Hieronimo shows in
a moment). The Old Man is virtually silent, unable to connect the past to

From *ELH* 39 (1972). © 1972 by The Johns Hopkins University Press.

the present through speech, and in a play rife with language this figure of silence holds a special position. He also holds a special meaning, for the face of the silent Old Man becomes for Hieronimo the location of mysterious signs. In that face Hieronimo sees the image of his dead son ("Sweet boy, how art thou chang'd in death's black shade!"—III.xii.146), then the image of a fury from hell ("What, not my son? thou, then, a fury art"), and finally the image of himself ("Thou art the lively image of my grief"). This collocation of the murdered son, outraged father, and vengeful fury—this gathering of images from Hieronimo's deepest experience into the worldless presence of the Old Man—forms one of the fullest moments in the play; but it is a difficult moment to explain, and one must approach it from apparently remote angles.

I

The Old Man is not the only abstract figure in the play. He calls to mind an earlier character, the Spanish General, who also appears in only one scene and whose function is to narrate the battle between Spain and Portugal in which Don Andrea was killed. Both characters derive from the Senecan tradition (the Senex and the Nuntius), but in regard to language they are opposite figures. Where silence is the attitude of the Old Man in his private grief, the General acts only publicly and only through words.

The General's scene is a moment of high ceremony, a visual display of procession and heraldry organized around the central property of the Elizabethan stage, a raised and stately throne. The stage gives an image of order—political order primarily, although in Elizabethan thought political order readily has religious implications. When the General brings word of victory, the King responds by referring the issue to heaven—"Then blest be heaven, and guider of the heavens, / From whose fair influence such justice flows" (I.ii.10–11)—and the Duke of Castile quickly fulfills the ceremonial possibilities of the event by showing (in Latin) the King's alignment with God (12–14). Within the context of this heady political idealism the General is invited to perform his account of the battle, and his elaborate speech— second longest in this play of long speeches, informed by the figures of rhetoric, touched by literary allusions—becomes the center of decorum for the high ceremony of the Spanish court.

As Jonas Barish points out in his excellent essay on rhetoric in the play, language of this order and design amounts to a reimagining of the event described, turning the battle into a "nearly heraldic formality":

> Where Spain and Portingale do jointly knit
> Their frontiers, leaning on each other's bound,
> There met our armies in their proud array,
> Both furnish'd well, both full of hope and fear,
> Both menacing alike with daring shows,
> Both vaunting sundry colours of device,
> Both cheerly sounding trumpets, drums and fifes,
> Both raising dreadful clamours to the sky.
>
> $\qquad\qquad\qquad\qquad\qquad\qquad$ (I.ii.22–29)

The repetitive structure of the clauses places the armies as mirror versions of one another, establishing a mutual formality between them. All is action and reaction, movement and counter-movement; even the border between the warring nations is "jointly knit." And as the General proceeds to describe the violence of battle once erupted, it is the careful response of literary echo that gives control to his language:

> Now while Bellona rageth here and there,
> Thick storms of bullets rain like winter's hail,
> And shiver'd lances dark the troubled air.
> $\qquad\quad$ *Pede pes et cuspide cuspis,*
> *Arma sonant armis, vir petiturque viro.*
>
> $\qquad\qquad\qquad\qquad\qquad\qquad$ (I.ii.52–56)

It is Garnier's description of the battle of Thapsus (*Cornélie*, Act V), itself derived from Lucan, which shapes the narration here, along with suggestions of Virgil, Statius, and Curtius. The speech sets forth the battle as a symmetrical form and then offers it as a type which has been turned to eloquence by other poets; and in both cases the General's rhetoric transforms the event which it purports to describe into a formality of language suitable to the ceremonial moment in which it is offered.

This accomplishment of language draws from the King the strongest idealization of words—the idealization that words and action form a unity, that the General's language and the victory it describes stand in apposition to one another: "These words, these deeds, become thy person well." A moment later, the victorious army itself appears, passing twice in review, and the King responds to the General's words and deeds by bestowing on every soldier two ducats, and on every leader ten.

The General's speech is the leading example of a motif which runs through the first act of the play. Two other characters tell of the same battle in answer to formal requests, and in both cases, although the situations of their speeches are different, their speeches are similar to the General's in answering primarily to their situations. The clearest example of this intention of language toward the present moment of performance is Villuppo's tale to the Viceroy of Portugal (I.ii.59–71), in which he fabricates the death of Balthazar at the hands of Alexandro. His speech lacks rhetorical fulness, of course, for the ceremony before the throne of Portugal is one of defeat and personal loss, and the perfect lie requires little eloquence anyhow. Villuppo merely reports his version of the battlefield incident, falsely describing the past in order to gain advantage from the present situation. As in the previous scene in the Spanish court, a bestowal (the Viceroy's reward to Villuppo) concludes the narrative account.

The other report about the battle is more interesting because it intends, like the General's speech, to be truthful. In his first intimate scene with Bel-imperia, a forward-looking girl who would spend a moment hearing about the past, Horatio tells of her lover's death in battle (I.iv.1–43). What is really happening in the scene, however, has more to do with the new relationship between Horatio and Bel-imperia than it does with the battle being described or the death of an old lover. As Wolfgang Clemen observes, it is in this careful recapitulation of Andrea's death, conducted in the slow tempo of formal speech, that a relationship between prospective lovers begins to cohere. As in the earlier two examples, a bestowal from the listener to the speaker (the bestowal of Andrea's scarf upon Horatio) indicates that the narration of the past has taken effect in the present situation. Language has served not so much to examine the past as to participate in the forming of present relationships and the opening of future possibilities.

These three narrations of the battle have seemed somewhat of a nuisance to modern readers ("this superfluity of narrative clogs the wheels of the action in the opening scenes"), but in noticing certain similarities among the three reports, we ought to allow that Kyd, rather than merely venting his Senecan enthusiasm, was shaping this part of the play toward a particular effect. All of the first act is organized with the battle as the steady point of reference. No fewer than six witnesses to the battle figure in these scenes; along with the three whose speeches have been described, Lorenzo, Balthazar, and the Ghost of Andrea are also ready to put their own versions of the event into words. To a modern student this multiplicity of views toward a single event might resemble the narrative technique prominent in prose fiction, where various points of view accumulate toward an effect of psychological relativism and the question is raised of whether the past can or should be known objectively. That is not Kyd's interest at all. While certain differences occur in the several versions of the battle which fill Act I, Kyd's interest centers on the enactment of the speeches rather than on discrepancies in their content. What Act I implies is that the past can be controlled and brought into present meanings through acts of speech. As the General's words turn the event of battle into an eloquent part of a royal ceremony, as Villuppo's words turn that event into a fabrication for self-gain, as Horatio's words turn that event into a slow overture for Bel-imperia to quicken, the impression forms that the past, accessible to a speaker's intentions, can through language be modified into essential parts of present relationships.

The "truthful" speeches—the General's and Horatio's—seem to evoke a leading Renaissance idealization of time and language. Particularly in a dominantly Christian society, in which the linear progression of time seems to be made coherent through the Word of God, language is recognized as a creative mediator in man's temporal experience. Exactly what the General attempts to perform in his speech—a re-imagining of battle into a simulacrum of order—accords with much Renaissance theory about verbal mimesis. In the humanist tradition, the achievement of eloquence expresses man's proper relationship to God, and since man's proper relationship to God finds its political reflection in the ceremonies of established authority, the General has every reason to fashion the past into a rhetorical shape for his king. What the General offers to the King, or Horatio to Bel-imperia, is the enactment of a crucial humanist assumption: that through language the past can be brought into present ceremonies of politics and love.

This idealization of time and language, however, is denied by the villains of the play. Villuppo's lie casts a shadow on any humanist ideal, of course, but the more interesting denial belongs to Lorenzo. Lorenzo is the close-worker of the play, adhering outwardly to the ceremonies of politics and language which he inwardly neglects. When he addresses himself to the past he lies, and toward the future he has only the strategist's outlook of manipulating others toward calculable results. He seems to be helping Balthazar in his courtship of Bel-imperia, but this is a fraudulent motive. Lorenzo wants nothing—no loyalties, no bonds, no ideals—beyond his own willfulness. He seeks complete self-sufficiency and has no social intention, not even a socially destructive intention, for his network of scheming. More than Iago, who is at least willing to talk about the possibilities, Lorenzo is motiveless—and he disguises even that point by stating it in an Italian couplet which means in translation: "and what I want, no-one knows; I understand, and that's enough for me" (III.iv.87–88).

Toward language Lorenzo is the ultimate cynic. Words are merely a way, and one of the less effective ways, of controlling others. He cares "not to spend the time in trifling words" (II.i.44), but to work upon men with objects, objects which can be held close in the hand as a lure or a threat. "Not with fair words, but store of golden coin" (II.i.52) does he bribe Pedringano to reveal the name of Bel-imperia's suitor, and when that proves unsuccessful he draws a sword and forces the information. The sword then becomes a cross for swearing Pedringano to silence—"Swear on this cross, that what thou say'st is true, / And that thou wilt conceal what thou hast told"—and then he seals the bargain by offering gold again. This effectiveness with objects goes together with scorn for language, for the cynical Lorenzo assumes (and the play does not deny his view) that behind the facade of ceremony and eloquence by which the public life of Spain pretends to be organized, men are actually motivated and commanded by the properties of wealth and power: "Where words prevail not, violence prevails: / But gold doth more than either of them both" (II.i.108–109).

Like others who seek self-sufficiency, and like others who manipulate men through objects, Lorenzo is a severe ironist. His perfect achievement would consist of arranging an object to control others in his absence, a potentially comic situation. Kyd provides both the situation and a peculiar version of its comedy in the scene of Pedringano's execution, where the object is nothing more than an empty box held by a japing boy. Pedringano, believing that the box contains his pardon, struts a bit on the scaffold and taunts the executioner until suddenly he is hung. A grim joke, one might think, but a joke nevertheless; murder has been trivialized into a jest with an empty box, and the self-sufficient ironist need not appear to control the tone of the scene. A boy can do it.

Lorenzo's effectiveness in irony, however, does not diminish his thorough viciousness. Instead, it serves as a reminder that the really vicious man—the theatrical tradition of the Vice bears out the point—will make others look silly even as he performs his serious business. In the scene which turns the play into Hieronimo's tragedy, Lorenzo is the central actor. It is his knife, another hand-held object, which first stabs Horatio, and the brutality of the act is very stark. Horatio is hung from the arbor, and as Lorenzo drives his knife into the helpless body he marks each blow with a word: "Ay, *thus*, and *thus*, these are the fruits of love" (II.iv.55). Language has come down to a naked demonstrative, a "thus" which subserves the object of the knife and the act of murder. And when the act of murder is over, Lorenzo reverts to his favorite language of debasing irony: "Although his life were still ambitious proud, / Yet is he at the highest now he is dead." It is an object of his own making which gives Lorenzo this contemptuous satisfaction—a corpse, raised on the arbor and pierced, emblematic of crucifixion.

If one motive of the earlier scenes, therefore, concerns the humanist ideal of narrative language, the clarifying of present relationships by recitations of the past, another motive is Lorenzo's denial of that ideal by his manipulations of objects and language to serve his own will. In the humanist view, past and present form a coherent process of time in which man participates through language. In the cynical view, past and present are merely dimensions for an ability at timing. Lorenzo's ability at timing turns men into victims, and nothing in the play suggests that his activity can be controlled by the humanist motive. Indeed, the play itself is a matter of timing in which victimization occurs. Kyd's combination of two plots, in which subordinate events at the court of Portugal are juxtaposed to the main action at the court of Spain, results in an ironic alteration of time sequences and turns one character from the sub-plot, the Portugese Viceroy, into the epitome of victimization.

The Viceroy appears in only three scenes, and in each his longest speech is a formal lament. He does not initiate action; he suffers reactions, and his sufferings take the form of set speeches. His first lament has an important effect. It follows upon the ceremony of victory at the Spanish court, replacing the idealism of that scene with a different order of expression. G. K. Hunter aptly calls the new language the "frantic poetry of loss" and goes on to note that this father, lamenting the supposed death of a son, prepares the way for Hieronimo's similar kind of expression after he discovers the corpse of Horatio. Both bereaved fathers express their grief in the language of formal lament, and in their outspoken sorrow both seem helpless before the dishonesty of manipulators like Lorenzo and Villuppo. What makes the Viceroy a victim in the temporal progression of the play, however, is that at the time of his first lament he is wrong. His son has not died, and his impassioned rhetoric of grief responds only to an error. This discontinuity between event and language makes room for Villuppo's fabrications, and so the villain turns the past into a lie for which the Viceroy's lament has established the groundwork. Victimization would seem to be complete at this point, but Kyd rarely lets go of a favorite idea. After the Viceroy's second lament (III.i. 1–14), news arrives that Balthazar in fact lives, and the Viceroy is permitted a moment of joy—exactly after his son has given rise to another father's lamentation by helping to murder Horatio. Always the Viceroy responds, and always his responses are outrun by events; time is beyond his earnest language. Finally he beholds his son directly—acting in a play, it would seem, but really dying in a revenge plot. The cause of his earlier laments has suddenly been realized, and as he speaks the final words of the play from the human realm, the Viceroy recognizes that he has become the symbolic figure of helplessness:

> Take up our hapless son, untimely slain:
> Set me with him, and he with woeful me,
> Upon the mainmast of a ship unmann'd,
> And let the wind and tide haul me along.
>
> (IV.iv.210–213)

But the idea of human helplessness toward time is not only presented through such a character as the Viceroy. It is also present from the beginning in the control of Revenge, the allegorical figure who remains on the edge of the human action, knowing the direction that all events will take and possessing the only understanding of the past validated by the play. He knows that the central past event of the battle will have one necessary effect upon the human society of the play—the effect of retribution for the death of Andrea—and that the ceremonies which various speakers attempt to create through their narrative addresses toward the past, as well as Lorenzo's manipulations of objects and language, will be precisely destroyed by that retribution. Only Revenge knows that these events at the courts of Spain and Portugal are a scheme in time, a scheme which cannot be affected by any form of humanist eloquence or by any degree of Lorenzo's ironic strategy. It is a scheme of the underworld which takes effect in human actions but which cannot be touched by the rational discriminations of language and will. The time of Revenge is autonomous, making victims of all who speak as though the past can be brought into present relationships or who act as though the future is open to their own intentions.

That is why the Old Man, virtually wordless, incapable of addressing the past, presents the human condition in this play. He is the emblem of the victim, but he allows Hieronimo a moment of imaginative freedom, a moment which holds apart from the autonomy of time. What Hieronimo sees in the Old Man's face has no dimension into past or future. It is only in the bewilderment of an enclosed present that the images of murdered son, hellish fury, and outraged father gather on the silent face. "Horatio, thou art older than thy father," Hieronimo cries when he thinks he sees his son, and the conceit has validity not in the progression of time but in the presence of loss. Eventually, returning to time, he will enact the meaning of those images—he will summon a hellish fury to avenge himself for his murdered son—but that is not a consequence of this encounter with the Old Man; instead it is the temporal version of that encounter, its enactment in the time-scheme of Revenge. The encounter itself has no consequence. It has meaning only as it gathers the energies of revenge into visual images which can be seen by the sudden imagination, in silence and out of time.

II

During Act I, with its weight of narrative recitation about the past, Hieronimo plays only a slight role—slight but consistent. He makes only two appearances in these scenes, and in each he acts simply as a functionary of the court. In the ceremonial scene of victory over Portugal he attends the King silently until it becomes clear that Horatio was the hero of the battle, and then he is called into play because of his son's accomplishment: "But now Knight Marshal, frolic with thy king, / For 'tis thy son that wins this battle's prize" (I.ii.96–97). All of his speeches in the rest of the scene relate to Horatio, suggesting that the initial definition of his role depends strictly upon his gladness as father to this valorous son. His other appearance in Act I is equally simple, although the emphasis is different. When the Spanish King entertains the Portuguese Ambassador at a banquet, it is Hieronimo who is called upon to stage a series of dumb shows, slight dramatic emblems of the mutual accord between nations that is supposed to have been formed from the battle. So in his two appearances in the opening scenes, Hieronimo acts only at the bidding of the King, and his role is defined by two functions: his pride in a valorous son and his skill at devising pageants. Both functions return in terribly changed form at the end of the action, when Hieronimo stages a murderous playlet before his King and then reveals the object which has driven him to ruin the ceremonies of Spain, the corpse of his murdered son.

This serviceable man of the early scenes is not the memorable Hieronimo, not the character famous enough to be echoed and parodied throughout the Elizabethan theatrical age. The functionary of Act I turns radically different in his next appearance, the night-time scene in which Horatio is murdered. The world of the play changes abruptly at this point. From the throne-centered ceremonies of Act I, where eloquence and public response seemed to go together, the stage becomes an area of darkness and brutality where a man is hung from an arbor and, in a silence broken only by shrieks and commands, is stabbed to death. In response to those shrieks—"What outcries pluck me from my naked bed"—Hieronimo comes to the arbor and discovers his son. At this moment the pressure of immediate experience enters his role for the first time, and the result is a radical disruption of identity. The foundations of his earlier performance are ruined by the murder of Horatio, for the comfortable father now has lost his son and the useful court functionary—he is Knight Marshal, and the point is important—must become the seeker for justice instead of justice's administrator. He is suddenly helpless before the cynical effectiveness of Lorenzo, for the object of the hung man which Lorenzo has arranged for his own delight turns Hieronimo's past role to an emptiness and forces the old man to seek a new sense of himself.

In a way, the problem of the character coincides at this point with the problem of the actor of the role. The socially integrated part he has played during Act I has provided the actor with no basis of emotion and language from which to develop Hieronimo's passionate response to his son's murder. The passionate response must come as a matter of the actor's sudden invention, playing through the increased rhetoric of the role; like Hieronimo, the player must make a new beginning. The bizarre theatricality of madness would provide an effective way to perform such a transformed role, and in the revised version of the scene that first appeared in the quarto of 1602, Hieronimo has an extra forty lines of incipient madness to act upon. As Philip Edwards notes in his edition, however, the additions of the 1602 text somewhat obscure the play's original design, and in this case the original design connects Hieronimo's transformed role, his need for a new sense of himself, not so clearly to madness as to the central intellectual terms of the play: justice and revenge.

Justice is profoundly ceremonial, partaking of that world of apparent eloquence and royal response presented in Act I. Hieronimo does not speak of this ceremonial ideal in his immediate reaction to the murder of Horatio—he speaks of revenge instead—but a significant appeal to justice is made by his wife Isabella:

> The heavens are just, murder cannot be hid,
> Time is the author both of truth and right,
> And time will bring this treachery to light.
>   (II.v.57–59)

These are important lines. They derive from an adage familiar to Kyd's audience—"Truth is the daughter of Time"—and they also epitomize the ideal of justice which would have fashioned Hieronimo's office of Knight Marshal. Justice originates with Heaven and operates through the established agencies of an ordered human society. Time is the providential medium in which this operation of justice occurs. Hence both time and justice are beyond the will of any individual; by recourse to the established forms of law and by an attitude of Christian patience, the wronged man will experience the ceremony of justice. Revenge—at least as it is presented in this play—is the precise opposite of this ideal. It is the seizing of justice into one's own grasp, the rejecting of public ceremony in favor of private ritual, the violating of eloquence to the point where silence becomes equivalent to language in expressiveness. Hieronimo will eventually take the way of silence, ritual, and revenge, but it is important to realize that at this moment when the need for a new sense of identity is forced upon him, the ideal of justice is voiced in Isabella's unmistakably Christian terms. It is an ideal to which Hieronimo will seek access in subsequent scenes.

His immediate response, however, contains no word about justice. His own thoughts open only to revenge, and at once certain motives become apparent which will eventually coalesce into the ritual of vengeance—motives of language and of objects. His decision to retain the corpse of his son and the handkerchief soaked in blood indicates an awareness that revenge will ultimately be a display of these properties. And his language turns toward formal incomprehensibility. Before carrying away the corpse. he speaks a Latin dirge for his son, fourteen lines loosely affiliated with classical verse and (even before an Elizabethan audience) difficult to understand in a theatre. On the stage, the clearest impression would come not from the content of the speech but from the gesture of the speaker, the gesture of formal emotional expression whose meaning is largely held private. Eventually Hieronimo will stage his ritual of revenge in four foreign languages—eventually he will mutilate his own tongue—and the Latin dirge adumbrates those strange inventions.

But this scene poses a more challenging consideration than that. Such immediate prefigurations of ritual and revenge originate in the deepest of psychic moments, the moment of self-loss. In the corpse of his son, Hieronimo sees his own death. The feeling of exchanged identity at a moment of death is not a rare idea in the Renaissance, but *The Spanish Tragedy* is unusual in carrying the idea through to an enacted conclusion. At first the point remains theatrically obscure, for Hieronimo's identification with his dead son is buried in the Latin dirge:

> *Omnia perpetiar, lethum quoque, dum semel omnis*
> *Noster in extincto moriatur pectore sensus.*
> *Ergo tuos oculos nunquam, mea vita, videbo,*
> *Et tua perpetuus sepelivit lumina somnus?*
> *Emoriar tecum. . . .*
>
> (II.v.74–78)

But later this realization becomes the crux of the scene with the Old Man, whose face Hieronimo sees as the mirror first of Horatio and then of himself; and it becomes precisely verbal in the achievement of revenge, as Hieronimo completes his ritual with the disclosure of the corpse: "From forth these wounds came breath that gave me life, / They murder'd me that made these fatal marks" (IV.iv.96–97). This sudden recognition of dying must be understood as an essential motive in Hieronimo's action. With self-loss as the new condition of his experience, life becomes—as Hieronimo says—a "lively form of death" (III.ii.2), and the only question that remains for him is how best to enact this sense of a personal ending in time in such a way as to redress the murder of Horatio. To say that Hieronimo is obsessed by his son's murder or that he becomes mad under this pressure is to set the problem in poor focus; both statements imply that he could have acted in some normal and approvable manner. The play is more difficult than that. It presents a man who discovers death as the figure of his experience and who carries that figure through—of course he is obsessed, of course he seems mad—to its realization.

In the immediacy of the murder scene, then, the motive of revenge involves the experience of self-loss and a private, ritual sense of language and objects. It occurs in a moment of personal disintegration, when the foundations of a banal and serviceable career become useless and when a new role, answerable to this radical experience of loss and injustice, must be improvised. What complicates the play, what perhaps makes it true to extreme experience, is Hieronimo's inability to sustain this complex motive of revenge as a ground of action in itself, without resorting to the opposite idea of justice in a futile endeavor to renew the terms of his previous career. Having expressed the complex terms of revenge in the immediacy of the murder scene, he now pursues the idea of justice and tries, through a surfeit of eloquence, to declare himself toward the Christian conception of social order in which time is the author both of truth and right.

The surfeit of eloquence occurs in his next several appearances, and it is here that the famous language of Hieronimo becomes most distinct:

> O eyes, no eyes, but fountains fraught with tears;
> O life, no life, but lively form of death;
> O world, no world, but mass of public wrongs,
> Confus'd and fill'd with murder and misdeeds;
> O sacred heavens! if this unhallow'd deed,
> If this inhuman and barbarous attempt,
> If this incomparable murder thus
> Of mine, but now no more my son,
> Shall unreveal'd and unrevenged pass,
> How should we term your dealings to be just,
> If you unjustly deal with those that in your justice trust?
>   (III.ii.1–11)

The feeling of self-loss—eyes as fountains, life as a form of death—continues to prompt these words, but the elaborate rhetoric of the speech suggests the type of public eloquence which should participate in the social order of justice. In part the speech seeks to become a highly-wrought ceremony in itself, the kind of eloquent gesture which the General offered in Act I. It would demand a formal public response, it would demand justice, to indicate that order in this world prevails. Yet there is nothing public about the situation of the speech (it is soliloquy), and the rhetoric is strained by an awareness that these words and this grief will be forced to remain private and frustrate, like the laments of the Portuguese Viceroy. The result is language which offers itself as the eloquent cause for public justice and which also becomes strained toward fulsomeness by the apprehension that justice will prove inaccessible. The exaggeration of rhyme in the final couplet quoted above is an open signal of what is wrong, the redundancy of sound echoing back on itself through an extrametrical line to indicate the reflexive strain of the speech and the situation. Hieronimo is himself supposed to be chief justice of the court from which justice seems to be absent.

In this access of figurative language, Hieronimo is helpless. His isolation seems complete, a compound of political alienation and personal solitude. Politically, he is the victim of Lorenzo, the ironist who reduces words to the service of gold and the sword and who puts away everyone who could understand Hieronimo's outrage. The personal solitude comes from Hieronimo's experience with death. The man who has encountered the figuration of self-loss and still must do something about it is radically separate from other men, who will not know what he is talking about. His words seem to participate in nature and seem to penetrate hell, for in both nature and hell death is a persistent condition:

> The blust'ring winds, conspiring with my words,
> At my lament have mov'd the leaveless trees,
> Disrob'd the meadows of their flower'd green,
> Made mountains marsh with spring-tides of my tears,
> And broken through the brazen gates of hell.
>
> (III.vii.5–9)

But eloquence is a social endeavor, man's civilized way of relating to human order and eventually to divine order, and the most specific meaning of Hieronimo's isolation is that his words will not reach these locations of life:

> Yet still tormented is my tortur'd soul
> With broken sighs and restless passions,
> That winged mount, and, hovering in the air,
> Beat at the windows of the brightest heavens,

Soliciting for justice and revenge:
But they are plac'd in those empyreal heights
Where, countermur'd with walls of diamond,
I find the place impregnable, and they
Resist my woes, and give my words no way.
                                          (III.vii.10–18)

So the ceremony of language fails. The effort to summon eloquence toward the ideal of justice comes to nothing; the words have "no way." This is not Hieronimo's last speech about justice, for after receiving accidental confirmation of the murderers' identities, he intends to seek redress from the King himself; but by then "justice" has become an isolated word, unconnected with the figures of rhetoric, and Hieronimo's final motive forms instead around the private and decisive irrationality of revenge.

The revenge-motive is realized in objects rather than in ideals. Just before meeting the King, Hieronimo has a soliloquy which focuses on two objects—a dagger and a halter—for which the context of the play provides a specific meaning. The dagger and halter are the instruments which Lorenzo used together to kill Horatio (death by hanging and stabbing), and they are also the instruments which Hieronimo will later plan to use together to kill Lorenzo and himself (he stabs Lorenzo and intends to hang himself). In short, Lorenzo's instruments of furtive murder would eventually become Hieronimo's instruments of ritualized revenge. At this point, however, before the revenge motive has been fully renewed and while he awaits the futility of crying "justice" to the King, Hieronimo has turned desperate (the dagger and halter are also the traditional emblems of despair), and he views these objects as suicidal avenues to hell, where the real "judge" is to be found:

Away, Hieronimo, to him be gone:
He'll do thee justice for Horatio's death.
Turn down this path [the halter], thou shalt be with him straight,
Or this [the dagger], and then thou need'st not take thy breath:
This way, or that way? Soft and fair, not so:
For if I hang or kill myself, let's know
Who will revenge Horatio's murder then?
No, no! fie, no! pardon me, I'll none of that:
                    He flings away the dagger and halter.
This way I'll take, and this way comes the king,
                    He takes them up again.
And here I'll have a fling at him, that's flat.

                                          (III.xii.12–21)

The rejection of the objects is significant. In seeing them as ways of suicide, Hieronimo would give himself over to the simplest meaning of self-loss and would lose the possibility of combining death with a ritual action of revenge. To kill himself with the dagger or the halter at this stage would give perfect satisfaction to Lorenzo, whose earlier efficiency with such objects controls their meaning. Flinging away the instruments suggests a violation of Lorenzo's objective control, and seizing them again, as Hieronimo does one line later, suggests that they will become apt for new intentions. Toward the King he then advances, a bewildering supplicant with "justice" on his lips and the dagger and halter in his hands, the image forming a precise combination of the antithetical terms of the play, but the King does not notice anything. He is busy with another of his state ceremonies, the approaching marriage between Bel-imperia and Balthazar, one further formalization of the league between Spain and Portugal; and Lorenzo is able to manipulate matters so that Hieronimo, now turning distracted, goes by unnoticed. It is a brilliant theatrical scene, this hurrying on to new ceremonies while the maddening Hieronimo turns aside, for it visualizes the political failure which makes justice inaccessible and renews motives for revenge. The range of authority has closed into its own political preoccupations, leaving a former functionary, now a man of private danger, outside and unheard.

At once Hieronimo's irrationality breaks out in a bizarre gesture toward ritual and revenge. He digs into the ground with the dagger, a frenzied effort to make the knife a device for reaching and revealing the corpse of his son:

> Give me my son! You shall not ransom him.
> Away! I'll rip the bowels of the earth,
> *He diggeth with his dagger.*
> And ferry over to th'Elysian plains,
> And bring my son to show his deadly wounds.
>
> (III.xii.71–73)

This desire to penetrate the earth then becomes an open threat of revenge, which entails a rejection of his office as Marshal:

> I'll make a pickaxe of my poniard,
> And here surrender up my marshalship:
> For I'll go marshal up the fiends in hell,
> To be avenged on you all for this.
>
> (III.xii.75–78)

Hieronimo has found his final role at this point. Before the uncomprehending eyes of the King, he summons a fury of acting in which gesture and language coincide. The old man will find his son in some private location, an area of hell where the furies pay heed to outrage, an area of the irrational mind where self-loss and revenge are known to be one; he will find his son whose death is his own and will disclose this object of the past where even the blind King will have to recognize it.

Language cannot long make raids upon the inarticulate, and in this range of experience words become inessential—a convenience, but not a ground of action. When the Old Man enters a few minutes later, this figure of silence makes apparent the images of son, fury, and self which the revenger will eventually act upon, but these images are grounded on death rather than on language. As his tradition in Christian typology indicates, the Old Man is death-bound. The face on which appear the images of revenge is in its own physicality a masquerade for dying, life turning clotted and pale:

> Within thy face, my sorrows I may see.
> Thy eyes are gumm'd with tears, thy cheeks are wan,
> Thy forehead troubled, and thy mutt'ring lips
> Murmur sad words abruptly broken off.
>   (III.xiii.163–166)

The scene is insistently physical and desolate. Unable to give corporal speech to an outrage which "began in blood," the Old Man must resort to the objects of writing:

>   could my woes
>   Give way unto my most distressful words,
>   Then should I not in paper, as you see,
>   With ink bewray what blood began in me.
>   (III.xiii.74–77)

At once Hieronimo draws out the handkerchief dipped in Horatio's wounds— he touches the blood of his son—and this object of revenge, held in contrast to the inked document of legal supplication, releases a tide of speech which carries beyond sense to cry out on the wordless forces of nature, of waves, of an elemental power sought by the human revenger:

>   If love's effects so strives in lesser things,
>   If love enforce such moods in meaner wits,
>   If love express such power in poor estates:

> Hieronimo, whenas a raging sea,
> Toss'd with the wind and tide, o'erturneth then
> The upper billows, course of waves to keep,
> Whilst lesser waters labour in the deep:
> Then sham'st thou not, Hieronimo, to neglect
> The sweet revenge of thy Horatio?
>
> (III.xiii.99–107)

Editors would emend this speech to make sense of it, but as it stands it is not out of place. Answering to the grief of blood, it is a corporal utterance in which some of the rhythms of Hieronimo's earlier speeches about justice can be felt, but increasing here toward the indiscriminate movements of waves and shame rather than toward the discriminations of eloquence. In this moment cleared from the autonomy of time, language tends toward immediacy, like the images of the Old Man's face; and as the ordinary mediations of language and vision give way, all things become possible. It is no less fitting for Hieronimo to tear the Old Man's written supplication— that is what the language of law comes to now—than it is for him to compare himself, powerless, to Hercules (lll) and the Old Man, mute, to Orpheus (117).

It is Hieronimo, however, who is associated with Orpheus by the end of the play (IV.v.23), and this transfer of reference from the Old Man to the revenger occurs through the information that in his younger days Hieronimo was a poet. This last-minute exposition makes the play barbarous to Renaissance beliefs about language, reducing even poetry to an instrument of revenge and eventually to the conditions of silence. Hieronimo's poetic craft is the drama (Kyd brings barbarity home to his own activity), and his play of "Soliman and Perseda" changes the most public of the literary arts into a piece of uncanny solipsism. The poet-revenger holds to the example of Babel. He renders the language of his play incomprehensible by casting it in a mixture of foreign tongues, and he renders the action of his play incomprehensible by having the performers of this confusion die rather than act. The royal spectators have been given the playbook so that they might follow the plot, but in fact Hieronimo has locked them from the drama as securely as he has locked them from the stage. Scanning the playbook while the performance turns into strange tongues, and celebrating a political marriage while the performance turns into the deaths of the betrothed, the royal spectators are discovering the gap between the clarity of the world they expect and the outspoken incomprehensibility of the world the poet-revenger creates.

This "Soliman and Perseda" has designs upon the past, for the plot repeats the situation of Horatio's murder. Others have noticed the analogues to the love-triangle in which Horatio died: Perseda stands in the place of Bel-imperia (the inamorata); Soliman, in the place of Balthazar (the unsuccessful suitor); Erastus, in the place of Horatio (the lover); and the Bashaw, in the place of Lorenzo (the schemer and murderer). But an analogue between real and fictive situations is not Hieronimo's goal. The fictive situation must become real too, through careful casting which keeps Balthazar and Bel-imperia in their original relation to each other, while Lorenzo is forced into the place of the murdered Horatio, and Hieronimo steps into the place of the murderer Lorenzo—all of them to die in a ritual repetition of the past.

Frank Kermode has distinguished between myth and fiction by saying that myth "operates within the diagrams of ritual" as "a sequence of radically unchangeable gestures," while "fictions are for finding things out, and they change as the needs of sense-making change." Hamlet's play-within-the-play, for example, is a fiction in precisely this sense; in imitating the murder of the King (both the past murder of King Hamlet by the agency of poison and the future murder of King Claudius by the agency of a nephew), the fiction finds things out by connecting the dimensions of time, a partially known past to a partially expected future. Like all fictions, it participates in the continuity of time. Hieronimo, acting in a scheme of Revenge which makes time autonomous to human will, performs a different operation. In the present he repeats a situation of the past, but there is nothing imitative or fictive about this performance, and it has no future dimension. It is, strictly speaking, a re-action rather than an imitation, and in a series of radically unchangeable gestures, it comes to an ending in time.

More precisely, it comes to the disclosure of the corpse of Horatio, the ritual object preserved from the past and brought into the present to offer its meaning now. In a last-minute reassertion of rhetorical form, Hieronimo makes the present react upon the past; for the present is "here" in each clause, "here" is the corpse now displayed, and what is "here" expresses only the past in which the deaths of the father and son coincide:

> See here my show, look on this spectacle:
> Here lay my hope, and here my hope hath end:
> Here lay my heart, and here my heart was slain:
> Here lay my treasure, here my treasure lost:
> Here lay my bliss, and here my bliss bereft:
> But hope, heart, treasure, joy and bliss,
> All fled, fail'd, died, yea, all decay'd with this.

From forth these wounds came breath that gave me life,
They murder'd me that made these fatal marks.

(IV.iv.89–97)

There is nothing in those lines for people of courts to understand. Court people like to believe in a future, and even with their children dead at their feet they will call for effective instruments to probe into the reasons for these events. They will torture the poet-revenger to learn what is happening. Hieronimo tells them what is happening in some fifty lines of remarkably patient explanation under the circumstances (98–145), but this final narrative speech, in a play which began as a series of narrative ceremonies, no one from the court understands. And when Hieronimo goes on to say that he has vowed to keep his motives silent, (187–188), he does not contradict himself in the face of his own narrative explanation, as many readers have felt, any more than he inaccurately saw his son, his fury, and himself on the face of the Old Man. In the solipsism of his ritual, language and silence come to the same point in the end, a point of identity where the present reacts upon the past and where acting and dying are figures of each other. His ritual has extended the images of the Old Man's face into the world of court ceremonies, narrative recreations, political marriages, and villainous plots, putting it all to an end. The court people are left with nothing to work on, and as they depart—their separate dead marches marking the political isolation of Spain from Portugal—they have no future to speak of, aside from mourning and lament. Only Revenge and the ghost of Andrea can speak to close the play. Time is at their disposal, and the future is open to their view. As for Hieronimo, he has turned into the wordless old man by the act of mutilating his tongue, and then he has turned into the silent old man by the act of killing himself. What the Old Man is, he has become.

PETER SACKS

Where Words Prevail Not: Grief, Revenge, and Language in Kyd and Shakespeare

Where words prevail not, violence prevails.
The Spanish Tragedy (II.1.110)

The mere word's a slave,
Debauch'd on every tomb, on every grave
A lying trophy; and as oft is dumb
Where dust and damn'd oblivion is the tomb
Of honour'd bones indeed. What should be said?
—*All's Well That Ends Well* (II.3.135–39)

T oward the end of the sixteenth century, the question of "what should be said" in the face of suffering and death had become particularly vexing. For when supposedly immutable principles of divine, human, and natural order were increasingly suspected of being no more than figural impositions on an essentially intractable reality, the traditional means of consolation were robbed of their protective charm. As Thomas Nashe spelled it out in 1592, "Hell's executioner / Hath no ears for to hear / What vain art can reply."

Many poems of the time offer moving testimony to this predicament. But it is in such plays as *The Spanish Tragedy, Titus Andronicus*, and *Hamlet* that one finds the most moving dramatization of the dilemmas that ensure when man's need for consolation or redress is obstructed by his loss of faith in the power of art's reply. By "art" I here understand not only such fictions as those of pastoral elegy, but also the no less artificial mediations of justice

From *ELH* 49 (1982). © 1982 by The Johns Hopkins University Press.

and the law. These plays reveal that no work of mourning can be successfully completed without positive recourse to various forms of such mediation; and while they offer penetrating views of melancholics and revengers, they invite us to study these failed mourners not as pure phenomena, but rather in their inescapable and unhappy relation to such artful fabrics as those of language and the law.

Since revengers are, in a sense, elegists manqués, and since many revenge tragedies refer to the perversion of a consoling pastoral world, it is worth preceding a study of the plays by noticing the contemporary decline of the traditional pastoral elegy. So, too, revengers are unsuccessful plaintiffs, and we should also look briefly at some of the current problems besetting the principle of justice, particularly with regard to revenge.

Admittedly, elegies have always questioned the adequacy of their own utterance. But Spenser's antiphonal hovering over "verses vaine, (yet verses are not vaine)" is far more radical than Moschus' "If I too had such power with the pipe, / I should myself sing before Pluteus." Moschus doubted only his ability to match the song of Bion, whereas Spenser apparently doubts the efficacy of song itself. In "Astrophel" the comforting pastoral matrix, and hence the very locus of elegy, is shown to be so vulnerable to the violence of history that Spenser can only salvage the image of pastoral by a forceful critique and a bold Neoplatonic revision of its fictions.

Few of Spenser's contemporaries and followers, however, could match his odd blend of faith on the one hand, and skeptical poetic sophistication on the other; and the pastoral form was increasingly rejected as a fictional resource for consolation. Ellen Lambert has shown, for example, how the elegies of Drayton employed pastoral motifs as mere decor, while those of Basse and Browne explicitly rejected the old conventions. As Basse declared with the leaden solemnity which so often marked the current elegist's lack of power:

> Not (like as when some triviall discontents
> First taught my raw and luckless youth to rue)
> Do I to Flockes, now, utter my laments,
> Nor choose a tree, or streame, to mourn unto:
> My weightier Sorrow now (Dear Sir) presents
> These hir afflicted features to your view.

We may recall Guiderius' mockery of his brother's elegiac strewings in *Cymbeline*: "Prithee have done, / And do not play in wench-like words with that / Which is so serious" (IV.2.230–32). In each case, the question returns, "What should be said?" For it seems that the mythos of the vegetation deity, with its attendant imagery of resurrection, has shrunk like the merest flower, much as Spenser's Clorinda had insisted. In Ben Jonson's beautiful lyric, "Slow, Slow, Fresh Fount," a voice, singing of Narcissus, laments that "Nature's pride is now a withered daffodil." The very sign, therefore, of consolatory transformation and renewal has been superseded by a withered version of itself. And the singer, after all, is Echo.

As Ruth Wallerstein has well demonstrated, the solacing powers of pastoral continued to diminish as the political and religious uncertainties of the age deepened; and by 1637, "Lycidas" alone among the more than thirty poems for Edward King was written as a pastoral elegy. Not surprisingly, the dominant motifs of the entire collection were those of the felt inadequacy of language, coupled with a hesitant groping for an obscured principle of justice.

For not only the fictions of *pastoral* had lost their power to console. A similar onset of skepticism had undermined trust in the divinely guaranteed nature of *justice*, leaving in its wake not merely the sense of an exclusively mundane and fallible system of human law, but a suspicion that the "Justice" which had now departed to heaven had perhaps never been more than a fiction, dependent for its "presence" on such figures as the personification *Astraea*. Ovid had depicted the forlorn ascent of *Astraea*, last of the divinities to forsake the fallen world; and by the end of the sixteenth century, there was a widespread return to Ovid's scenario. In *The Spanish Tragedy*, *The Faerie Queene*, and *Titus Andronicus*, one finds only three of the many complaints that "justice is exiled from the earth."

Part of the reason for this loss of faith in the existence or operation of justice was the entire climate of unhingement between sacred principles and secular practices. By the mid-sixteenth century in England, parliament had taken responsibility for many judgments that had been previously left to the absolute monarch, thus introducing a sense of justice as a matter of inter-pretation and human vote, rather than of heaven-sent verdicts. So too, the judiciary itself had become far more bureaucratic, with a proliferation of courts and jurors, a kind of swell of mediations which delayed and made increasingly opaque the actual administration of justice. (Hamlet's catalogue of torments, we recall, included "the law's delay.") It must have been well nigh impossible to preserve a sense of the divine nature of justice while being sent from court to court in a procedure which might in many cases last for well over a year.

This loss of faith in legal justice, together with the doubts as to the existence of a divine justice, even in the next world, had a severe effect on any mourner seeking consolation, especially for an "unjust" death. From the frantic complaints of Videna in *Gorboduc* (1561), questioning the abeyance of "Jove's just judgment," to Milton's turn to a powerfully reposited "all-judging Jove" in "Lycidas" (1637), the relation between justice and consolation is close and troubled, and some of the most vivid literary presentations of grief and, in particular, of unsuccessful mourning, are those which also address the problem of an absent or imperfect principle of justice.

Obviously a crucial element of consolation is the belief that the deceased has died for a just reason and will somehow receive his just reward in the next world. But there is a further connection between justice and mourning—one which relates more to the just administration of revenge in *this* world. As both anthropologists and readers of the ancient classics have noticed, an act of retribution commonly attends a funeral in tribal or ancient societies. In *The Elementary Forms of the Religious Life*, Emile Durkheim writes in survey of tribal funerary practices:

> it should be pointed out . . . how it [the vendetta] is connected with the rites of mourning, whose end it announces.

> If every death is attributed to some magic charm, and for this reason it is believed that the dead man ought to be avenged, it is because men must find a victim at any price, upon whom the collective pain and anger may be discharged.

Durkheim goes on to show how the anger and self-mortification of the survivors are turned upon the victims of a frequently inexact revenge. Indeed, retribution is sought regardless of whether or not the deceased had been murdered. Thus seen, revenge is a crucial marshalling of anger, but more significantly, an action in which the survivor assumes *for himself* the power that has bereaved him. It is perhaps in this sense that Bacon wrote "Revenge conquers Death." The violence suffered is returned, paid back; the griever has shifted the burden of loss and anger to another bearer, thus, by some strangely arithmetical tally, cancelling out his sense of violation and passivity.

Since the end of the fourteenth century, however, the individual had had to yield this act of revenge to the agents of the state. His anger would have to find indirect satisfaction in the official execution of the law. When, therefore, the principle and operation of justice were found wanting, the revenger would be faced not only with the original burden of his anger, but with an intensely privatized version of that anger. He would find himself suddenly outside the law, hence outside society, and frequently, as we shall see, outside the public institution of language. With his language itself tending toward the impossible and self-defeating condition of privacy, the issue of his madness would be close at hand, and this, together with his role as passionate definer and critic of the boundaries of public domain, made him an intriguingly dramatic figure for an audience so nervously self-conscious about the altering relation between the individual and his society.

Vengeful anger may, of course, be displaced in other media than that of legal retribution. As a variety of elegies show, from Theocritus' "First Idyll" to "Lycidas" and "Adonais," vindictive wrath may be mediated by literary language. But when doubt is cast upon language and its figures, when its function as a medium is diminished, it is natural to find unbound anger flowing back towards less mediated expression. In regressing toward violence, therefore, the revenger has invariably found himself at odds not only with the law, but also with a language that seems to have grown equally opaque, reduced, as Hamlet says, to "words, words, words"; or to mere papers, as Hieronimo furiously tries to *show* by tearing up legal petitions with his teeth. Almost every revenge tragedy, therefore, includes a trial and violation of language. And it is worth noticing the frequency with which acts of vengeance are performed in ways which apparently make use of a theatrical or verbal mediation only to disrupt it.

The Spanish Tragedy begins with a shuffle of judgment in the next world, implying that even there justice may be a problem. The three-fold judge pronounces conflicting opinions as to whether the ghost of Andrea should be committed to the afterworld of lovers, or of soldiers. In a referral to another court, so typical of the late Elizabethan age, Andrea's case is presented to Pluto, who in turn allows Proserpine to summon Revenge. Revenge leads Andrea through the gates of horn ("Where dreams have passage in the silent night"), to view the ensuing action on earth. The suggestion is, therefore, that the entire play to come is but a dead man's dream.

We move to the court of Spain, to hear the King rejoicing over his victory against Portugal: "Then blessed be heaven and guider of the heavens, / From whose fair influence such justice flows" (I.2.9–10). His words, echoing the traditional view of justice, will of course be ironized throughout the play, as the heavenly source of influence is shown to be in fact a diamond-hard wall, impervious to the words or needs of man. As though to introduce the problem, the king is immediately embroiled in a scene of judgment where he must decide between the claims of Horatio and Lorenzo, rival captors of the Portuguese prince Balthazar, who had slain Andrea. His words, "Then, by my judgment, thus your strife shall end," will also be ironized by the following conflict.

It is probably unnecessary to rehearse the plot, except to notice the persistent slighting of language at crucial moments of its development. Bellimperia, in love now with Horatio, rejects Balthazar's suit: "these are but words of course." And her brother, Lorenzo, in league with Balthazar, bribes Pedringano "not with fair words, but store of golden coin" to assist in the murder of Horatio. Lorenzo has, after all, decided that "where words prevail not, violence prevails."

The murder of Horatio is a vicious rupture and perversion of a miniature pastoral world. "The court were dangerous, that place is safe," said Bellimperia, referring as a rendezvous to "the pleasant bow'r the field" of Horatio's father. Yet it is in this allegedly idyllic spot, "made for pleasure, not for death," that Horatio is hung up in the trees and stabbed to death: " 'What, will you murder me?' 'Ay, thus and thus: these are the fruits of love.' " This perverse substitution of death for fruit is echoed much later by one of Hieronimo's laments for his son:

> This was the tree; I set it of a kernel:
>
> It grew a gallows, and did bear our son
> It bore thy fruit and mine—O wicked, wicked plant!
>> (III. 12.64–72)

And the motif culminates in the extraordinary scene in which Isabella, insane with grief, destroys the remnants of this pastoral world.

Isabella's rampage is a literal *enactment* of the elegiac verbal curse against nature, or of the pathetic fallacy which asserts nature's suffering. For Isabella has none of the elegist's necessary trust in words. She has heard and said enough:

> Tell me no more!
> Since neither piety nor pity moves
> The king to justice or compassion,
> I will revenge myself upon this place
> Where thus they murder'd my beloved son.
>> [She cuts down the arbour.]
>> (IV.2.1–5)

We notice the "thus" of the revenger. She destroys the trees "in the same way as" the murderer had killed her son.

> Down with them Isabella; rent them up,
> And burn the roots from whence the rest is sprung.
> I will not leave a root, a stalk, a tree,

> A bough, a branch, a blossom, nor a leaf,
> No, not an herb within this garden-plot—:
> Accursed complot of my misery.
> Fruitless for ever may this garden be.
>
> (IV.2.10–16)

Isabella's literalization of the language of elegy, her inability to rest content with the mere words, will of course be matched by her husband's similar refusal to allow theatrical pretense to remain mere pretense. Her destruction of the pastoral setting is followed by her own suicide, another actual performance of the kind of "breast-wounding" or "piercing" that we encounter only figuratively in elegies.

It is, however, Hieronimo who most claims our attention, for it is he who most suffers from a sense of the inadequacy of language and from an attendant loss of faith in justice:

> O sacred heav'ns! if this unhallow'd deed,
>
> Shall unreveal'd and unrevenged pass,
> How should we term your dealings to be just,
> If you unjustly deal with those that in your justice trust?
>
> (III.2.5–11)

> Yet still tormented is my tortur'd soul
> With broken sighs and restless passions,
> That winged mount; and, hov'ring in the air,
> Beat at the windows of the brightest heavens,
> Soliciting for justice and revenge:
> But they are plac'd in those empyreal heights,
> Where, countermur'd with walls of diamond,
> I find the place impregnable; and they
> Resist my woes, and give my words no way.
>
> (III.7.10–19)

Here then, for Hieronimo, is the essential failure of language to serve as an intermediary agent of justice or compensation. The human court is equally impregnable, leaving him to circle desperately, calling for "Justice, O, Justice to Hieronimo . . . Justice, O, justice, justice, gentle king." By its very repetition, the word is losing valency, becoming a mere sound.

In a crucial scene Hieronimo receives the petition of an old man seeking redress for the murder of a son. Declaring that "on this earth justice will

not be found," Hieronimo proposes a quest in which the old man will act
as his Orphic courier:

> I'll down to hell, and in this passion
> Knock at the dismal gates of Pluto's court,
>
> Yet lest the triple-headed porter should
> Deny my passage to the slimy strand,
> The Thracian poet thou shalt counterfeit:
> Come on, old father, be my Orpheus,
> And if thou canst no notes upon the harp,
> Then sound the burden of thy sore heart's-grief,
> Till we do gain that Proserpine may grant
> Revenge on them that murdered my son.
> Then will I rent and tear them, thus and thus,
> Shiv'ring their limbs in pieces with my teeth.
>   [Tears the papers.]
>   (III. 13. 108–22)

Since Moschus' elegy for Bion, the figure of Orpheus has been close to
the consciousness of many mourners, but that closeness is by no means
unequivocal. On the one hand, Orpheus is an attractive figure, having the
power to enchant not only the natural world, but also the guardians of the
threshold to the world of death. On the other hand, as Ovid emphasizes,
he is also a negative model for the mourner. For Orpheus insists on rescuing
his *actual* wife from death, rather than a figure or substitute for her. His
looking back, and her subsequent return to the underworld are proof that
she herself can never be revived. And it is Orpheus' failure to reattach his
affections elsewhere that brings about his martyrdom. The resentful women
tear him apart precisely because of his refusal to turn away from the dead.

Like Orpheus, Hieronimo will die for his refusal to accept what might
be considered the mediated forms of consolation. His final transgression will
be to literalize the actions of what is supposed to be a play within the play,
to kill *in fact* the victims whose "killing" he might only have *represented* in
theater. In the light of this association of Hieronimo with Orpheus, we
understand more fully, perhaps, why it is that he is finally led in the next
world to the fields "where Orpheus plays." For the moment, however, we
are left with the image of Hieronimo, in his role as Chief Justice of Spain,
literally ripping apart what represents the fabric of language and the law,
in fact avenging himself against it with the same "thus and thus" equation
that his wife makes in the arbor.

Before concluding with the play within the play, it is worth noticing how the "painter scene" affords yet another example of the ways in which Hieronimo constantly defines the limits of *any* intermediary signs or representations. He demands a painted narration of his loss, but does so in a way that would completely overtax the painter's medium:

> "Canst paint a doleful cry?"
> "Seemingly, sir."
> "Nay it should cry. . . . "
> (III. 12. 127–29)

The rejection of illusion *per se* is thus paired with the demand for an unavailable language or cry. And the merely painted cry, like that of Lucrece's painted Hecuba, served only to mock the mourning viewer's own lack of effective utterance. Nor is this all. "Stretch thine art," Hieronimo insists, commissioning a representation of noises, speeches, and successive events, which are designed finally to abolish the difference between the viewer and his painted image, having on the former the therapeutic effect that is to be depicted on the latter:

> Make me curse, make me rave, make me cry, make me mad,
> make me well again, make me curse hell, invocate heaven, and
> in the end leave me in a trance—and so forth.
>
> (III. 12. 161–3)

With an ironic sense of the impossibility of these demands, the painter asks "And is this the end?" to which Hieronimo, in one of the great moments of the play, admits that there can be no rest for him within any kind of medium: "O no, there is no end: the end / Is death and madness."

At Hieronimo's insistence, the play within the play is enacted in various languages, as though to emphasize his sense of the opacity of *any* language, and to "breed confusion," an impossibility of interpretation such that action itself will seem to have the only meaning. After the killings, he disabuses the audience by explaining how the mediate has in fact been made immediate ("Haply you think—but bootless are your thoughts— / That this is fabulously counterfeit"). Significantly, Hieronimo concludes his entire war against language, expressing the "rupture of [his] part," by biting out his tongue. And as if this were not yet sufficient proof of how consistently his violence has been assaulting language itself, he makes signs for a knife to mend his pen, but instead uses the knife to stab the Duke of Castile and at last to kill himself.

One cannot forget that Kyd has framed his play by the suggestion of its being Andrea's dream, and by the fact that it is viewed by Andrea and Revenge as audience, like ourselves. Kyd thus implies that, although imperceptible to the benighted Hieronimo, there *is* contact between the diamantine heavens and the fallen world. Hieronimo's words do penetrate above, and the principle of Revenge does watch over events. But this is paradoxical, for there would have been no revenge had not Hieronimo felt the absence of justly enforced retribution and had he not felt compelled to take justice into his own hands. However much one may invoke theories about the so-called "scourge of god" attitude, Hieronimo is plagued by his very *separation* from an impersonal or transcendent authority. Indeed, by having Hieronimo become insanely violent, killing even the innocent Duke, Kyd suggests that the instruments of revenge are themselves always imperfect, and that there may be some flaw in the actual embodiment or vehicle of this now dubious principle we see personified as leaning over the play.

Critics have nevertheless argued that Kyd is deliberately portraying the aberrations of a man who loses faith in justice, and who abandons spiritual hope. But the hapless, mournfully secular nature of the action and language of the play nevertheless goes a long way towards shaking our belief that there *is* another, "higher" level other than merely that which is shared by the dramatist and spectator. Indeed, when we recall that Revenge is the usher of Andrea's dream, we see these two inhabitants of that "upper" realm as little more than versions of the playwright and his audience. And as we turn to *Titus Andronicus* we find that the personification of Revenge, supposedly arriving from some extra-mundane world, is presented only as a fraudulent impostor—the villainous Tamora in fancy dress. In fact it is Shakespeare's destruction of personification, and of the transcendent realm to which it may refer, that is a primary ingredient of that play's unmitigated darkness.

HAROLD E. TOLIVER

The Shoemakers' Holiday:
Theme and Image

Thomas Dekker will not likely share the lot of rediscovered minor figures. *The Shoemakers' Holiday*, to be sure, frequently appears in selections of Elizabethan comedy; but Dekker had the misfortune of being overmatched by Jonson in satire and overshadowed by Shakespeare in romantic comedy. An uncertain canon sprinkled with collaborations has made him more attractive to textual studies than to criticism. Like the rest of Dekker's comedies, *The Shoemakers' Holiday* is occasionally commended for its delightful realism, or in Mary Leland Hunt's words, for being "the most attractive picture of citizen life presented on the Elizabethan stage, and perhaps . . . the truest," and for manifesting Dekkers' "sane, sweet, and democratic mind." But the implication is that the "picture" is spontaneous, untidy, and without enduring significance for an age which does not turn excitedly to a drama of sweetness and sanity.

I think, however, that the play's vagabond madness has a method and that its lighthearted "democracy" has a shape and coherence which might tend to raise our estimation of Dekker's craftsmanship if observed. The thematic goal of the play is not to exalt one segment of Elizabethan society above others, to be a trade manual for shoemaker apprentices, or to offer a guidebook to late fifteenth-century London; rather, it is to show that the deficiencies of various social levels are symptomatic of enduring human faults, faults which may be remedied by the right kind of discipline and the right kind of holiday freedom. The special areas of deficiency and their remedies may be divided into a few imagistic and thematic categories. The shoemakers,

From *Boston University Studies in English* 5, no. 4 (Winter 1961). © 1961 by The Trustees of Boston University.

especially Firk, are addicted to sensual 'feasting' while those of higher standing entertain at a falsely civil and arid table; these two are transcended in
the ceremonial-sensuous banquet which Simon Eyre, the shoemaker-mayor,
serves the King. A false love for position and wealth threatens the two central
love affairs from above while poverty threatens them from below; these
dangers are dissolved in love matches-with-blessings. Likewise, a false sense
of honor seems momentarily to promise rewards while true honor results
only in a crippling lameness and a life of hardship. This condition, the world
being what it is, cannot be entirely cured, but is set straight as far as possible.
And last, in the shoemakers' lives a holiday atmosphere of irresponsible
festivity and the crude necessities of life stand opposed; this condition, too,
is ameliorated by the power of the King in conjunction with the shoemaker-
mayor. If any of these is central, it would seem to be the last, though the
opposition might be more broadly phrased as a struggle between the exigencies imposed upon one's free will by a life of commodity and compromise,
and the desire to escape these necessities, to be an entirely free and romantic
agent perpetually on a "holiday."

Freedom is not entirely dependent upon money: even those with money
must learn to compromise and the unpropertied can find a way to direct
their own affairs and to have their own means of creating holidays. "Prince
am I none," Simon says, "yet am I princely born," receiving his proper
inheritance as the "sole" son of a shoemaker. Honor can in fact be gained
in a life of commodity: "I am a handicraftsman," he adds, "yet my heart is
without craft" (v.v.10). But the conflict between life as it is and life as the
romantic spirit would have it be is nevertheless intimately involved in the
differences between social and economic levels, as the two contrasting songs
which serve as prelude suggest in their own oblique way. The first of the
two combines natural harmony and serenity with comic lowness:

> Now the Nightingale, the pretty Nightingale,
> The sweetest singer in all the forest's choir,
> Entreats thee, sweet Peggy, to hear thy true love's tale;
> Lo, yonder she sitteth, her breast against a brier.
>
> But O, I spy the Cuckoo, the Cuckoo, the Cuckoo;
> See where she sitteth: come away, my joy;
> Come away, I prithee, I do not like the Cuckoo
> Should sing where my Peggy and I kiss and toy.'
>
> O the month of May, the merry month of May,
> So frolic, so gay, and so green, so green, so green!

> And then did I unto my true love say:
> 'Sweet Peg, thou shalt be my summer's queen!'

The poetry of the love holiday is thus 'impure.' Merely setting a romantic "true-love's tale" in the context of the "brier" would not in itself make it so—the holiday atmosphere of romantic comedy is customarily intensified by a token resistance which, it is apparent from the beginning, will be overcome. But romance is confronted also by the formidable challenge of the cuckoo, which, unlike the aristocratic "sweetest singer" of the forest, is common, bourgeois, and a little absurd: love can withstand rich uncles, but can it survive domestication? The singer, at any rate, apparently fears not; he must take his joy "away" from the cuckoo's song. An uncomfortable awareness of creaturely realities impinges itself upon lovers even as they "kiss and toy," which predicts what the play itself will demonstrate, namely, that romantic loves like that of "Rose" and "Lacy" must be considered in the context of the more prosaic life of the shoemakers, especially the marital life of Simon and Margery and the sensual life of Firk.

These two views of love are part of a complex of interrelated class levels and "planes of reality" (in E. M. W. Tillyard's phrase) which the play presents. But other kinds of love besides these two are also possible. The second song resolves the conflict between romantic merriment and disenchanted reality by proposing a spirited resignation and an open-eyed love (reminiscent of Jane's and Ralph's, as we shall see later):

> Trowl the bowl, the jolly nut-brown bowl,
>   And here, kind mate, to thee:
> Let's sing a dirge for Saint Hugh's soul,
>   And down it merrily.

> Cold's the wind, and wet's the rain,
>   Saint Hugh be our good speed:
> Ill is the weather that bringeth no gain,
>   Nor helps good hearts in need.

If romance is tested by comic realism in the first song, in the second indoor security and warmth contain a measure of sorrow and necessity. Desire for an ideal "summer's queen" and fear of a wife who might make the cuckoos sing are both exchanged for a stable bond with a "kind mate"—an endearing but well-tried love. Likewise, nature's spontaneous tutelary powers are exchanged for society's martyr (Saint Hugh being the patron saint of shoemakers) and the light-hearted songs of the May for trowling of the bowl and a "dirge." It is not the best of all possible worlds but festivity is possible—"sing a dirge," but "down it merrily."

The season itself, which is thus a mixture of winter cold and summer merriment, is to be judged partly by what can be "gained" from it. Perhaps the free and light of heart can afford to have the nightingale for a patron, but the shoemakers need Saint Hugh, or as the prologue suggests to the Queen, a goddess who will care for her "meanest vassals," as the King cares for Simon (the implication being that the Elizabethan theater, like Simon's banquet hall, is also a kind of festive meeting place where, "on bended knees," the shoemakers may properly ask for tribute).

The theme of gain is immediately taken up in the first scene by Lincoln and Lord Mayor Oteley, whose feasting together has become a mere outward form, as indeed love and honor have also. Though they are decidedly not "good hearts" in need, money is a commanding power capable of arousing distrust between them. "Poor citizens must not with courtiers wed" (I.i.12) who will spend more in a year on "silks and gay apparel" than the mayor is worth. To make the point sure, Lincoln describes at length the dissolute spending of his nephew, who has become the lowest of the humble, a shoemaker in Wittenberg, "A goodly science for a gentlemen / Of such descent!" (I.i.30). Rose, the object of Lacy's love, Lincoln describes as a "gay, wanton, painted citizen" though, as we discover, she presents the only opportunity for Lacy to exchange the bright scarves, the "bunch of feathers," and "the monstrous garters" which characterize his affectation, for the true garland of festivity (I.ii.1). She in turn is enabled by him to be bound "prentice to the Gentle Trade" (III.iii.87). His disguise as a shoemaker is in a sense his own creation of identity; paradoxically, only by becoming a shoemaker can he and Rose share in the "frolic, so gay, and so green, so green. . . . " To this extent, his love takes on the qualities which modify the romantic spirit of the second song—his disguise is a symbolic acquisition of the sturdiness of the lower classes.

The issue is more clearly drawn in Lincoln's instructions to Lacy (I.i.7f.). The Lord Mayor, "this churl . . . in the height of scorn," according to this Polonius in the height of worldly wisdom, has attempted to 'buy' Lacy off. Honor, family position, and the image one puts before the world hinge upon defining love in the 'proper' way, not, as the King will tell Lincoln, as that which "respects no blood, / Cares not for difference of birth or state" (V.v.104), but as the essence and achievement of birth and state:

> Remember, coz,
> What honourable fortunes wait on thee:

> Increase the king's love, which so brightly shines,
> And gilds thy hopes. I have no heir but thee,—
> And yet not thee, if with a wayward spirit
> Thou start from the true bias of my love.
>
> (I.i.80)

The implications are that a "mixture" of bloods will destroy the social hierarchy rather than bestowing benefits on each level; the King's love functions to "gild" one's personal hopes with an external grace; and "my love" has the "true bias," which cannot be left for the wayward infatuation of romantic love without incurring the risk of disinheritance. As a comparatively free aristocrat, Lincoln misses all the advantages of his station and acquires the disadvantages of those who by necessity must be concerned for "gain." When Lacy falls into the game, Lincoln rewards him with "thirty Portigues" for his fair words of acquiescence. And while Lacy secretly rejects Lincoln's command to seek "fair Honour in her loftiest eminence" in the wars in France, policy is as yet his only remedy for policy. He implicitly endorses a superficial sense of values, while self-flagellation for not living up to them stifles festivity as surely as parental authority and false honor could have. Love is powerful only in changing "High birth to baseness, and a nobler mind / To the mean semblance of a shoemaker!" (I.iii.10). But he also sees another side of things which will develop in the course of the play until the threat of disinheritance ceases to matter:

> Then cheer my hoping spirits, be not dismay'd,
> Thou canst not want, do Fortune what she can,
> The Gentle Craft is living for a man.

Simon Eyre's version of the last line shows "living" to mean not only possessing the minimum necessities but having real life. According to the standards of Lincoln, missing the war in France to become a shoemaker-lover is not to gain a way of living but to kill the real man, the "name": "Lacy, thy name / Liv'd once in honour, now 'tis dead in shame" (II.iv.52). It is to destroy the self and the bankbook, as though identical, in the same fire, "The fire of that love's lunacy" in which Lacy has "burnt up himself, consum'd his credit" (II.iv.41). But Lincoln's economics of love are gradually turned against him. Lacy becomes "surfeit with excess of joy" and is made happy by Rose's "rich perfection," which pays "sweet interest" to his hopes and "redoubles love on love":

> let me once more
> Like to a bold-fac'd debtor crave of thee,
> This night to steal abroad . . .
>
> (IV.iii. 12)

Only by the sweet theft of love can important debts be paid. In spite of her father's anger and his uncle's hate ("This traffic of hot love shall yield cold gains," IV.iv.139), trading false honor for love can be consummated in "happy nuptials" blessed by the King himself. As Firk aptly says of this "humble" marriage of the new shoemaker, "They shall be knit like a pair of stockings in matrimony."

The love of Ralph and Jane, on the other hand, is beset more by necessity than by false honor; shoemakers go to France because pressed into service, not to gain a name but to lose the full use of their limbs. The intercession of Simon is not sufficient to keep the newly married couple together, but even shoemakers can be worthy soldiers if forced to be: "take him, brave men; Hector of Troy was an hackney to him, Hercules and Termagant scoundrels." Simon's advice is somewhat more sound if less delicate than Lincoln's to Lacy; it is not, of course, without its own concern for social class and honor:

> fight for the honour of the Gentle Craft, for the gentlemen shoe-
> makers, the courageous cordwainers, the flower of St. Martin's,
> the mad knaves of Bedlam, Fleet Street, Tower Street and White-
> chapel; crack me the crowns of the French knaves, a pox on them,
> crack them; fight, by the Lord Ludgate, fight, my fine boy!
>
> (I.i.211)

(And as Firk shows, shoemakers can also turn necessity to gain: "God send thee to cram thy slops [pockets] with French crowns, and thy enemies' bellies with bullets," I.i.221.)

Ralph himself understands clearly the contrast between the poor and the rich as they go to war. Rich men "give their wives rich gifts, / Jewels and rings, to grace their lily hands," while those of his trade make "rings for women's heels." His gift of a pair of shoes, besides being practical, becomes a symbol of fidelity and humbleness. It offers a metaphorical language for the poor to talk about love without ostentation ("These true-love knots I prick'd; I hold my life, / By this old shoe I shall find out my wife"), though to Firk love sentiments are but an "ague-fit of foolishness" (IV.ii.46). And by the shoes Ralph is enabled to find Jane as she is about to accept a countergift of Hammon's "rings," which will give her a chance to have "lily hands" of grace rather than the working hands of craft pompously described by Eyre: "Let me see thy hand, Jane. This fine hand, this white hand, these pretty fingers must spin, must card, must work; work, you bombast-cotton-queen; work for your living . . . " (I.i.208).

It is Jane, in fact, who is most clearly faced with the choice between an honorable poverty and a fair name. Her dilemma is this: to choose wealth is to sacrifice romance, but to choose romance is perhaps to destroy it, for it cannot survive without holidays. Hammon would make festivity possible by buying her "hand"; but she finds festivity and necessity incompatible: "I cannot *live* by keeping holiday" (III.iv.31). She would rather, she asserts, be wife of a poor man "than a king's whore" (III.iv.79), and, if her breath will make him "rich," Ralph's death makes her "poor" (III.iv.124). When set between the crippled Ralph and Hammon, like Everyman between vice and virtue, and forced to distinguish between false and true honor, she has little difficulty in choosing, but the choice, considered in context, is not a facile one. "Whom should I choose? Whom should my thoughts affect / But him whom Heaven hath made to be my love?" she asks, turning to Ralph; "Thou art my husband, and these humble weeds / Make thee more beautiful than all his wealth" (v.ii.53). The dilemma is dissolved by submission to a higher order ("for wedding and hanging goes by destiny," Firk remarks) and by a discovery of values in keeping with that order. While it is not possible to achieve an unrestricted self-fulfillment, one can acquiesce in providence and grasp whatever beauty exists in "humble weeds." The original choice lay with heaven, perhaps, but it can be endorsed by an act of free will which, within the limits of contingency, is an act of self-determination. Neither Jane nor Ralph is quite complete until this choice is made, but afterward they alone require no gifts from the King. Hammon is left as he began, requiring the "sunny eyes" of a kind mate to warm a "cold heart" but achieving nothing. His position in the cold street outside Jane's warm (and thoroughly honest) shop in which she sits, "a light burning by her," has revealed symbolically a 'winter' nature which finds love a "lunacy" when it makes a single look "as rich . . . as a king's crown" (III.iv.12 f.).

Hammon's attempt to deter Ralph with "fair gold" offers a way to bring the virtues of the gentle trade into the love-honor-money complex: "dost thou think a shoemaker is so base to be a bawd to his own wife for commodity? Take thy gold, choke with it! Were I not lame, I would make thee eat thy words" (v.ii.82). A choking "feast" of gold and words might be more appropriate for Lincoln, but the point is well made, and properly conditioned by necessity—"were I not lame. . . . " Fidelity and honor, having survived the test, get their reward and the tables are turned upon their false counterparts. Oteley and Lincoln, mistaking appearance for reality, rush in to "unmask" what is, of course, no disguise but the genuine 'article.' Rather than easing "her blindness," theirs is lifted:

> LINCOLN.   O base wretch!
> Nay, hide thy face, the horror of thy guilt
> Can hardly be wash'd off. Where are thy powers?
> What battles have you made? O yes, I see,
> Thou fought'st with Shame, and Shame hath conquer'd thee.
> This lameness will not serve.
>
> (v.ii.121)

Ironically, he speaks more truly than he knows. Real guilt cannot indeed be "washed off" like gilt, and lameness will not "serve" one, though, in another sense, this lameness has served the state, and without a visible entourage of "powers."

In the symmetrical cross-referencing of the two love plots, Jane rejects Hammon for someone lower in the social scale while Rose rejects him for someone higher pretending to be lower; both reject him not because he is personally undesirable—by and large he is sympathetically portrayed to remove that possibility—but because "summer love" cannot be arranged or politic. The democracy of shoemakers, with its levelling of social barriers, would seem to win in both cases. Actually, a countersatire operates throughout which shows that commodity and authority inevitably have their place and that shoemakers as well as courtiers can exalt these things beyond their due. Simon's conveniently quick return on an investment enables him to spread the affectations of the rich thinly over a crude, good-hearted sensuousness. It is significantly a shipload of sweet wares, enough "prunes, almonds, and sugar-candy" to send Firk into raptures and Margery into a French hood, which makes him Lord Mayor. If Margery feels "honour creep upon" her and "a certain rising" in her flesh, meaning a rise in nobility, Firk can correctly interpret it as simply growing fat: "Rising in your flesh do you feel, say you? Ay, you may be with child. . . . But you are such a shrew, you'll soon pull him down" (II.iii.136). While putting on as much finery as the "pishery-pashery" of "those silken fellows, . . . painted beings, outsides, outsides," whose "inner linings are torn," she is quick to reprove Ralph's mourning with a glib morality: "Ralph, why doest thou weep? Thou knowest that naked we came out of our mother's womb, and naked we must return; and, therefore, thank God for all things" (III.ii.91).

Firk himself is not entirely immune to the money-disease, but, like Simon, he is more apt to err on the side of crudity than on that of "finery."

True festivity, as we learn from the last scene, should not be entirely without discipline, as he tends to make it: the banquet over which the new mayor and the King preside, like the love of Ralph and Jane, has an appointed order and time. That Simon is both shoemaker and mayor, the King both supreme ruler and 'feaster,' is significant. And "when all our sports and banquetings are done, / Wars must right wrongs which Frenchmen have begun" (v.v.190): holidays, by the nature of things, cannot last forever. To be sure, both Simon's democracy and his discipline cease when he deals with his wife, and his feast of language is anything but a gourmet's dish: "Away, you Islington whitepot! hence, you hopperarse! you barley-pudding full of maggots! you broil'd carbonado!"; but he is not merely an irresponsible king of misrule designed to carry off subversive and aberrant impulses. Though he is a "wild ruffian," even noblemen praise him as a man "as serious, provident, and wise, / As full of gravity amongst the grave, / As any mayor hath been these many years."

Perhaps the nature of the final compromise, which brings out the best in the social hierarchy as well as in love, honor, and the working-festive life of the "gentle craft," can best be seen in the feasting imagery, some examples of which I have already quoted. There have been several false starts toward the final concept of the communal banquet. The only agreement Lincoln and Mayor Oteley can achieve over their "sundry" feasts, as we have seen, is that it is a "shame / To join a Lacy with an Oteley's name." Hammon, the hunter of his "dear," having lost his venison, expects to "find a wife," only to become ironically the prey at Oteley's "hunter's feast." Switching the hunt to Jane, his "poor famish'd eyes do feed on that / Which made them famish" (III.iv.5), but he is finally excluded altogether from the shoe-makers' banquet, as he is excluded from the harmony and festivity of love itself (v.ii.91), because he has not been willing to sacrifice station to love. His is a false quest, not without appeal, but clearly misdirected. Before the final banquet a preliminary feast is held during which Eyre dominates and becomes the envy of those who have more money but less gaiety. Margery's suggestion to "put on gravity " (III.iii.11) is found unacceptable and Rose is advised to marry "a grocer, " since "grocer is a sweet trade: plums, plums." And so Hodge and Firk, as I have indicated, conceive of the feast of life in sensual terms only:

HODGE. Let's feed and be fat with my lord's bounty.

FIRK. O musical bell, still! O Hodge, O my brethren! There's

> cheer for the heavens: venison pasties walk up and down
> piping hot, like sergeants; beef and brewis comes
> marching in dry-fats, fritters and pancakes comes
> trowling in in wheel-barrows; hens and oranges hopping
> in porters' baskets, collops and eggs in scuttles, and tarts
> and custards comes quavering in in malt-shovels.
>
> (v.ii.187)

This kind of dream, so full of childlike personification, is, of course, quite different from the aristocratic dream of ideal love, but it, too, rests on the borderline between innocence and irresponsibility. The final shoemakers' banquet, while satisfying these appetites and giving gaiety its due, places controls upon the impulse to take a prolonged vacation. When the pancake bell rings, the shoemakers can be "as free as my lord mayor," shut up their shops, and make holiday, and it may seem that the holiday will "continue for ever"; but in fact it will cease and come again under the cyclical restrictions and discipline of nature and under the sanctions of a social decorum. Except for Ralph, Jane, and Hammon, everyone comes to the banquet to receive his proper reward or retribution. "Care and cold lodgings bring white hairs" (v.v.31), but "mirth lengtheneth long life," as Dekker says in the dedicatory epistle to "all good fellows . . . of the Gentle Craft"; and it causes the King to rule by the promptings of the heart rather than by the promptings of the senior citizens. He perhaps speaks better than he knows when telling Simon that it does him good to see the mayor in a merry mood, as though among his shoemakers (v.v.15). He sends Rose and Lacy to bed and by simple commandment redeems lost honor to one willing to "stoop / To bare necessity," and, forgetting courtly pleasures, to gain love by becoming a shoemaker. As the temporal head of social order, he asserts his power against false divisions. No hand on earth "should dare untie / The sacred knot, knit by God's majesty" which unites unequals "in holy nuptial bands" (v.v.63). God's majesty at the spiritual head of all hierarchies joins with the shoemakers to sustain that democratic union. Not all India's wealth would cause Lacy to forgo his love; for Rose to leave him would be like a separation of body and soul. Festive celebration thus depends upon a harmonious community which fulfills the demands of body and soul through the legal bonds of the "sacred knot," rather than through factitious differences of birth or state, or a sensual indulgence in the feast as such. Finally, even Lincoln and the former mayor are made more or less content in the general harmony.

"Ill is the weather that bringeth no gain," however, and so Simon uses

the festive occasion to win a concession from the King allowing the shoemakers to buy and sell leather in the mayor's new hall twice a week. With
that gift, the banquet may be concluded. In an exchange of courtesies, Simon
asks the King to taste of his "poor banquet" which "stands sweetly waiting"
his "sweet presence," served by none but shoemakers:

> Yet add more honour to the Gentle Trade,
> Taste of Eyre's banquet, Simon's happy made.
>
> (v.v. 182)

In the semiritualistic mixture of prose and poetry and in the gesture of the
King eating from the shoemakers' holiday table, feast and work, nobility
and the gentle trade, honor and love, find their festive blessing and their
"gain."

ALVIN B. KERNAN

Tragical Satire in The Malcontent

In formal satire the satirist has a tendency to play the tempter. He leads his victims on and encourages them in their foolishness only to reveal them for what they are and scourge them. In his three early comical satires Jonson made use of this trait of the satirist to bring his plays to a conclusion. It simply remained for some playwright to perceive that the satirist could be made an intriguer throughout a play, not just at the conclusion, and that the plot of the play, either serious or comic, could be the satirist's attempts to expose the fools and villains. The chief advantage of such a method would be that the satirist could be given relatively unlimited time to rail, since the railing would now become the chief motive force in the plot. Marston's *The Malcontent* (1604) is perhaps the most interesting of the many Jacobean plays constructed on this principle.

Briefly, *The Malcontent* tells the story of Altofronto, former Duke of Genoa, who has been deposed by Pietro with the aid of the citizenry and the Duke of Florence. At the point the play begins, Altofronto disguised as Malevole, a malcontent, returns to Genoa and undertakes a series of intrigues which first place Mendoza, a Machiavellian schemer, in the ducal palace and finally bring about his overthrow and the return of Altofronto to his rightful throne, once again with the aid of the fickle mob.

Malevole is the satirist of the play, and a few examples of his language and activities will establish his conventional character. When asked for news by Ferrardo, Malevole responds in the usual snarling tone: "Common news! why, common words are, God save ye, fare ye well; common actions, flattery

From *The Cankered Muse.* © 1959 by Yale University Press. Originally entitled "Tragical Satire."

and cozenage; common things, women and cuckolds" (I.1.60–2). On other occasions he employs the typical soaring rhetoric and displays his profound pessimism. "World! 'tis the only region of death, the greatest shop of the devil; the cruelest prison of men, out of the which none pass without paying their dearest breath for a fee; there's nothing perfect in it but extreme, extreme calamity" (IV.2.25–9). Act I, scene 1, where Malevole greets each member of the court in turn and makes scathing comments on their appearances and morals, is, with the exception of a few bits of dialogue, in the exact pattern of formal verse satire where the satirist stands in a crowded place and describes the passersby. Finally, Pietro describes Malevole in terms which specifically identify him as the traditional satirist:

> This Malevole is one of the most prodigious affections that ever conversed with nature: a man, or rather a monster; more discontent than Lucifer when he was thrust out of the presence. His appetite is unsatiable as the grave; as far from any content as from heaven: his highest delight is to procure others vexation, and therein he thinks he truly serves heaven; for 'tis his position, whosoever in this earth can be contented is a slave and damned; therefore does he afflict all in that to which they are most affected. The elements struggle within him; his own soul is at variance within herself; his speech is halter-worthy at all hours. . . . See, he comes. Now shall you hear the extremity of a malcontent: he is as free as air; he blows over every man.
>
> (I.1.26–42)

Malevole never lets an opportunity pass to anatomize and flay any villain or fool he sees, and his railing now has an added function: it not only opens up moral infection but becomes the instrument which Altofronto uses to regain his dukedom. The two functions of satirist and intriguer are neatly combined in the following speech in which Malevole tells Pietro that his Duchess is having an affair with Mendoza, the scheming Machiavel of the play:

> PIETRO. Death and damnation!
> MAL. Lightning and thunder!
> PIETRO. Vengeance and torture!
> MAL. Catso!
> PIETRO. O, revenge!
> MAL. Nay, to select among ten thousand fairs
>   A lady far inferior to the most,
>   In fair proportion both of limb and soul;

> To meet her spirit in a nimble kiss,
> Distilling panting ardour to her heart;
> True to her sheets, nay, diets strong his blood,
> To give her height of hymeneal sweets,—
> PIETRO. O God!
> MAL. Whilst she lisps, and gives him some court-*quelquechose*,
> Made only to provoke, not satiate:
> And yet even then the thaw of her delight
> Flows from lewd heat of apprehension,
> Only from strange imagination's rankness,
> That forms the adulterer's presence in her soul,
> And makes her think she clips the foul knave's loins.
> PIETRO. Affliction to my blood's root!
>
> (I. 1. 144–68)

Malevole plays his part here with extreme shrewdness. He is on the surface playing the traditional role of the satirist who uncovers hidden vice without regard for personal danger. His subject is a favorite one with the satirist, the lewdness of woman, and in order to render vice ugly he describes it in exact and vivid terms. At the same time there is a certain lip-smacking interest in the elaboration on the details of the sexual act which suggests the usual prurience of the satirist. But, while the speech may be an excellent piece of satire, it is simultaneously a fine bit of intrigue. Every word is carefully chosen to inflame the imagination of the jealous husband, and his anger is carefully fed bit by bit to bring him to visualize the act itself. So thoroughly does Malevole control Pietro by the end of these lines that he can go on to a final piece of impudence in which he describes how Mendoza may beget a bastard son on the Duchess who may in the course of time marry an acknowledged child of Mendoza. Pietro is properly shocked and exclaims "Hideous imagination!" But then Malevole thoroughly bewilders him by proceeding to show that adultery, though a terrible sin, is not so bad as simony! The satirist is playing with his victim, and the results are all he could desire. Pietro breaks with Mendoza. Mendoza soon recovers, however, and Malevole uses the same technique of simultaneously satirizing and setting the villains at odds again, and encourages Mendoza to murder Pietro. In this way satire becomes a potent political weapon, and Malevole describes his technique in this way:

> Discord to malcontents is very manna:
> When the ranks are burst, then scuffle, Altofront.
>
> (I. 1. 250–1)

Malevole's efforts are successful, and the play ends with the overthrow of Mendoza, the banishment of the fools, and Malevole's restoration to power as Altofronto. Pietro and Aurelia, the usurpers, are brought through Malevole's satire to recognition of what their lives have been, and when Malevole effects the cure by telling Pietro bitter, harsh truths, he employs the medical imagery of the satirist and justifies his methods with the conventional explanation:

> PIETRO. Thou pinchest too deep; art too keen upon me.
> MAL. Tut, a pitiful surgeon makes a dangerous sore: I'll
>   tent thee to the ground. Thinkest I'll sustain
>   myself by flattering thee, because thou art a
>   prince? I had rather follow a drunkard, and live
>   by licking up his vomit, than by servile flattery.
>
> (IV.2.93–99)

The Malcontent is filled with satiric speeches and incidents of the kind discussed above, and Marston lavished more attention on satiric utterances and situations here than in any of his other plays. We might conclude then, as many have, that the play is merely a vehicle for popular satirical rant and lurid scenes of debauchery in an Italian palace, and that the disguise of Altofronto as Malevole is no more than a successful way of coupling an exciting intrigue pattern with a large amount of railing. While *The Malcontent* is certainly this, it is something more as well. We can best understand its additional dimensions by exploring the relationship between the disguise and the character, Malevole and Altofronto.

Altofronto was originally a Duke of a most free and open nature. He describes his former state in this manner:

> Behold forever-banish'd Altofront,
> This Genoa's last year's duke. O truly noble!
> I wanted those old instruments of state,
> Dissemblance and suspect: I could not time it, Celso;
> My throne stood like a point midst of a circle,
> To all of equal nearness; bore with none;
> Rein'd all alike; so slept in fearless virtue,
> Suspectless, too suspectless.
>
> (I.1.219–26)

Like Timon, Altofronto once idealized man, and traces of this attitude linger in his malcontent speeches. For example, in speaking of the evil of Pietro's Duchess, Aurelia, Malevole argues that a man makes a woman "commandress of a better essence / Than is the gorgeous world, even of a man." Disillusionment overtook him however, when Pietro, Aurelia, and Mendoza banded together with the citizenry, "Still lickorous of untried novelties," and overthrew and banished him. His Duchess, Maria, was imprisoned, and the court became a nest of Machiavellian intrigues for power, sexual corruption, and plain idiocy, where villain and fool strove only to gratify their lusts. To say that "it became" this is not quite correct, for since the characters of the play were the courtiers during Altofronto's reign as well, and the citizenry he ruled and the mob which overthrew him were one and the same, the implication is that the state of Genoa and the world which it mirrors, were always the same. What has changed is Altofronto's point of view. He now sees the palace and city as a banished Duke who has been treated to a full view of human depravity. So Altofronto becomes Malevole.

Malevole is not only a disguise assumed for the political purpose of cleansing the state, but a facet of Altofronto's character as well. He, like other satirists and other men, has been disenchanted: having thought man a god and justice the rule of the world, he has discovered that Fortune and chance play a large part in human affairs, that men follow their selfish desires rather than right, and that virtue can be defeated by cunning. When Altofronto speaks in his own person to those few who know him, or in an aside, he reflects on the world's depravity in deeply pessimistic but restrained terms:

> How smooth to him that is in state of grace,
> How servile is the rugged'st courtier's face!
> What profit, nay, what nature would keep down,
> Are heav'd to them are minions to a crown.
> Envious ambition never sates his thirst,
> Till sucking all, he swells and swells, and burst.
>
> (I.1.288–93)

But in the role of Malevole the satirist, Altofronto gives full and violent expression to the despair and loathing of man which he feels because of his misfortunes. He can go the extreme of declaring all life to be nothing but corruption and rottenness:

> Think this:—this earth is the only grave and Golgotha wherein all things that live must rot; 'tis but the draught wherein the heavenly bodies discharge their corruption; the very muck-hill on which the sublunary orbs cast their excrements: man is the slime of this dung-pit, and princes are the governors of these men.
>
> (IV.2.141–7)

Or, using the license of the satirist, he can abandon all restraint in dealing with the fools, as he does in this greeting of the white-haired rake Bilioso: "And how does my old muckhill, overspread with fresh snow? thou half a man, half a goat, all a beast! how does thy young wife, old huddle?" (I.1.76–9).

But the satirist's view of the world and his reaction to it are not allowed to stand unchallenged. Malevole's "scuffling" methods do bring about the overthrow of the usurpers, and his savage descriptions of the fools and villains are accurate, but they are shown to be excessive. By the end of the play he has "cured" Pietro and Aurelia, and he discovers that no enticements can force his own imprisoned wife, Maria, to yield to Mendoza, who is now Duke. Maquerelle, the old bawd who has accompanied Malevole to tempt Maria, expresses a view of womankind to which he would have acquiesced at the beginning of the play, "Why, are ye ignorant that 'tis said a squeamish affected niceness is natural to women, and that the excuse of their yielding is only, forsooth, the difficulty obtaining? You must put her to't: women are flax, and will fire in a moment" (v.2.144–8). But Maria's steadfastness has convinced Malevole that though some women are bad, all are not depraved:

> now I see,
> Sooner earth's fire heaven itself shall waste,
> Than all with heat can melt a mind that's chaste.
> (v.2.155–7)

Under the impact of repeated demonstrations of virtue he arrives slowly at a more balanced view of the world. The process continues, and when he finds out that "the castle's captain stands for me, the people pray for me," he can add, "and the great leader of the just stands for me" (v.2.281–3). In the concluding scene he sums up the transition he has undergone:

> O, I have seen strange accidents of state!
> The flatterer, like the ivy, clip the oak,
> And waste it to the heart; lust so confirm'd,
> That the black act of sin itself not sham'd
> To be term'd courtship.
> O, they that are as great as be their sins,
> Let them remember that th' inconstant people
> Love many princes merely for their faces
> And outward shows; and they do covet more

To have a sight of these than of their virtues.
Yet thus much let the great ones still conceive,
When they observe not heaven's impos'd conditions,
They are no kings, but forfeit their commissions.

(v.3.180–93)

The speech sums up the progress of the satirist who happens in this case also to be a Duke. Having looked at the world and found it dirt rather than fire, he falls into an extreme pessimism which finds relief in railing. But having seen evidence of virtue in a few, he returns to belief in the ultimate necessity of moral conduct, with the qualifying knowledge, however, that most men are base. The response of the satirist to the world's evils is clearly shown to be an exaggerated view, and here we see in another way that the satirist was not conceived of by Marston as an absolute extension of his own personality, but as a creature with an overly intense and unwarranted reaction to what is, nevertheless, very real and powerful evil.

ALVIN B. KERNAN

Tragical Satire in The Dutchess of Malfi

In the "satiric tragedies" we have looked at, the scene has always been more complex than it is in Juvenalian formal satire. Human nature has been sufficiently ambiguous, or there have been enough good men, or the world itself has shown enough evidence of a moral tendency, to challenge the satirist's simplified image of the human scene. But in *The Duchess of Malfi* (1613) the almost totally depraved and decaying world which the satirist postulates is brought to life in the ducal palace at Amalfi and in the episcopal palace at Milan. The Duchess and Antonio are surrounded by men and women whose lives are no more than a struggle for power, for gold, for satisfaction of lust. The metaphors which the satirist traditionally uses to describe the filthiness and idiocy of mankind now become literal realities before our eyes. Ferdinand stalking the Duchess in her chambers is more wolf than man, and he contracts lycanthropia before the play is ended and becomes a wolf in all but outward form. Julia demanding immediate sexual satisfaction from Bosola is no longer woman but a rutting bitch. The images of insanity which the satirist uses as metaphors for man's lack of reason are translated here to the dance of the madmen, the frenzies of Ferdinand, and the mad vision of the Cardinal. Disease is everywhere, and the rotting flesh and physical functions which so fascinate the satirist pervade the play. Even the Duchess cannot escape carnal involvement and the continuing process of corruption in which all life is caught up:

> our Duchesse
> Is sick a dayes, she puykes, her stomacke seethes,

From *The Cankered Muse.* © 1959 by Yale University Press. Originally entitled "Tragical Satire."

> The fins of her eie-lids looke most teeming blew,
> She waines i'th' cheeke, and waxes fat i'th' flanke.
>
> (II. 1.65–8)

This world is the natural habitat of the satirist, and Webster provides one, Bosola, who is a textbook model. He has every peculiarity of the satiric character, every trick of speech, every trait which had become traditional in the preceding years. Here, very near the end of the satirist's appearance in the theater, we find the "ideal" Elizabethan satirist, the pure satyr, and it will be worthwhile to catalogue his traits before going on to see what use Webster made of him in his tragic scheme.

"Sometimes the Divell doth preach," says Bosola, when in one of those flickering moments of revelation the satirist is prone to, he, like Kinsayder commenting on his "squint-eyed sight," recognizes his own twisted nature while attempting to justify his railing at the world's deformities. But ordinarily Bosola keeps such knowledge to himself, or forgets it, and attempts to keep to the world the face which the satirist traditionally claims to be the true image of his character, the face of an honest, fearless, straightforward man who calls "a spade a spade" because his moral uprightness and zeal for truth will not allow him to flatter and pretend that villainy is virtue. "Let me be simply honest," he cries; advises his Duchess when she appears to be angry with Antonio that this alone was "an honest states-man to a Prince" among a rout of parasites and rogues; and still playing the part of the honest counsellor tells the savagely dangerous Ferdinand, who has boasted of his unfathomable policy, "You are your owne Chronicle too much: and grosly flatter your selfe." On the world at large Bosola rails with true satiric disgust and with equally true satiric facility for finding the vivid phrase and the repellent metaphor. The first scene of Act II provides a good example of his railing. Here he attacks, in what he calls his "rough-caste phrase," a number of standard targets: the courtier, the judge, women and their painting. His description of a woman's cosmetic closet is in the old style: "One would suspect it for a shop of witch-craft, to finde in it the fat of Serpents; spawne of Snakes, Jewes Spittle, and their yong children['s] ordures—and all these for the face: I would sooner eate a dead pidgeon, taken from the soles of the feete of one sicke of the plague, then kisse one of you fasting . . . I do wonder you doe not loath yourselves" (lines 37–45). Aware that he is putting on a first-rate performance, Bosola proudly advises his auditors, "observe my meditation now," and turns from attacking specific follies to a rousing general denunciation of the human animal:

> What thing is in this outward forme of man
> To be belov'd? we account it ominous,
> If Nature doe produce a Colt, or Lambe,
> A Fawne, or Goate, in any limbe resembling
> A Man; and flye from't as a prodegy.
> Man stands amaz'd to see his deformity,
> In any other Creature but himselfe.
> But in our owne flesh, though we beare diseases
> Which have their true names onely tane from beasts,
> As the most ulcerous Woolfe, and swinish Meazeall;
> Though we are eaten up of lice, and wormes,
> And though continually we beare about us
> A rotten and dead body, we delight
> To hide it in rich tissew.
>
> (lines 47–60)

All of the satirist's rhetorical tricks, his typical language and imagery, and his attitudes are in these lines, and this is but one of the many star performances which Bosola provides.

While Bosola is aware from time to time of his own unpleasant and twisted nature, on the whole he is enchanted by his own words and deceives himself into believing that he is the Tamburlaine of Vice acting from the purest motives. For example, he discovers that the Duchess has secretly had a child, and callously informs on her, for profit, to her mad brothers. This act is the basest kind of betrayal, but Bosola exultantly presents it as a praiseworthy example of the satirist's heroic quest for hidden sin, and smugly characterizes the Duchess' "failing" in a sententious manner:

> *Though Lust doe masque in ne{'e}r so strange disguise,*
> *She's oft found witty, but is never wise.*
>
> (II.392–3)

The other characters of the play, however, are not taken in by Bosola's mask of honest piety; they understand him as we have, with the author's help, understood other satirists. Their comments seek out the traditional ambiguities of the character, find the tensions, and assign other motives to the railing than saeva indignatio. Antonio observes that Bosola's

> rayling
> Is not for simple love of Piety:
> Indeede he rayles at those things which he wants,

> Would be as leacherous, covetous, or proud,
> Bloody, or envious, as any man,
> If he had meanes to be so.
>
> (I.1.24–9)

Envy, which is mentioned several times, is, however, only one of the usual complex of twisted motives attributed to Bosola. His "old garbe of melencholly" is spoken of by Ferdinand, and Antonio fears that Bosola's "foul mellancholly will poyson all his goodnesse." His diseased state of mind compounded of envy and melancholy is thought to arise from two conventional sources: lack of suitable employment and too curious study as a young man. "Want of action," Antonio tells us with reference to Bosola,

> Breeds all blacke male-contents, and their close rearing
> (Like mothers in cloath) doe hurt for want of wearing.
>
> (I.1.82–3)

At Padua Bosola was as much "a fantasticall scholler" as Chrisoganus, Lampatho Doria, and similar pedants,

> who studdy to know how many knots
> Was in *Hercules* club, of what colour *Achilles* beard was,
> Or whether Hector were not troubled with the tooth-ach—
> He hath studied himselfe halfe bleare-ei'd, to know
> The true semitry of *Caesars* nose by a shooing-horne.
>
> (III.3.51–6)

And all this he did, Delio explains, not for love of learning but "to gaine the name of a speculative man."

But melancholy, envy, lack of employment, and fantastic studies are in themselves fairly conventional explanations for the satiric character. Bosola, like other satirists, has darker and more twisted forces at work in the deeps of his character which appear only obliquely in his language and actions, and are glimpsed by the other characters only in moments of crisis. The Duchess sees him truly for an instant when he is berating Antonio in a pious fashion and wishes she could "beat that counterfeit face, into thy other" (III.5.142), but she breaks off without describing the darkness into which she has looked. Antonio too perceives that beneath the mask of "Let me be simply honest" Bosola has a monstrous pride, is "puff'd up with . . . preferment" (II.1.88), and tells him bluntly, "I do understand your inside." And at the conclusion of the play when death has washed away all disguises, one of the courtiers characterizes the dying Bosola as "Thou wretched thing of blood" (v.5.116). These brief lines are no more than half-formed insights into Bosola's characteristic satiric pride, his loathing of man and his works, his psychotic hatred of the flesh which is mixed with fascination, his sick concentration on disease and the bodily processes, and his sadistic joy in torturing others. All of these qualities float to the surface in his language and find partial expression in his delight in tormenting his victims, particularly the Duchess who in her purity and determination to remain "human" resists his persistent attempts to involve her in the general madness, bestiality, and decay of flesh which he believes to be the normal state of the world. Although a modern psychiatrist would not be completely satisfied with his explanation, Webster provides a source for Bosola's perverted nature. He has been betrayed and brutalized by the world. At some time in the past he has committed a murder for the Cardinal, who then abandoned him. As a result Bosola was sentenced to the bestial life of a galley slave. His only comment on the experience is the laconic "for two yeares together, I wore two Towells in stead of a shirt," but he has been marked. He has seen the world from the under side, and his life of brutality, treachery, and disappointment has permanently warped a character that was none too straight in the beginning, for he had been the Cardinal's bravo before being chained to a galley bench.

Bosola combines in himself, and gives full expression to, all the peculiarities of the Elizabethan satyr, but Webster does not employ him in a conventional manner. The other dramatic satirists no matter how tainted their natures and how suspect their motives have not willingly and actively engaged in evil, though the end effect of their railing may be further to infect an already sick world. But Bosola, who is an intriguer like Malevole, becomes the villain of the play by selling his talents to Ferdinand and the Cardinal, and knowingly using his railing to do their business and ultimately line his own pockets. His intrigues, which result in the exposure of the secret marriage of the Duchess and Antonio and put them in the power of her mad "Aragonian" brothers, need no recounting, and one example will show the way he works. After the Duchess has been captured, Ferdinand wants to drive her insane, so he and Bosola arrange a series of macabre scenes—each of which is an emblem of the play as a whole—in which Bosola appears disguised as a tomb-maker. Ironically, the intended disguise reveals his true nature which is concealed by his normal "face." Satire is Bosola's weapon, and he attempts with all the satirist's rhetorical skill to force on the Duchess the extreme satiric sense of life, to make her see herself and the world through his eyes as no more than slimy bestiality:

Thou art a box of worme-seede, at best, but a salvatory of greene mummey: what's this flesh? a little cruded milke, phantasticall

puffe-paste: our bodies are weaker then those paper prisons boyes
use to keepe flies in: more contemptible: since ours is to preserve
earth-wormes: didst thou ever see a Larke in a cage? such is the
soule in the body: this world is like her little turfe of grasse, and
the Heaven ore our heades, like her looking glasse, onely gives
us a miserable knowledge of the small compasse of our prison.

(IV.2.123–31)

Even in this fantastic scene Bosola does not abandon his sanctimoniousness,
but despite the reference to the soul and the obvious relation of the speech
to the tradition of Christian asceticism, the emphasis here is on despair, and
it is on this aspect of the satiric character that Webster capitalized in con-
structing his play.

Bosola has despaired of man and of honesty at the beginning of *The
Duchess of Malfi*. The world is no more than a hospital "where this mans
head lies at that mans foote, and so lower, and lower." Since every man is
an arrant knave, why not become a flattering pander and "hang on the eares"
of the great "like a horse-leach" until full of blood, and "then drop offe?"
The despair inherent in the satiric sense of life, not saeva indignatio, thus
becomes Bosola's principal motive, although the mask of righteous indignation is still worn and the pretense of working a cure is maintained.

But *The Duchess of Malfi* is not finally a satiric play existing only as a
vehicle for Bosola and his criticisms of humanity. The satiric scene may have
become the dramatic scene, but there remains in Webster's scheme the
possibility of tragic dignity for individuals caught in a mad and bestial
world. The Duchess cannot deny or conquer in any material sense the evil
which destroys her family and her body, but she can refuse to submit to it,
to become a Bosola herself, and she can maintain simply that she is "Duchesse
of *Malfy* still." And the "Duchesse of Malfy" is not only a nobly born
woman, but, as language and scenes reveal, the very spirit of love, life, joy,
and society. Bosola stands in direct contrast to the Duchess. He too has felt
the dark, blasting power of hatred and unchained individualism, the killing
forces embodied in Ferdinand and the Cardinal. But his reaction has been
despair, cynicism, and railing. In this way the tragic reaction to an undisputedly mad world is counterpointed with a satiric reaction, and the sinister
aspects of the latter are underscored by allowing the satirist to follow his
baser instincts and become the mere creature of those forces which have
destroyed him once and bring him at last to his confused and miserable
death, which contrasts so strongly with the quiet and dignified manner in
which the Duchess faces her death at the hands of the strangler.

The conflict between the tragic and satiric attitudes is the ground of the play, and it is manifested not only outwardly in the struggle between the Duchess and Bosola, but inwardly in the soul of the satirist. His conflict is neither so intricate nor so deep as Hamlet's, but somewhat like Hamlet, Bosola combines in himself a cynical acceptance of the vicious world and a nagging conscience which demands that he resist in some way what he feels to be wrong. Acceptance is his way for the most part. His acquiescence with Ferdinand's plan to use him as a spy, "I am your creature," is as simple and straightforward as the tragic statement, "I am the Duchesse of *Malfy* still." But when he is paid off with the job of master of the stables he can cynically note that his corruption "grew out of horse doong." After the death of the Duchess, in which he has been chief agent, Bosola's conscience urges him even more strongly, and his attempts to cope with it while still keeping his feet on the "slippery yce-pavements" of the court result in the sudden reversals of his character which have long troubled critics. His final decision to kill the Cardinal remains appropriately ambiguous, springing partly from a desire to help Antonio and partly from a desire to save himself from the vicious Cardinal, who after employing him to kill Antonio has now decided to be rid of his agent. In the confused and bloody melee of the concluding scene Bosola kills Antonio *by mistake* and then destroys Ferdinand and the Cardinal at the cost of his own life. The ending is a typical blood-revenge conclusion emblematic of the savage and disordered life of the principals, and Bosola's state of mind at this point is particularly interesting since it is the final judgment of the Jacobean theater on the satirist and the satiric sense of life. Webster having made his point through Bosola's activities that satire is essentially a negative and selfish approach to an undisputedly rotten world, an approach which denies man's "owne good nature," attempts in Bosola's last speeches to show the confusion and darkness of the satiric mind. Bosola ends with a platitudinous warning to mankind,

> Let worthy minds nere stagger in distrust
> To suffer death, or shame, for what is just.
> (v.5.127–8)

But his language suggests that he himself is lost in a world and in a death which he has not understood. He killed, he tells us, "in a mist" and "unwittingly," and speaks of the world as "gloomy," "a shadow," and a "deepe pit of darkenesse." His own life, and those of the other villains, leaves no mark on the world but is like "dead wals, or vaulted graves, / That ruin'd, yeildes no eccho." He can describe his dying as no more than holding his "weary soule" in his teeth, and his only cause for exultation is that he has accomplished the destruction of the Cardinal. The emptiness and sterility of the satirist's way is made clear even in this, the most pessimistic Jacobean play, and Webster's rejection of the extreme satiric view of the world is in keeping with the general Elizabethan and Jacobean attitude.

About 1615 the satyr satirist in his purest form disappeared from the theater. There remained, of course, characters, usually villains, who shared the satirist's despairing view of the world and who occasionally described human depravity in tones reminiscent of the satirists of Nashe, Marston, and Hall. Satiric drama continued to flourish in the hands of Jonson, Middleton, and Massinger, but it now was Menippean in form, and the satiric end of scourging the fools was achieved by allowing them to reveal their fundamental ridiculousness in their own speeches and actions. But the old satiric commentator, guilty himself of all the sins he attacks, torn by psychic disorders, and ready in an instant either to describe some particular fool in foul but striking terms or deliver a gorgeous and elaborate tirade on the dirtiness of mankind and the present Age of Iron, was no longer employed by the dramatists. In a theater where sensational characters came and went the satirist had no doubt become passé by this time—he had held the stage for fifteen years or more—but the real reason for his disappearance must be sought outside the fickle tastes of the audience.

G. WILSON KNIGHT

The Duchess of Malfi

I have often written of the Shakespearian play as "set spatially as well as temporally" in the mind, analyzing its area of imagistic and symbolic suggestion. *The Duchess of Malfi* shows an even thicker clustering of such impressions than Shakespeare. A brake is applied to the action by it, as with the stickiness of Hardy's prose, like a wet ploughed field, organically retarding the clogged and fettered progress of his unhappy people. Numerous, often conflicting, colours interthread Shakespeare's carpets: in *The Duchess of Malfi*, though there are certain tableaux of colour, the toning of thought and image is more level: black, brown, grey, a spurt of flame occasionally, but, for the rest, hardly a purple.

Many ordinary and rather uninteresting man-made objects are mentioned, as a group nearly, and yet not precisely, fitted by the term "mechanical." These contribute to the dun tonings generally: such as "touch-wood," "rough-cast," "spectacles," "shoeing-horn," "glass-house," a "dirty stirrup riveted," a "false key," a "rusty watch," a "heavy lump of lead," breasts "hoop'd with adamant," "three fair medals cast in one figure." The work of artisans is often suggested, sometimes their trades named: "tradesmen," "rope-maker," "soap-boiler," "picture-maker," a "curious artist" taking a watch to pieces in order to mend it, a "curious master" in the "quality" of making wax figures, a "strong-thigh'd bargeman," the "galley-slave" at his oar. Often we touch the specifically scientific or mechanical: that "fantastic glass made by Galileo," safety "runs upon engenous wheels," death's door goes on "strange geometrical hinges." "Mathematics," "geometry," "corasive," "perspective," "curious engine" come in naturally. Here is a more

From *The Malahat Review* 4 (October 1967). © 1967 by *The Malahat Review*.

extended example: "I would have a mathematical instrument made for her face, that she might not laugh out of compass"; or

> When Fortune's wheel is over-charg'd with princes,
> The weight makes it move swift.
>
> (III, v, 112)

An age-old image given a more scientific twist. Webster, like many seventeenth-century poets, often uses the mathematical, geometrical, or scientific drive in an abstract judgment: "as if he was ballass'd with quicksilver" is typical. The list is unShakespearian in its comparative emphasis and is only slightly foreshadowed in Marlowe. It reflects town rather than country life; is homely, realistic, and a little depressing. Sometimes there is a predominant cast of cynicism, often something of a hard, dry, humour.

Nor is war here romantic: rather its modern engines come in for unpicturesque stress; no flashing shields of knightly armour. There is talk of "great battles," "towns of garrison," "a new fortification," a "fort-bridge." Servants speak of a switzer "with a pistol in his great cod-piece," the "moulds" of whose buttons were "leaden bullets"; "paper bullets" are used in the Shakespearian sense of "witticisms"; the Duchess images herself "shot to death with pearls"; Bosola compares the Cardinal and Ferdinand to "two chain'd bullets." Fire may be suggested: "a hollow bullet filled with unquenchable wild-fire." Pistols play a part in the action. Impressions of gunpowder and cannon occur. Though Count Malateste "has worn gun-powder in his hollow tooth for the tooth-ache," he is afraid the smell of gun-powder will spoil the perfume of his mistress's scarf. There is a powdery, sulphurous smell over the play:

> PESCARA: The Lord Ferdinand laughs.
> DELIO: Like a deadly cannon
> That lightens ere it smokes.
>
> (III, iii, 65)

The Duchess imagines herself as standing on a mine about to blow up; and again

> O misery: like a rusty o'ercharg'd cannon
> Shall I never fly in pieces?
>
> (III, v, 121)

A good instance of the unromantic yet sulphurous threat of this play's impressions. The action moves in a world of "touch-holes" and "fire-locks," there is a background of human enmity and smouldering danger. It is part of Webster's stock-in-trade: you get as much, or more, in *The White Devil*. Talk of war is frequent: some of the chief persons are, or have been, at the wars; and at a central point, the Cardinal, chief villain of the piece, is installed as a soldier. Renaissance war here is realistic, mechanical and sulphurous, blending with other hell-tonings to be observed later: there is little or none of Shakespeare's "pride, pomp and circumstance of glorious war."

From this realistic and often drab toning certain references to rich stones unhappily and ineffectually shine out. There is satire on gold as in the Apothecary scene of *Romeo and Juliet*. The Duchess dreams of the diamonds on her coronet of state being changed to pearls, forecasting tears. Riches are thus, in one way or another, toned evilly as when Julia talks of "stealing a diamond." They are, as it were, smothered by the palling smoke and muffled thunder of the impregnating condemnation that constricts our world. Asked by Bosola if the cords of execution do not terrify, the Duchess answers:

> What would it pleasure me, to have my throat cut
> With diamonds? or to be smothered
> With cassia? or to be shot to death with pearls?
>   (IV, ii, 222)

The ultimate worthlessness of riches is intrinsic to the thought: such references, in their contexts, intensify the gloom.

I pass from such man-warm objects or implements to observe nature references, seeing how they blend in with our other impressions. There are, as in *King Lear*, many animals, usually unpicturesque. Often they are felt in a semi-human way: the "political dormouse," "irregular crab," "abortive hedge-hog," "impudent snake," "old fox," "tame elephant." We have flatterers compared to "lice," foxes carrying fire among crops, servants as "vipers," children as "young wolves." Suffering is often in some fashion suggested: a "bear in a ring," a leveret dying "without resistance," a mouse uncomfortably housed "in a cat's ear" (a typical macabre stroke of humour), English mastiffs grown fierce with being tied up, a bird's wings clipped, birds entrapped, a spider's "black web." Subtle torture is in this:

> the bee
> When he hath shot his sting into your hand
> May then play with your eye-lid.
>   (IV, i, 92)

There is mad Ferdinand's self-inflicted penance of driving "six snails" before him to Moscow as a trial of patience, a ludicrous touch recalling Lear's madness. Most of the animals are ugly or fearsome either directly or through superstitious associations: the mule, the mole, "dogs and monkeys," para-queto, scorpions, porcupines, crows, jackdaws, starlings, magpies, cater-pillars, glow-worms, worms (especially in association with death), wolves and owls (both frequent). A man lifts his nose like "a foul porpoise before a storm." The madmen's dirge concerns "ravens, screech-owls, bulls and bears." The frequent man-animal association in varied guise is important. "This mole does undermine me" is pure Webster. In a strange speech at II, i, 47–60 animals are used to suggest disease ("the most ulcerous wolf and swinish meazle") and harmless quiet beasts are mentioned in contrast to human "deformity." Ferdinand ends up digging graves, a man's leg on his shoulder, howls and says he is a wolf. Aptly in such a play where man's nature is so ruthless the chief villain descends to this wolvish horror. *King Lear* is often suggested, and Swift continually forecast. . . .

Once the "spheres" are mentioned, but the universal nature is mostly shut out, dimmed by pressing agonies, distorted by wolvish actions, the best smeared and overlaid by human and pessimistic thinking and super-stition. There are more nature references of the *Euphues* sort used with a sense of legendary belief: such as the cedar tree made firm by shaking; or we may have, once, reminiscence of Greek myth, persons transformed to pleasant natural objects. These have only a secondary, literary reality, similar to the salamanders, basilisks, and cockatrices elsewhere. "I have this night digged up a mandrake" is a good Websterian scene-opening. But never, or seldom, is nature directly seen or felt in and for itself as a preliminary to its use for a more general poetic purpose. Our animals are mostly thick-coated with superstition, or used mainly, more evidently than in Shakespeare, as man-comparisons. They have less rights on their own as animals; that is not normally relevant here. Much of Webster's impressionism is rooted in medieval pseudo-science. Always, as it were, to quote Tennyson's *In Memoriam*, a "web is woven across the sky" of direct sight. Exact analysis and weighing of his imagistic quality leads to this important result: Webster's world is a mind-world; his nature, a studied nature; his horrors, mind-horrors, saturated in conventional superstition. The saturation is part of the horror. Each touch is pondered and weighty, the superstition heavy with accumulated centuries of fear.

Astrology plays an important part. There is talk about "setting a figure for the nativity" of the Duchess' child. Bosola reads out in detail the cal-culations: "The lord of the first house, being combust in the ascendant, signifies short life . . . " and so on. Elsewhere, told that some hold that all things are written in the stars, Bosola characteristically replies: "Yes, if we could find spectacles to read them." We hear of a soldier who fights by the

almanack shunning "critical" days. Stars are naturally here impregnated with
such pseudo-scientific superstitions, their native glory unfelt:

> We are merely the stars tennis-balls, strook and bandied
> Which way please them.
>
> (V, iv, 63)

The air is heavy with superstition. Sometimes it is criticized, as when
Ferdinand wonders if love-potions are more than the fraud of mountebanks,
or the Duchess calls Cariola a "superstitious fool" for disliking the irreverence
of a pretended pilgrimage. But there is too the Duchess's dream of pearls
and Antonio's grim interpretation. Superstition is felt powerfully, whatever
is said. Here is the quality distilled:

> How superstitiously we mind our evils!
> The throwing down salt, or crossing of a hare;
> Bleeding at nose, the stumbling of a horse,
> Or singing of a cricket, are of power
> To daunt whole man in us.
>
> (II, ii, 80)

How quiet, yet how ominously weighted the simple, limping, accents fall:
this is a philosophic, inactive world, paralyzed by fears of all sorts. Witches
are often referred to. They give the Devil suck, convey man through the air
on whirl-winds, whisper charms in a "deformed" silence, stick needles into
wax figures: the normal and traditional beliefs.

An orthodox belief in Hell is therefore natural. All the chief persons
express a dim faith in an after-existence, though the phrases are mostly
cheerless. Hell-tonings are to be expected. Fire is here evil. I have already
noticed the cannon-references. There is violent fire observed in Ferdinand's
villainous eye; the Cardinal, talking to Bosola, considers their evil scheme
as a fire well-burning; Ferdinand would have the Duchess and Antonio burned
in a stopped-up coal pit, so that their smoke might not rise to Heaven, or
wrapped in their own sheets saturated in "pitch or sulphur," then lighted.
Fire is evilly impregnated:

> I have this Cardinal in the forge already,
> Now I'll bring him to the hammer.
>
> (V, iv, 92)

Notice the mechanic work-shop suggestion: the whole play is something of
a devil's smithy. The world is a hell:

Th' heaven o'er my head seems made of molten brass,
The earth of flaming sulphur, yet I am not mad . . .
                                                    (IV, ii, 27)

The Cardinal at the end is puzzled concerning the "material fire" of Hell; and soon after sees a figure "armed with a rake," recalling Dante. Nearly all the fire-images are hellish, as the stars are threatening: fire or light as a cosmic and optimistic force is almost unknown. Hell and the Devil are on everyone's lips: "Those houses that are haunted are most still till the Devil be up." "Deep groans and terrible ghastly looks" are usual impressions. One of the few classical touches in this medieval horror, is that of Charon's boat conveying dead souls "o'er the dismall lake." And even the more sanctified religious colourings, outwardly Christian and orthodox, are likely to be fateful.

We hear of "Doom's-day," a "solemn vow," a "sacrament o' the church," etc. The Cardinal is a central figure; and the shrine of My Lady of Loretto an important scene, with the entrance of pilgrims. Ferdinand is met "behind St. Mark's church," come from digging up bodies in the graveyard. There is the echo-scene among ancient ruins of an abbey and talk of its long past, and the men buried there. Religion here often suggests an eternity of tomb-like death: traditional Christianity is as much a matter of death as Lyly's Hellenic piety of life. Often a dark religion is ranged against simple love. The Cardinal and the Duchess are the final human antagonists. Bosola suggests the Duchess be given "a penitential garment" with "beads and a prayer-book" for having married Antonio: the opposition is imaginatively explicit. She herself asks why she should be "cas'd up as a holy relic" since she has "youth and a little beauty": notice how the understatement of her claim reflects the stifling of the grimly religious gloom. And yet the religious tonings have their own sombre, grave-like magic. The person's words, their questions and plaintive half-worded hopes, linger wanderingly as about the vaults of some vast, ruined cathedral of a universe, echoing, self-answered, no more. Or maybe it is rather the "suburbs of hell" we are in—delightful phrase! Once a sweeter Christianity is shadowed: as when Bosola, told by the Duchess of her marriage, for love, to a simple steward, calls her bed a "fair seminary of peace," says how "unbenefic'd" scholars will pray for her, Turks and Moors turn Christian; a strange tangled but of course mainly hypocritical speech (III, 2, 324–341) associating Christianity with simple love. Even so, it is in its context ironic. Religion is usually a matter of wicked cardinals, stone ruins or tombs; or, if blessed, an otherworldly eternity:

> In the eternal church, sir,
> I do hope we shall not part thus.
> (III, v, 84)

Webster's ghostly phrase strikes like a chill and a doubt even when it would seem most to comfort.

It is a world of disease: no impression is more powerful than that of disease. Physicians and midwives, poisons and medicines, hospitals—medical terms of all sorts pile up amazingly from a close inspection. Here are some of the ailments: small-pox, leprosy, ague, apoplexy, frenzy, melancholy (considered as a physical ailment), palsy; and here some medicines (or poisons): a deadly honey-dew, "Balsamum," "desperate physic," poisoned apricots, poisoned pills, "possets to procure sleep," lemon pills, "lenitive poisons," a "lingering poison," "rhubarb" to purge "choler." We hear of a "sick man's urine," a "sick liver," "one in physic," galls overflowing livers, mad folk "from the common hospital," "broken sleeps." The plague is especially frequent: "one sick of the plague," "give out she died o' the plague," cities "plagued with plagues," plagues that "make lanes through largest families." Princes' images are made "as if they died of the toothache," death is a "mandragora" to make the Duchess sleep, Ferdinand suffers from a "very pestilent disease" called lycanthropia. Seeing Julia of whom he is tired the Cardinal remarks prettily, "Yond's my lingering consumption" and later makes her kiss a poisoned Bible. Pain, we are told, is removed by fear of worse, as tooth-ache by sight of the operating "barber." Wisdom is a "foul tetter" running over the body. Places at court are like beds at a "hospital," one man's head at another's foot. We hear how physicians applying horse-leeches to a swelling cut off their tails to led the blood run through. A great physician cured the Pope by making him laugh so that the "imposthume" broke. Childbirth is inverted to a sickness: the Duchess "is sick a days, she pukes, her stomach seethes . . . " Notice with what sickly cynicism or fatalism these impressions and the way they are used soak our play's texture. It positively drips with diseases. This is how people talk of anger:

> FERDINAND: Have not you My palsy?
> CARDINAL: Yes—I can be angry
>   Without this rupture—there is not in nature
>   A thing, that makes man so deform'd, so beastly,
>   As doth intemperate anger.
> (II, v, 71)

Webster seems to feel man as by nature deformed:

> Man stands amaz'd to see his deformity
> In any other creature but himself.
> But in our own flesh, though we bear diseases,
> Which have their true names only ta'en from beasts,
> As the most ulcerous wolf, and swinish meazle;
> Though we are eaten up of lice and worms,
> And though continually we bear about us
> A rotten and dead body, we delight
> To hide it in rich tissue.
>
> (II, i, 52)

A revealing, Swiftian, speech. Death and disease go hand in hand. Told by
Bosola he is come to make her tomb, the Duchess asks, "Dost thou perceive
me sick?" Almost her last words are that her little boy be given "some syrop
for his cold," a touch losing something of the pathos a less disease-ridden
context might give out; and she forgives her executioners since human actions
of cruelty are only bubbles on that vast sea of world-disease which the play
reveals: "the apoplexy, cathar, or cough o' the lungs would do as much as
they do." When someone says

> Come: I'll be out of this ague;
> For to live thus, is not indeed to live
>
> (V,iii, 59)

we tend to endorse the statement; and one of the last impressions to linger
is

> Pleasure of life, what is't? Only the good hours
> Of an ague . . .
>
> (V, iv, 78)

Life is a living death.

So the play is weighty with death. As the climax of the Duchess' murder approaches there is insistence on every detail. Bosola is come to make
her "tomb"; has with him a coffin, cords and bell; acts the part of the
fatal bellman. Webster depicts not a murder but a carefully explicated
dramatization of the hideous *quality* of death. Bosola, high priest of the
occasion, so often a voice to the play's movement, speaks the moral of it
all:

> Thou art a box of worm-seed, at best but a salvatory of green
> mummy. What's this flesh? A little curded milk, fantastical puff-

paste. Our bodies are weaker than those paper prisons boys use
to keep flies in: more contemptible: since ours is to preserve earth-
worms.

(IV, ii, 123)

Though he may talk of the soul in the body as a caged lark the stress is far
heavier on the body's death than the soul's life. Indeed, it scarcely exists,
the body-soul dualism being to a Renaissance poet a thought but not a lived
and felt actuality. Death here is a "general storm of terror." Men suffering
from lycanthropia "steal forth to churchyards in the dead of night and dig
dead bodies up." Asked to take up Julia's body Bosola remarks

I think I shall
Shortly grow the common bier for church-yards:

(V, ii, 344)

The Duchess and Bosola play with the idea of tombs, of what stuff will he
make hers?

> BOSOLA: Nay, resolve me first of what fashion?
> DUCHESS: Why do we grow fantastical in our death-bed?
>   Do we affect fashion in the grave?

(IV, ii, 150)

Tombs are usual: "And wherefore should you lay fair marble colours upon
your rotten purposes to me?" and "Think you your bosom will be a grave
dark and obscure enough for such a secret?" and—

> You have a pair of hearts are hollow graves
> Rotten, and rotting others.

(IV, ii, 345)

This all blends into images of ruin. The Duchess is like "some reverend
monument whose ruins even are pitied," a phrase strangely feeling the pathos
of the inanimate in decay. In his last speech Bosola says

> We are only like dead walls, or vaulted graves,
> That ruin'd, yields no eche.

(V, v, 121)

The whole tragic action of the play—indeed almost the play itself—is once
referred to as a "noble ruin." But best of all is the fine description earlier
of the "ruins of an ancient abbey" now, significantly, a "fortification":

I do love these ancient ruins.
We never tread upon them but we set
Our foot upon some reverend history.
And questionless, here in this open court
(Which now lies naked to the injuries
Of stormy weather), some men lie interr'd
Lov'd the Church so well, and gave so largely to it,
They thought it should have canopied their bones
Till Doom's-day. But all things have their end.
Churches and cities (which have diseases like to men)
Must have like death that we have.

                                                    (V, iii, 10)

Webster's impressionism feels the Renaissance as the ruins of a past age,
not the birth—and we can remember Webster's sickly view of birth—of a
new one. His poetry points consistently back, as Shakespeare's does not.
The Shakespearian phrase has an immediate sap in it that keeps it taut,
erect, whatever its explicit content; whereas Webster's limping rhythms only
add to the nerveless horror or pathos of his meaning. His death-horrors are
the traditional ones: graves, worms, mouldering flesh; ruins and decay. It is
an intellectual horror at certain sense-impressions, totally negative, and, in
its way, conventional, an inborn convention, that is, of the human mind in
general: it is not, necessarily, rational. Although orthodox tonings suit well
here—and the inevitability of the association is of almost terrifying significance—yet none of it is Christian in the Gospel sense: "Let the dead bury
their dead." The Gospel feeling for immediate and forward-thrusting life is
a positive for which we must go to Shakespeare or the Hellenists, Lyly,
Elizabethan lyric and the Romantics; or, as I shall show, certain aspects of
Webster's human understanding as distinguished from his close net of sickly-
traditional impressions, sweet only with the sweetness of death.

There is no warmth of human joy here; instead, a freezing cold:

'Tis even like him that in a winter night
Takes a long slumber o'er a dying fire
As loth to part from it: yet parts thence as cold
As when he first sat down.

                                                    (III, ii, 237)

A lovely instance of the recurrent Websterian movement: a few lines succeeded by a limping, half-line, close. Cold dominates, in association with
negations, in opposition to love; as when Ferdinand's tears of pity were
"frozen up" by his evil nature whilst the Duchess lived, or the single life is

compared to Anaxarete, "frozen into marble." "I'll not freeze i' the business"
is a more general, obvious phrase; and so, too, this fine miniature:

> I must look to my footing;
> In such slippery ice-pavements, men had need
> To be frost-nail'd well . . .
>
> (V, ii, 367)

But in both cold is hostile. There is a cold horror often. The very incidents
build it. Holding the dead hand (supposedly Antonio's) in the dark the
Duchess says: "You are very cold." Icy, corpse-like horror. Again, seeing
the supposed dead bodies of Antonio and his children, she would join the
frozen group:

> If they would bind me to that lifeless trunk
> And let me freeze to death.
>
> (IV, i, 79)

"A cold tomb-stone o'er his bones" is the most anyone here can wish for.
There are "anatomies" set by doctors "i' th' cold yonder in barber chirurgeon's
hall." Russia, to the writers of this period a word of wintry suggestion (we
may remember its use in *The Winter's Tale*), occurs three times. There is
mention of a "slave-born Russian"; there is Ferdinand's driving his team of
snails to Moscow; and the Duchess cursing

> those three smiling seasons of the year
> Into a Russian winter: nay, the world
> To its first chaos.
>
> (IV, i, 117)

Winter: chaos: death. A certain stillness freezes Webster's stage: it is paralyzed by a horror till horror itself shakes paralysis to a keener agony. Flames
give no warmth here: both its sulphurous and icy tonings derive from medieval, Dantesque, hells such as those in Claudio's fearful death-speech. We
"seem to sweat in ice and freeze in fire," says Bosola. "A cold sweat" is a
phrase occurring more than once. So the cold has nothing of Marlowe's Swiss-
holiday imagery of scintillating sun-flashing crystals. The play significantly
closes with the sun coming out to dispel the snow-step recollections of our
wintry horror. But during the action there is only cold of a corpse-like pallor,
a frozen horror, and thoughts of an eternity icy as the stony vaultings of a
ruin'd church. Here it is all summed up:

> that speech
> Came from a dying father: your kiss is colder
> Than I have seen an holy anchorite
> Give to a dead man's skull.
>
> (III, v, 102)

On the one side, human love; on the other, holiness, orthodox religious colourings, a skull, icy death. Again, the associations, and still more their compact and organically satisfying result, is of insistent significance.

For Webster's associative technique is of an unswerving precision. If a man stuffs up his ears here it is with black cotton-wool. His area of choice may be limited but the variations within that area are subtle, coherent, and organic. There is nothing like Marlowe's jarring imaginative inconsequences and arbitrary oppositions. Whatever Webster's references to artisans and mechanic trades or objects, there is no mechanical journey-man work in his artistic structure. *The Duchess of Malfi* has as perfect an organic life as anything in our literature, every tissue is in its place. And therefore it, finally, delivers negatively the exact message which Lyly delivers positively: their statements, necessarily, converge. His substance may be different, but his art obeys the same inevitable logic of associative law. Marlowe, whose *Faustus* presents a conflict of the erotic and the medieval, gives you neither in clarity; his work expresses neither, nor therefore their conflict, satisfactorily. But also there is always a close philosophy within Webster's imaginative precisions. We see how the newly human is impressionistically smothered by the traditional and medieval: by orthodox tonings of all sorts, age-old superstitions, mouldering ruins of the mind of man. And this blends into his harsh, bitter realism concerning the present: as though the past was now a revolting corpse; and the present merely a hideous, insentient, intruder, desecrating with its own disease the ruins of the past. In this world is set the action and its conflict; in this world the Duchess placed to champion the trust in humanity, especially woman, that beats in Lyly's Pandora and Shakespeare's Cleopatra.

II

To pass now to Webster's more specifically human exposition. I have noticed references to trades and artisans. What might be called middle-class professions come in for far more notice than in Shakespeare, the general effect tending to satire. Lawyers are not heavily attacked but legal terms occur in association with Antonio's stewardship. The law is associated with prisons and suitors, and called a "foul black cobweb," and we hear of a "lawyer's mule" and a Vicar going to law for a tithe-pig to "undo" his neighbours; though judge and jury and the ceremonial of a law-court once receive respectful notice. Besides the Vicar just noticed, ecclesiastical reference is varied and thick: the Cardinal as a pillar of the Church exists as a bitter comment. Astrology and physic are suggested continually and often critically. These more learned professions are those represented by the four speaking madmen, according to F. L. Lucas's identification, in the ghoulish mask. From which we see how close is the organic coherence of the whole. This masque is at the play's heart, summing or tying up many elsewhere dominant strands into a significant symbolism: the madmen are not just a means to torment the heroine but are themselves important. They indicate a world gone mad in study, recalling Swift's "projectors" at Lagado. There is the Astrologer drawing Doom's-day close with a "perspective"; the Lawyer and his vision of Hell, though I cannot see in his first remark a direct professional reference; the Priest and his parish amours, his talk of damnation, his play with "wenches" in the midst of "tombs," a significant opposition; and the Doctor whose making of a "soap-boiler" "costive" was his "masterpiece." Doctors are elsewhere satirized, especially in the ludicrous play between the over-confident Doctor and mad Ferdinand. Both come off poorly: "Are you out of your princely wits?" says the Doctor. The "forty urinals filled with rose-water," the "anatomies" in "barber-chirurgeon's hall" are satirically toned, and the Doctor is knocked down for his pains. All this points ahead to Swift and Shaw. Webster's scientific interest is all along clear from his imagery, but he does not seem very fond of scientists. Academic literary learning gets a lash. We hear of "fantastical" scholars who study to know

> how many knots
> Was in Hercules' club, of what colour Achilles' beard was,
> Or whether Hector were not troubled with the tooth-ache.
>
> (III, iii, 51)

—all to gain the reputation of a "speculative man." The satire touches that of certain passages in Pope's *Dunciad*. Webster's satiric by-products of his vast and properly non-satiric whole have often a modern application. . . .

These prevailing thoughts relate to the main human figures of our drama and the main conflict. Satire on place and supposed "honour" blends with the family pride of the Cardinal and Ferdinand, which is the originating spring of hostile and evil action. Love is opposed by a rotten social code. Her family resent the Duchess' marriage both, it is suggested, for greed of gold and because Antonio is a commoner. Their jealousy is a complex of antipathies. It is not a worn-out problem: there is, perhaps must be, an eternal opposition between the familial and the sexual, often taking the shape of social objection, and here in addition incurring an accusation of lust. The Duchess' love is smirched by unjust suggestions: to wed twice is "luxurious," a matter of "lustful pleasures," though "honour" in her husband might excuse it. It is all totally irrational, but not out of date. Hamlet himself was guilty of a similar nonsequitur. Antonio is called the Duchess' "lecher" to be shut in a cell such as "anchorites" put to "holier use": again observe the opposition. Bosola suggests the Duchess' "delicate skin" be tormented by a "penitential garment." The body is a "prison," "sin" is in man's "conception": can bodily pleasure be pure? The Duchess asks why marriage is forbidden her, ironically observing that she is starting "no new custom." Against her is her brothers' puritanical disgust, like that of Mr. Barrett in *The Barretts of Wimpole Street*. A false idealism based on greed and outward "place" gives birth to a perverted puritanism. Webster presents a crucial family condensation of the disease of the modern western world, aptly remarking how "kindred" commonly agree worse than strangers. Sex here is often crudely and puritanically phrased: courtezans, strumpets, whores, are often mentioned. The princely Cardinal himself, centre of the play's social structure, inconsistently keeps a mistress. It is all there, the usual insincerities, the usual desecrations. Secondary values crush primary ones, it is a decadent social and family system desecrating a wholesome love. In this diseased society a puritanical religion, greed for wealth, and social respectability are all ranged against the Duchess' choice.

Though the impressionism is so often medievalist and supernatural, the main persons themselves, as distinguished from any general attitude to society, are conceived with a Renaissance realism and insight. Webster is, in his own fashion, inside his persons. They are all individuals with a certain stage dignity, at least to start with, and a strange static sort of direction, pointing if not progressing. They are conceived, especially the three villains, with a Shakespearian sense of force, together with a certain warmth of sympathy. No one is wholly evil. The fiery and haughty Ferdinand repents after the Duchess' death. His eyes "dazzle"; he slinks off to hunt badgers by owl-light; and goes mad. There is nothing quite like Iago's perfect and baffling unity. These villains, as in the Cardinal's phantasma of a "thing arm'd with a rake," tend to condemn themselves, like Richard III after seeing ghosts and Lady Macbeth in sleep. But, like Richard III and Macbeth himself, Ferdinand dies with a super-confidence not readily to be analyzed:

> I will vault credit and affect high pleasures
> Beyond death.
>
> (V, v, 86)

His words recall the similar, even stronger, human confidence in *The White Devil*. It is a trust in the individual's native human force, irrespective of morality. We find it pre-eminently in Shakespeare and *The White Devil*; it is here, less vividly, in *The Duchess of Malfi*.

Webster's two great plays revolve round the central women. Whatever puritanical essences appear in his work, his *human creation* is planted firmly in the positive love-trust celebrated so differently in Lyly. He has a wholesome unromantic faith, far from the eye-lust and aestheticism of Marlowe. Webster's own mind starts with no innate sex-conflict at all: the terrific figure of Vittoria Corrombona, her womanly power and attraction, the irrelevance of moral categories in our judgement of her, indicate this. Webster's negations are not, finally, sexual. I deduce this most important result: having got straight, as it were, on the matter of sex, he is in a position to attack the next great problem, death, with its subsidiaries of evil and suffering, as Marlowe or Milton could never have done.

The play must be given a Renaissance understanding. The motor-force of evil in action comes at first sight mostly from a person or persons, more evidently than in *King Lear* where Edmund dissolves into the universalized suffering of the whole, yet not so precisely as in *Othello*, where Iago is so humanly particularized and evidently responsible. I used to wonder how Webster's universal poetry on fate and death could blend as it does with so human and exceptional an evil: the Duchess seemed to be unlucky in her brothers, that was all. But to the Renaissance mind a traditionally supernatural evil may often be humanized: the divine is seen in human terms, as in Shakespeare's Desdemona, Cleopatra, and Hermione; the devil may take the shape of Iago, or be split into a trinity of villains in *The Duchess of Malfi*. In *Macbeth*, however, evil is supernatural. In *The Duchess of Malfi*, though the impressionism recalls *Macbeth* and is full of religious colourings, mouldy superstitions and hauntings, no single supernatural figure or event, no witches, no ghost, here takes the stage; and, though there was certainly a ghost in *The White Devil*, it would somehow be strange if one did. This massive play, more than any one work of Shakespeare, splits its universal negations of suffering, evil and death into a close-inwoven variety of medieval colourings and Renaissance psychology that contains all that a poet of his day knows or feels about them. Shakespeare takes different directions in turn: this one play contains, or at least suggests, all. Responsibility cannot be definitely located; rather it pervades the whole. We are not invited to allot blame.

The movement from a medieval to a humanist conception, the Devil becoming Iago, is here compacted in the opposition of a supernatural impressionism and a wholly naturalistic humanism.

Ferdinand is a straight human study: aristocratic, fiery, unprincipled. The Cardinal is more mysterious. He is "able to possess the greatest devil and make him worse"; again, "He is a melancholy churchman. The spring in his face is nothing but the engendering of toads"; yet—and coming as it does curtly at the end of a speech on his "dark and devilish nature" it is a truly Shakespearian touch—"some good he hath done." He stands icily cold, a background figure, setting the action, though himself, like the Duchess' passivity against which the action is directed, rather motionless. There is in him a semblance to the Church he represents as seen by Webster, but he cannot be wholly so equated. A central piece of stage pageantry shows his installation as a soldier, which may be related to the Echo scene on an ancient disused abbey, now turned into a "fortification." Both incidents reflect that smouldering Renaissance war-threat Webster feels to be rising among the ruins of a dead or dying faith.

Bosola is our most complex person. Often he is a choric voice to the action, which he directs and comments on throughout, both criminal and avenger in one. He is a born moralist, though a professional murderer. His blend of pity with a scientific interest in another's suffering and stern conscience saddled to an un-moral nature reflect Webster's own artistic and creative, almost scientific, psychology and that in the Renaissance mind that gives us the dispassionate human analyses of Machiavelli and Bacon. He is unfailingly honest with himself. He knows that an intelligencer is a "quaint invisible devil," that "place and riches" are "bribes of shame." At first he refuses Ferdinand's offer, then accepts. He can wholeheartedly pursue the evil which he also paradoxically hates.

He is a cynic and his cynicism, like Iago's, takes a Manichean form. His conversation with the old lady strangely parallels Hamlet's with Ophelia: her "painting" is to him a "scurvy face-physic." He continues with two speeches loaded with physical nausea (smallpox, ordure, spittle, plague) and pronounces a formal Swiftian denunciation of man's "deformity." His attitude to the Duchess' pregnancy is coarse. But he can speak profoundly of the limitations of wisdom and counsel "simple honesty." He easily recognizes goodness, without following it: he speaks with religious fervour of the Duchess' love, then meditates on his own duplicity. His satire on princes and flatterers is continual and sincere. Those flatterers who now insult Antonio at his fall are "lice." Above all, he is a student of humanity. He talks to the Duchess of Antonio's low birth in order to observe her reaction, his short phrases winning each an interesting and expected speech in reply. He describes with sensitivity the Duchess' state in imprisonment to Ferdinand, her resignation to death, nobility in adversity and loveliness in tears appealing strongly to him: "She will muse four hours together . . . " Ferdinand, as usual impatient, prefers to study no longer "in the book of another's heart." Bosola can enjoy showing the Duchess the supposedly dead Antonio, ironically stimulating her grief with "Come, you must live," and "O fie, Despair? Remember you are a Christian." He may be partly sincere. He is giving religious counsel. When he says that he pities her, we are baffled: it may be so. He asks Ferdinand *why* he torments her—again so interested—and suggests that he go no farther. He himself will not visit her again in his own shape, but goes disguised readily enough, talking of the body's corruption, bringing bell, coffin and cords of execution, leading her "by degrees to mortification." Again, he is giving ghostly counsel. Her courage amazes him:

> Yet, methinks,
> The manner of your death should much afflict you.
> This cord should terrify you?
>
> (IV, ii, 219)

It is a laboratory of suffering, Bosola the vivisecting scientist. On Ferdinand's entry he turns his attention on him, asking how the children have offended, telling him to fix his eye steadily on their and the Duchess' dead bodies, transferring his former technique to his master, this time with more success. Denied his reward for crime he repents explicitly and irrevocably. We now feel that he all along hated his evil course: maybe he did; but he found it fascinatingly interesting. More phrases now pour from him: conscience, innocence, hell and so on. He becomes the avenger.

> The weakest arm is strong enough that strikes
> With the sword of justice.
>
> (V, ii, 379)

During the final scene of violent murders Bosola acts as high-priest of the occasion still, chorus and chief actor in one. He is almost a projection of the author involved in his own play: at once pathologist, criminal, avenger, and penitent. An impersonal voice following all the twists and turns of the action, he yet remains a convincing person. He is a most striking conception, more complex than Iago, and with many touches of Hamlet. No other period could have made him.

In Bosola many of the play's dominant themes converge. He is its philosophy in action. The paradoxes of his nature can be best resolved by study of his Manichean strain fusing a semi-religious fervour with a life-denying negation. At the climax, just before the Duchess' death he, the criminal, rings his bell and pronounces, or chants, the religious moral of his crime:

> Of what is't fools make such vain keeping?
> Sin their conception, their birth, weeping:
> Their life, a general mist of error,
> Their death, a hideous storm of terror.
>
> (IV, ii, 188)

Here, and in the murders that directly follow, is twisted and finally knotted together the recurrent association of religion and death. The association is dramatized as murder, the imaginative logic exquisite.

Among these adverse forces is set to shine out as some rich jewel from a funereal velvet, the love of the Duchess and Antonio. This is presented without idealizations. Antonio is an accountant, the widow proposes to him. She can talk quite broadly of bed-pleasures, with a certain honest unreticence. She has no sense of sin, and seems untouched by that strong sense in the others. She approaches Shakespeare's sunlight heroines in her wit, especially during the death-scene: she is, despite differences, in the tradition of Lyly's girls, Rosalind, Portia, and certain strains in Cleopatra, a tradition seeing woman as a sweet force of humour, gentleness, strength and common-sense; and perhaps it is this more than anything else which the literature of the modern world adds to medieval Christianity. There is here a poor stage for her gifts, which are muffled and clouded by the dark forces. Yet marriage is beautifully felt: the "sacrament of marriage" is the "first good deed begun in the world" after the creation, says Antonio; it knows no purgatory, but contains either heaven or hell. Like everyone here, he can be critical:

> Say a man never marry, nor have children,
> What takes that from him? Only the bare name
> Of being a father, or the weak delight
> To see the little wanton ride a cock-horse
> Upon a painted stick, or hear him chatter
> Like a taught starling.
>
> (I, i, 456)

Even so, an uncritical simplicity and warmth burns through the idle phrases. The exquisite presentment of Giovanni in *The White Devil* witnesses Webster's love and understanding of children: and this quality is one with that proud unmoral faith which he gave to the creation of Vittoria Corrombona in *The White Devil*, like Shakespeare's to his Cleopatra, an erotic and feminine and non-moral trust without which love of children alone is, it may be, sentimentality. We find both in Webster. Less forceful than in *The White Devil*, they are yet fundamental in *The Duchess of Malfi*. The Duchess, Antonio, and the children are a passive group, defined more by what happens to them than by what they do; the Duchess is often a tragic voice only; but they, the Duchess especially, alone form the one side of our central conflict. They stand for human, especially feminine, love; for common-sense, for family peace, against a world and its society diseased and sick to death.

III

Webster's world is socially rotten, the very impulse of family instinct conflicting cruelly with family tradition; and all professions and grades in the community are satirically condemned. But the play is more than a social document. Love is here inherently luckless, the body of man itself a walking disease; and finally, there is death and its twin attendants, mouldering graves and icy-dark eternity. This death is perhaps neither good nor bad, but it is fearful, dark, and cold. What then, we may ask, is the final purpose of all this—the phrase is Webster's—"talk fit for a charnel"? What is the author doing? He is trying to express in warm action the freezing horror of a corpse; to give outward dramatic manifestation to what the play calls "not-being"; to express the quality of death in a sequence. That is why the Duchess must be "brought by degrees to mortification"; why we have the icy hand, the group of plaster corpses, the showing her of cords and coffin. Webster artificially loads on us and her all possible traditional elaborations of the horror of death. His people live death. The greatest torture of those in hell is that they "must live and cannot die"; to "live thus is not indeed to live"; the play is all "a sensible hell." Webster would make "not-being" live before our eyes. He refuses any supernatural action with a masterly reserve. But there is little positive sense-perception of bodies in health: the people are all ghosts, they have no proper bodies till they become corpses: they act in a sort of frozen stillness, are dead before the play starts. It is amazing that the thing is done at all. Webster's play is written from a ruling perception of death comparable to, but subtler than, that presented in Donne's sermons, Burton and Browne.

The Duchess remains unshaken by all attempts to fright her with her own death, asking how a more picturesque implement would benefit her, serenely and rationally facing the fact, unmoved by sense-horrors. Yet she is horrified at the hand and supposed group of corpses. Death is more fearful in those she loves than for herself. There is moreover a pervading stoical and resigned feeling that suffering may have a purpose. The fish's price is not known till it is near the fire; men are valued highest in misery; only "Heaven's scourge-stick" makes men go right; lovers are parted as a "curious artist" takes a clock or watch to pieces in order to mend it; men bruised like Cassia to get their perfume; we shall find excellent company in the other world. Is this the truth? Or this:

> all our wit
> And reading bring us to a truer sense
> Of sorrow.
>
> (III, v, 82)

Is man's best fate to be the "tann'd galley-slave" resigned to torment? To be the plaything "tennis-ball" of fateful stars? The answer is indecisive. The massed tonings suggest that death has the final say. But may death itself be kind? All the people, good or ill, feel some faint strangled and religious sense of a beyond, though these touches often seem no more than necessary constituents among so many others to the packed and varied exposition of traditional thinking on death. Julia dies with: "I go, I know not whither"; haughty Ferdinand will affect "high pleasures" beyond death; there is Bosola's bitter "mine is another voyage." Asked by the Duchess if we shall know one another in the next world, Cariola answers "Yes, out of question," the incident recalling Tess's question to Angel Clare on Stonehenge. The Duchess' death has religious direction: those who strangle will pull "heaven" down on her, she "kneels" for her entry. Maybe "in the eternal church" lovers part no more. This play's meticulous analysis of death in action, death in the tomb, death in the soul—for Ferdinand's and the Cardinal's hearts are "hollow graves rotten and rotting others"—is an attempt at death-penetration. It probes the question, hoping therein to find its own answer: "O that it were possible," says the Duchess, "to hold some two days conference with the dead," for that would teach us something we "never shall know here." This play is such a conference. It is a communing with death. The play elucidates its own problem, it contains its own answer. It implicitly asserts the final unreality of death, by speaking almost wholly in deathly terms. This forces both a phraseology and imagery of mouldering quality. I have shown how most of its associations, certainly all that refer to death, are traditional and conventional, often superstitious, expressing stock-reactions, worn by centuries of use: owls, wolves, graveyards, bones; or an eternity dark and inhumanly, icily, holy. The play's vast area presents a massive ruin scattered with mental *débris*. All the worst in folk-lore and orthodoxy is used and emphasized. But there is little direct and vital nature-contact: natural images of trees and birds tend either to be generalized or to smell of medieval oil, and the stars are thoroughly astrologized. There are no minute exactitudes of observation of the Shakespearian or Tennysonian sort; still less are there any vast natural or cosmic positives, such as the sea throughout Shakespeare, or the mountains in Goethe's *Faust* and Ibsen. Webster's world is too narrowly and inwardly human to be real; its infinities are the vast and accumulated poisons of fear, agony and evil in the human mind. It would appear that to talk of death well we must avoid actuality, that it is best defined in terms of the unreal. The play implicitly says this. The strange healthiness of *King Lear* is one with its avoidance of traditional eternity-thoughts and conventionalized horrors. *Macbeth* relates its superstitions directly to a moral and perverted evil, and they are dispelled in the end, as much by Macbeth as by Malcolm. Macbeth breaks free. Webster's action drives home the truth that evil, which is an aspect of death, contradicts itself. There is a perverse irony towards the end, almost a macabre humour. Bosola repents after the murder, the Duchess recovers, he is at the foot of heaven's mercy-seat, she dies. In error he kills Antonio, the one man he in his new repentance would give his life for. He, the implement of death, is a living contradiction: so are his actions and his fortunes alike. His very existence is a grim irony, and he knows it. The Cardinal, who arranged not to be interrupted while he disposed of a corpse, is not interrupted, through his own plan, while he becomes one. As for Ferdinand, his madness, horrible as it is, is almost as comic as horrible. The human forces of death contradict their own humanity, they tend to become de-individualized, paradoxical, comic. Their disintegration reflects Webster's human faith.

This thought applies to the whole play. The arrangement of action is heavily artificial. Unreal horrors are, if not central, yet approaches to the central horror: there is the supposed dead hand, the supposed group of corpses. What if the Duchess' own death, succeeding these, were equally a delusion? Certainly it causes her less suffering. Webster's horrors are aesthetic horrors, his imagery, so literary and backward in pedigree, "smells of mortality," to transpose a Shakespearian phrase; it is the result of a blackened thinking. The serene reason of life finds no home here: "for the subtlest folly proceeds from the subtlest wisdom." Is death itself such a folly? The Echo scene compresses that thought imaginatively. From these ancient ruins come back the grim words "like death that we have," "deadly accent," a "thing of sorrow," "thou art a dead thing." This scene is a miniature of Webster's universe. Every word is spoken first by Antonio and Delio. If you will walk among such ruins, you must expect an echo to interrupt your talk; and if you will end all your sentences with death, don't blame the echo. This is an interesting example of how imaginative architectonic may itself shadow an answer posed but insoluble, or at least left unsolved, on the plane of the author's explicit thought; just as Webster's creative human understanding is to be distinguished from his poetic impressionism.

The "problem" of death is, therefore, not to be answered in its own terms which continually dissolve as smoke under analysis, but rather by a concentration on forces of life; on those forces which flame with fitful violence in *The White Devil* and burn steadily, if dimly, in Webster's Duchess here.

The Duchess of Malfi has a harmony all its own. Its metaphysical contradictions are its imaginative truth, all false balances being redressed in the act of statement. Its horrors are sweetened by the author's fearless acceptance, his resigned artistic enjoyment: there is no *Macbeth* intensity, no Marlovian shiver of fear, but rather a passive relaxation. The negations have, more than in most dark worlds, a positive, harmonious quality. There is no violent conflict: if the Duchess were more vital, death-horrors would be unthroned from their centrality. The action unrolls with a pleasing inevitability and, twice, something of a colourful pomp. Both War and the Church are given incidents of pageantry, the Cardinal's ceremonial installation as a soldier, the pilgrims at the Shrine of Our Lady of Loretto. These contrast with the dun tone of the drama's thought and imagery; and still more with the more horrible events that follow; but there is a certain aesthetic richness about the horrible as well as the more obviously picturesque scenes, recalling that phrase in Flecker's *Hassan*: "Agony is a fine colour." The organic structure, the massed piling of event on event, though wanting occasionally in narrative logic, has a precise, if rough, imaginative coherence. On the picturesque is reared, mountainously, the pictorially gruesome: the tableau of death shown to the Duchess, the murder. The heart of the whole play is the Masque of Madmen and Bosola's entry with bell and coffin. The masque builds a grotesque harmony of dance and music into the central horror. Bosola rings his bell and chants

> Of what is't fools make such vain keeping?
> Sin their conception, their birth weeping.
>
> (IV, ii, 188)

There is a measured and ceremonial purpose, it is a controlled *ritual* of murder, with a certain ghoulish placidity to be distinguished from the middle scenes of conflict in *Macbeth* and *King Lear*. It is all strangely harmonious. After the Duchess' death the action descends. There is the disintegration of Ferdinand and the Cardinal, and the final murders. Except for the great Echo scene, perhaps the finest example of concentrated "atmosphere" in our drama, the movement might seem to droop. The drama follows the normal Shake-

spearian structure, the climax central, though with no sense of the Shakespearian ceremonial at the end; I think necessarily, considering the nature
of its statement. Moreover drooping is not here inorganic: disease is a dom-
inating impression, and the very blank-verse, yet colloquial, rhythms of its
speech tend continually to limp. Finally we can, if we please, see another
use in the falling action. The Duchess has been buried deep in her own play,
which next closes over her, her grave is heaped, not with earth but with
more death. Webster has thus his own consistent if funereal harmonics; his
play expands and balances in the mind like a massive and a weighty dream;
perhaps the most beautiful and profound creation of a mood in our literature.

JACKSON I. COPE

George Chapman: Myth
as Mask and Magic

If I correctly infer the implications of Eugene Waith's analyses, he indicates
that while the Herculean hero of the *trattatisti* and mythographers provided
materials from which many protagonists were erected from Tamburlaine to
Aureng-Zebe, it was only Chapman's titular figure in *Bussy D'Ambois* who
was conceived as symbol, as a paradoxical *Hercules redivivus* for "the more
sophisticated spectators" who might realize with the author that the play
"seems to be moving on two parallel lines, one of which is the adventures
of the historical Bussy, the other a progressive revelation of a mythic figure,
a Hercules disguised as Bussy." It is a likely conclusion, following from
what we have just noted about his Platonic heritage, that Chapman so veiled
another "mystery" in myth. But even so, the Herculean aspect of Bussy
hidden beneath the "pervial" surface of his court scandal serves ultimately,
in Waith's reading, only to emphasize "the moving dilemma of a great-
spirited man who attempts to live by a heroic code in a world dominated
by Machiavellian policy." In *The Gentleman Usher* Chapman adapted the
Herculean protagonist to even better effect, creating a truly Platonic Hercules
whose success is imaged through the transcendent magic of a vision which
sees the world as a masque of policy. And that which puts down policy is
the harmonious source of vision itself: patience.

The first scenes of the play are dedicated to theatrical spectacle, to
masque and grotesque anti-masque which serve as symbolic plays-within-
the-play. And yet there is a cross-current even here, as a prelude of prophetic
dream throws these carefully prepared shows strangely out of the focus of
manipulated control which is implied in symbolic spectacles.

From *The Theatre and the Dream*. © 1973 by The Johns Hopkins University Press.

The plot of *The Gentleman Usher* centers upon old Duke Alphonso's rivalry with his son Vincentio for the love of youthful Margaret, daughter of Earl Lasso. Into this perverse romantic situation are threaded the vicious, jealous pretensions of Margaret's aunt, Cortezza, and of three male witwoulds: Medice, evil counselor to the Duke; Poggio, hapless and witless nephew to Vincentio's friend Lord Strozza; and Bassiolo, "gentleman usher" to Margaret's father. But gradually it is Strozza, a manipulator who out-manipulates the schemers surrounding Vincentio and himself, who emerges as the protagonist. From the beginning through act IV the action centers upon plans for a boar hunt led by the Duke, a hunt which ends in a treacherous, nearly fatal attack upon Strozza by a minion of Medice. But in the earliest scenes the hunt is transmuted into the symbolic love hunt of a court masque through which the Duke woos Margaret, and it is still further delayed by an answering masque performed for the Duke's entertainment at the behest of Lasso.

In the opening scene the impending hunt is introduced in a nervous interview among Poggio, Strozza, and Strozza's wife Cynanche. Poggio has awakened late because of a dream of grotesque violence involving his horse, followed by another, equally grotesque, of love-servitude to Margaret. The tangential bearings of dream on reality are suggested when Poggio closes his account of equine disaster with the plaint, "Slud Aunt, what if my dreame had beene true (as it might haue beene for any thing I knew)." Strozza immediately associates the dream violence with the hunt through his ironic yet ambiguous epithet "furious" for the nephew (who closely approximates a type of childlike but prophetic fool popular on the stage at the time in all his individuations, from Lear's jester to Jonson's Bartholomew Cokes):

> Well said, my furious nephew: but I see
> You quite forget that we must rowse to day
> The sharp-tuskt Bore: and blaze our huntsmanship
> Before the duke.
>
> (I, i, 18–21)

As Poggio disappears to prepare, Cynanche moves his dream of violence a plane closer to the actual hunt with her own misgivings: "My Lord I fancie not these hunting sports"; "Take heede for Gods loue if you rowse the Bore / You come not neere him" (I, i, 49–62).

Reassured by Strozza, Cynanche leaves, to be replaced by Vincentio and the return of Poggio, in a highly excited state. He brings reports which again seem grotesque, yet are more discomforting as unnatural omens than the dreams which they translate into reality, completing the transition initiated by Cynanche. Strozza's hounds and horses have turned, "and *Kilbucke* being runne mad, bit *Ringwood* so by the left buttocks, you might haue turnd your nose in it" while simultaneously "your horse, Gray Strozza too haz the staggers, and haz strooke bay-Bettrice, your Barbary mare so, that shee goes halting" (I, i, 136–51). Before he was only amused by Poggio; now Strozza is inclined to think him ominous: "What poison blisters thy vnhappy tongue / Euermore braying forth vnhappy newes?"

The sense of nature gone wild is quieted immediately, however, by the entrance of Duke Alphonso to announce that

> Tis no true hunting we intend to day,
> But an inducement to a certaine shew,
> Wherewith we will present our beauteous loue.
>
> (I, i, 164–66)

The hunt is to be safely manipulated into a masque for Margaret, and this dramatized conceit becomes symbol when Strozza *ex tempore* narrates the show in which the Duke himself is brought before his mistress "bound" by Sylvanus the enchanter and attendant spirits. As in the portentous dreams, Chapman again tantalizingly maneuvers the masque-within-the-play in such a manner that Strozza is able to fashion a gloss which is both truth and fiction, in that it recounts the love hunt being enacted in the masque in terms of the boar hunt which has been the fictive mask for the masque:

> His Grace this morning visiting the woods,
> And straying farre, to finde game for the Chase,
> At last, out of a mirtle groue he rowsde
> A vast and dreadfull Boare, so sterne and fierce,
> As if the Feend fell Crueltie her selfe
> Had come to fright the woods in that strange shape.
>
> Horror held all vs Huntsmen from pursuit,
> Onely the Duke incenst with our cold feare,
> Incouragde like a second *Hercules*.
>
> Hunted the monster close, and chargde so fierce,
> That he inforc'd him (as our sence conceiu'd)
> To leape for soile into a cristall spring,
> Where on the suddaine strangely vanishing,
> Nimph-like for him, out of the waues arose
> Your sacred figure like *Diana* armde,

and (as in purpose of the beasts reuenge)
Dischargde an arrow through his Highnesse breast,
Whence yet no wound or any blood appearde:
And this Enchanter with his power of spirits,

. . . strooke vs sencelesse, while in these strange bands,
These cruell spirits thus inchainde his armes,

[*Enchanter*.] Bright Nimph, that Boare figur'd your crueltie,
Charged by loue, defended by your beautie.

(I, ii, 78–113)

Vincentio later protests to Strozza that his speech of interpretation has been too persuasive, benefiting Alphonso's cause before Margaret, and the Duke himself is clearly pleased. Neither, apparently, has listened attentively to the allegory. If Alphonso has been like a second Hercules, it has scarcely been in the classical pattern, for the boar has triumphed in metamorphosis. Alphonso's ultimate "release" by Margaret, which closes the masque, is a forced game urged by the Duke's supporters; it derives no more logically from Strozza's myth than does the Enchanter's conclusion. Indeed, the entire masque seems so distant from the Hercules legends that on the surface it suggests more strongly the Platonic *concordia discors* in which Venus arms herself with the weapons of Diana, and "the union of Chastity and Love through the mediation of Beauty is . . . expressed by one hybrid figure in which the two opposing goddesses . . . are merged into one."

The puzzlement is increased by the pageant which Lasso subsequently presents for his noble guest. Performed by rustic broom-men, rushmen, and bugs, with the simpleton Poggio as narrator, this actually functions as a comic anti-masque to the masque proper. But the moral of both is the same: if Margaret is invited to embrace the Duke at the end, it is (like Alphonso's release in the first masque) in spite of the lesson of the dance:

as our country girls held off,
And rudely did their lovers scoff;
Our Nymph likewise shall onely glaunce
By your faire eies, and looke askaunce
Vpon her feral friend that wooes her,

. . . though the rurall wilde and antike,
Abusde their loues as they were frantike;
Yet take you in your Iuory clutches,
This noble Duke, and be his Dutches.

(II, ii, 102–17)

Poggio's climactic broom speech not only supports the rejection of passion but asserts a bond with the first masque through an answering Herculean reference:

Grim *Hercules* swept a stable with a riuer,

Philosophy, that passion sweepes from thought,
Is the soules Broome, and by all braue wits sought,
Now if Philosophers but Broomemen are,
Each Broomeman then is a Philosopher.

(II, ii, 57–67)

I have called the presentation an anti-masque and this an "answering" allusion because it assigns to Hercules a role different from that he played in the masque of the love hunt. There he stood as the apparent victim, here as the symbol of victory over passion. If we turn to the mythographers whose compendia Chapman utilized, this apparent discrepancy in his Herculean symbolism disappears, to reappear as a familiar, traditional synthesis.

Invariably the mythographers devote several pages to the deeds and iconography of Hercules, that most exciting of the pagan gods. And if they differ in many particulars, none fails to focus a part of his exegesis upon Hercules as the great representative of man's spiritual triumph over the passions, often making him the exemplar of apotheosis through his deliberate rejection of the body. Vincenzo Cartari achieves a tour de force in explicating the labors and the traditional static iconography in a single brief and cohesive account which can stand for many other less economical versions:

[Hercules] was called a tamer of monsters; but because there are no uglier or more horrible monsters, nor tyrants more cruel among mortals than the vices of the spirit, some have wished to say that the strength of Hercules was not of the body but of the spirit, with which he overcame all those disordered appetites which, rebels against reason, disturb and harrass man continuously like ferocious monsters. And *apropos* of this Suidas writes that the ancients, in order to show that Hercules was a great lover of prudence and virtue, painted him dressed in a lion's skin, signifying greatness and generosity of spirit, and placed a club in his right hand, which signifies a desire for prudence and knowledge. With this they feigned the fable that he had smitten the fierce dragon and carried away three golden apples which it guarded. These he held in his left hand, signifying that he had overcome sensual appetite and thus had freed the three powers of the soul, ornamenting it with virtue and with just and honest deeds.

Cesare Ripa describes a number of Herculean icons under the rubric of *virtù* in his *Iconologia*, and one repeatedly meets the lion of spiritual fortitude and the boar of corporeal passion, each necessary and necessarily harnessed together by Hercules. There is one definition of heroic virtue in his exegeses which passes beyond the merely moralizing comments on the iconographic plates, however: "heroic virtue in man is that state in which reason has so overcome the sensitive affections that it arrives at a point whence it cannot be separated from virtuous means; one made so pure and illustrious transcends human excellence and draws near the ranks of the angels."

With the last phrase Hercules moves from the classical pantheon into the celestial choir of the Christian saints. It was not, of course, a recent journey, although one seldom reflected in the mythographic compendia. There had been those Fathers like Lactantius who dismissed Hercules as a barbarian who clearly had followed the opposite way from that of virtue. However, as the patristic tradition of attack succumbed in large part to neoplatonic syncretism in the Renaissance, even those commentators who took note of Hercules' lapses did so with an eye upon his eventual apotheosis.

That apotheosis is more prominent in the exegetes upon Ovid than in the compilers of mythic handbooks, since the former had the encouragement of the *Ovide moralisé* tradition and were also compelled to emphasize and explain the Nessus and Oeta episodes. We discover, for instance, in Giuseppe Horologgi's annotations to Giovanni Andrea dell' Anguillara's popular translation of the *Metamorphoses* a reconciliation of the two Herculeses—the passionate pagan sinner and Ripa's triumphant saint. Hercules, explains Horologgi, is the lover of glory who sees himself being robbed of his hard-earned fame (Deianira) through lasciviousness (the centaur). He kills this passion with an arrow dipped in his own virtue, but the poisonous shirt is the revenge which passion takes upon the man intent on glory. This allegory is but prelude to the climax of Horologgi's reading: "he burns himself and is rejuvenated, because as at first we pass from a lascivious, dishonest, and vicious life to one temperate, honorable, and praiseworthy by burning out the evil affections, so we return young again to virtue and to glory; and thence-forward we are lifted to Heaven again on wings of contemplation, and numbered among the Gods, who are those that have turned all their thoughts upon God, becoming Gods by participation, in the way the Psalm

says: 'I have said that you are Gods' [*Ho detto che voi sete Dei*]." Hercules
Oetaeus has become the very prototype of Christian promise: paradise well
lost that it may be regained upon a transcendent plane happier far. With
these reminders of an often-told history, we are equipped to examine those
resonances of the Herculean myth which couple masque and anti-masque,
and which finally structure the principal action of *The Gentleman Usher*.

The first masque deliberately confuses myth and, therefore, motive. It
seems to fall neatly into the tradition which associates Venus and venery,
love and the hunt, a pattern woven by Chapman's contemporary into *Venus
and Adonis* and *Twelfth Night*. But with the introduction of Hercules, the
hunt becomes, willy-nilly, symbolic of the control of passions, capture of
the rampant boar. And, willy-nilly, the boar turned upon the hunter becomes
Diana, to reaffirm the symbolic Herculean feat by which the monster was
brought to leash. It must be so, because Alphonso is the unnatural lover,
Hercules furens raging in passion's slavery, while the masque prophesies Hercules' transcendence of passion. The old Duke raging in the shirt of Nessus
is here promised that chastity he does not yet seek which will come, when
it comes, from one who is truly "a second Hercules," one who has learned
and teaches that "philosophy" which sweeps passion from the thoughts.

The contradictory confusions of the masques, the overtones of something
above controlled theatricality when dream disturbs the world of contrived
symbol—these aspects of the supranatural impinging upon the action are
supported by the strange markings upon the three wit-woulds. We have
noticed Poggio's dreams, his prophecies in nonsense, the repeated emphasis
upon his role as the innocent but inevitable carrier of bad news. If he speaks
folly, it is truth. "I am the veriest foole on you all," he cries, and "therein
thou art worth vs all, for thou knowst thy selfe," responds Vincentio (III,
ii, 219–21). Bassiolo, the "gentleman usher," is gulled through his own
vanity into uniting Vincentio and Margaret, and the scenes of his presump-
tuous intimacy with Vincentio strike notes strongly recalling Malvolio's
cross-garters. Yet the fact remains that he alone has joined with Strozza in
forwarding this natural union. And when, again like Malvolio, he stands
most mercilessly exposed before the court in his simpering claims upon
Vincentio, a reformed Alphonso refuses to be drawn to laughter or scorn,
but is bemused at a fool whose innocence improbably "saw the fitnes of the
match, / With freer and more noble eies then we" (V, iv, 175–76; cf. V,
iv, 162–64). These eerie marks are counterweighted by the unnatural pretensions of both Poggio and Bassiolo to a courtly status for which neither
is equipped; and the two strange extremes meet in the figure of Medice. For
if the pretensions are a focus of satire in Bassiolo and of farce in Poggio,

they flicker in a diabolic, pseudo-tragic light around Medice. Revealed in the denouement as the would-be murderer of Strozza, Medice is discovered to be Mendice, king of the gypsies, who was motivated in his intrigues by dark influences from "an old Sorceresse" (V, iv, 258 ff.). By this point we have already seen him grievously wound Strozza and Vincentio, the attack upon the latter being characterized as "blacke witchcraft . . . diuelish wrath of hell" (V, ii, 61–62). Unmasked publicly through Strozza's "diuine re-lation," Mendice finally flees the stage to "hide me from the sight of heauen" (V, iv, 277).

These strange butts, Poggio's strange dream, Cynanche's premonitions, the metamorphic vision of the first masque with its Enchanter, Mendice's sorcery—all these hover like indecisive shadows over the action of the drama until they are illuminated by the brilliant flash of Strozza's vision, a vision which makes him, indeed, as Schoell said, "a mixture of Christian mysticism and pagan stoicism." But Chapman urges us throughout to see him more specifically than this, as the mythic center in which these traditions merged, the Christian Hercules.

The turning point for Strozza, as for the play, is an incident which moves toward tragedy in a way unprecedented in Chapman's earlier comedies (if we discount the farcical murder of Prince Doricles in *The Blind Beggar of Alexandria*) and approached again only in *The Widow's Tears*. On the day following the masques Alphonso orders an actual hunt, in which Strozza is painfully wounded. As at the opening of the play, there is a sense of fatality when the hapless messenger of doom Poggio rushes on stage to announce this "accident" to his aunt, Cynanche. Almost immediately Strozza is carried in, overwhelmed by a desperate agony:

> Must we attend at deaths abhorred doore,
> The torturing delaies of slauish Nature?
> My life is in mine owne powers to dissolue:
> And why not then the paines that plague my life?
> Rise furies, and this furie of my bane,
> Assaile and conquer
>
> Resolue and rid me of this brutish life,
> Hasten the cowardly protracted cure
> Of all diseases: King of Phistians, death,
> Ile dig thee from this Mine of miserie.
>
>   (IV, i, 34–46)

His wife, more terrified by this desperation than by the physical wound, in order (as she soliloquizes) to "salue with Christian patience, Pagan sinne,"

attempts through "fained patience to recomfort him" when she offers Strozza
the reminder that

> afflictions bring to God,
> Because they make vs like him, drinking vp
> Ioyes that deforme vs with the lusts of sense,
> And turne our generall being into soule.
>   (IV, i, 62–65)

Her exhortations reach a climax with the proud assertion that "Patience in
torment, is a valure more / Then euer crownd *Th'Alcmenean* Conqueror" (IV,
i, 55–56). The allusion indicates the prototype of Strozza's anguished outcry
against the torture of a treacherous and incurable wound, as well as its
significance: it is "Hercules Oetaeus" burning in the shirt of Nessus.

Soon after Cynanche's expostulations with her husband we see them
together again; and the brief time that has elapsed has worked a miracle:
the wounded Strozza now volunteers a long panegyric upon the value of a
true wife, explaining that Cynanche's "diuine advice," her "heauenly words,"
have healed him:

> My free submission to the hand of heauen
> Makes it redeeme me from the rage of paine.
> For though I know the malice of my wound
> Shootes still the same distemper through my vaines,
> Yet the Iudiciall patience I embrace,
> (In which my minde spreads her impassive powres
> Through all my suffring parts;) expels their frailetie;
> And rendering vp their whole life to my soule,
> Leaues me nought else but soule.
>   (IV, iii, 43–51)

As Cynanche had proposed, affliction has turned his "general being into soule"
(IV, i, 65). Re-created in the fire of suffering sustained, Strozza experiences
in his person a paradox suggestive of the Herculean apotheosis—and of the
Christian:

> Humilitie hath raisde me to the starres;
> In which (as in a sort of Cristall Globes)
> I sit and see things hidde from humane sight.
>   (IV, iii, 61–63)

This holy vision becomes prophetic (through "that good Angell, / That by
diuine relation spake in me" [V, iv, 199–200]) in assuring him that on "the

seuenth day" the arrow will fall from his healed wound, a prophecy underlined
by Strozza's almost incantatory repetition of the magic number "seven." He
further amazes his skeptical audience when, rapt beyond their comprehension, he also sees a vision of mortal danger to Vincentio, who has left his
father's hunt in the hope of enjoying some stolen hours with Margaret. The
dream of danger is soon verified as Cortezza, the drunken sister of Lasso,
leads a suspicious Alphonso to the lover's tryst, reviving with perverted
emphasis the analogy between love and the hunt:

> Their confidence, that you are still a hunting,
> Will make your amorous sonne that stole from thence,
> Bold in his loue-sports; Come, come, a fresh chace,
> I hold this pickelocke, you shall hunt at view.
> What, do they thinke to scape? An old wiues eye
> Is a blew Cristall full of sorcerie.
>
> (IV, iv, 50–55)

Malevolent and lecherous, Cortezza joins the venomous Medice-Mendice in
setting up an imagistic counterpoint of diabolic sorcery, black magic, against
the divine benevolence of Strozza's healing powers and mystic visions. And
in the final act, set a week after the day of the near-tragic hunt, this
transcendent war between spiritual and demonic magic (up to this point a
muted battle which has gradually emerged from the early dreams of Poggio)
explicitly comes to dominate and to enlarge the action. Strozza, now mi-
raculously healed, assures his physician that

> t'was no frantike fancie,
> That made my tongue presage this head should fall
> Out of my wounded side the seuenth day;
> But an inspired rapture of my minde,
> Submitted and conioyned in patience,
> To my Creator, in whom I fore-saw
> (Like to an Angell) this diuine event.
>
> (V, ii, 1–7)

The good Doctor Benevenius glosses the lesson of this "right christian
president":

> What a most sacred medcine Patience is,
> That with the high thirst of our soules cleare fire
> Exhausts corporeall humour; and all paine,
> Casting our flesh off, while we it retaine.
>
> (V, ii, 10–13)

We have already met the transcendence of passion through suffering, the apotheosis of one "Submitted and conioynde in patience / To my Creator," in the Christianized Hercules Oetaeus of the commentators; let us further remind ourselves that patience is the lesson they, too, sometimes teach. As Sandys suggested, Nessus' shirt *"put on by* Hercules, *he broyls with heate, which subdues his fortitude with intollerable torments: who in his anguish disputes: with the Gods . . . (an impatience unto which the best of mortall men haue beene subiect . . .)."* By and large, Renaissance dramatists, following Seneca, emphasized this "impatience," but Chapman was no ordinary dramatist. He was, rather, as we have noted, an eclectic yet serious Platonist who drew his imagery as well as his vision from the legacy of Ficino's Florence. When we turn again to Ficino, this time as an interpreter of mythology, we discover an exclusive emphasis upon that *Hercules patiens* who succeeded and transcended *Hercules furens.* And we recover, too, the orientation of Strozza's magic dream vision.

For Ficino, Hercules was an exemplar of those victims of epilepsy who shared with other prophets the experience of self-transcendence, of leaving the body in life: "Quo excelluisse Hercules dicitur, Arabesque permulti, qui comitiali morbo corripiebantur." Suffering leads to God rather directly. And if we place this view of Hercules' significance within the total complex of Ficino's thought, it gives a light which clarifies Chapman's play, arguing from a reasoned system the supernal validity of dream. We know how Ficino reverses the perspective of society, teaching that only philosophers are awake to divine things while others dream in waking. The body, "things," constitute a shadow world which must be transcended by the divine rapture of knowing. Thus in dreams lie a responsibility and reality such as Strozza experiences after transcending the corporeal; or, to invert the equation in yet another dimension, man is "a dream / But of a shadow, summ'd with all his substance," as Chapman's Bussy reckons him. Those who, escaping the corporeal shadows, are able to see reality as dream and dream as reality are those who, like Hercules, are "rapt" beyond the Platonic cave of this world to a more direct communion with their "Creator" (it should not be forgotten that Ficino considered his *De raptu Pauli* important enough to translate it into Italian himself). But Ficino associated transcendent rapture with suffering: one emerged from time to time into the reality of the eternal dream through the interior ascent which begins in corporeal misery. So it was with Strozza and with Hercules.

The interior ascent toward an unmediated vision is articulable process as well as promise in Ficino's system, and the process is dependent upon that concept which has been echoing like a refrain through the speeches of

Strozza and Cynanche: "patience." It is this trait which focuses Ficino's discussion of the wise man's spiritual transcendence. "All other virtues consist in doing well; patience alone in suffering well," wrote Ficino. And to Antonio Cocchi he explained: "I think that patience prescribes mainly three things. First that you may be willing to suffer gladly evils which nature itself commands you to be unwilling to suffer. Secondly, that those things which fate has decided to be necessary you transform into voluntary ones. Thirdly, that you turn all evils into goods, which is God's task alone. [Patience, therefore] commands us . . . to make ourselves equal to God. . . . For only impatience causes misfortunes, which might be confined to external things and to the body alone, to pass into the soul as well." One can listen for the echoes of such a passage in Strozza's triumph over the physical agony of his wound, as when the doctor affirms the power of the "most sacred medicine Patience . . . Casting our flesh off, while we it retaine." But Ficino goes further in explaining just how man effects that visionary rapture which Strozza experiences as the reward of patience, understood in its root sense:

> Since it is impossible to approach the celestial seats with a corporeal bulk, the soul, taking thought as its guide, by the gift of philosophy, transcends through contemplation the nature of all things. . . . to speak comprehensively, since philosophy is a celestial gift, it drives earthly vices far away, bravely subdues fortune, admirably softens fate, safely uses mortal gifts, abundantly offers immortal gifts. . . . O sure guide of human life, who first defeats the monsters of vice entirely with the club of *Hercules*, then with the shield of Pallas avoids and overcomes the dangers of fortune, and finally takes human souls upon the shoulders of Atlas, frees them from this earthly exile, and returns them truly and happily to the celestial fatherland.

In Ficino's view, this is the path of divine patience by which *Hercules Oetaeus* arrives at the role of prophet in rapture, raised to the stars on the *scala* of suffering. And it is the path along which Strozza follows the Alcmenean conqueror of self.

In yet another comment on patience in suffering, Ficino said:

> Our body is attracted in a powerful attack by the body of the world through the forces of fate . . . and the power of fate does not penetrate our mind if our mind has not previously immersed itself in the body subject to fate. So no one should trust his own intelligence and strength enough to hope he can wholly avoid

the sicknesses of the body [*morbos corporis*] or the loss of things.
Every soul should retire from the pestilence of the body [*corporis
peste*] and withdraw into the mind, for then fortune will spend
its force on the body and not pass into the soul. A wise man will
not fight in vain against fate, but rather resist by fleeing. Misfortunes cannot be hunted down, but can only be fled.

The masque of Hercules and the chaste boar had been Alphonso's spectacle
of the frontal assault upon fate; *Hercules furens*, he had caught the arrow of
passion as the beast of the body turned upon him. And yet that beast had
been, in spite of his own will, a benevolent prey—as Strozza explains, passion
pursued becomes passion providentially spent. And when the same arrow of
misfortune pierces Strozza's side, he, wiser than the Duke, acted the role of
the divine philosopher, *Hercules patiens:* through his interior ascent from the
pestilent body he did, in fact, turn his "generall being into soule." In the
love hunt, symbolized by Strozza at its divine level, the victor is not the
hunter, but the prey.

If Chapman emphasizes illness, we can annotate his intentions here, too,
from Ficino's thought. Like the author of *The Gentleman Usher,* the Florentine
was obsessed with the medical, psychosomatic aspects of self-transcendence.
Soellner has traced the tradition of his interest, insofar as it relates specifically
to Herculean mythology, from the pseudo-Aristotelian *Problemata*, a handbook immensely popular in the Renaissance. There Hercules' madness was
attributed to epileptic melancholy, with the note that "epileptic afflictions
were called by the ancients 'the sacred disease,' after him"—Galen's νοσς
'Ηρακλειη, *Herculeus morbus*. But Soellner points out that "the Neoplatonists
of the Renaissance gave a new twist to the idea of the epilepsy of Hercules
by explaining it as something of a spiritual achievement. They fused a popular
medieval superstition about the prophetic gift of epileptics with the pseudo-
Aristotelian theory of the excellence of epileptic melancholiacs as exemplified
by Hercules." This new version of a medieval tradition owed a great deal
to Ficino's image of himself as a melancholiac seer whose power came from
morbidity. It is a self-portrait which is reflected in his extensive writings on
natural magic, and which permits us to refine more precisely the function
of Strozza in bringing into focus the theme of Chapman's play about the
absorption of artifice into vision and dream. Indeed, intentionally or not,
Strozza (in the milieu which Jacquot so felicitously tags "une Italie de rêve")
becomes not merely a modern Hercules, but imitator of that imitator of the
great epileptic of myth, an icon for Ficino himself.

Ficino insisted that he was a "Saturnine" victim of that ambiguous gift
of intellection which is marked by the stars as contemplative melancholy.

It was a gift which—as the "epileptic" diagnosis for Hercules supposes—
Ficino developed into a complex of physiologico-astrological magic that could
be rationalized as medicine. But he was undoubtedly influenced more by
familial tradition than by the horoscope he cast for himself because he
carefully reported in later life how both his father, a young physician, and
his mother gave him a personal legacy of prophetic visions and dreams. The
father, called to inspect an injured farmer, gave the man up as fatally
wounded. Returning home, he paused under an oak tree to rest, and there
experienced a vision in which a beautiful young woman accused him of
ingratitude to God for not employing his gift of healing more generously.
Three days later the farmer's father arrived to plead for the doctor's return.
When he did return, to his amazement he found the man still alive and was
able to cure him. Later he learned that the family had been praying to the
Virgin at the very moment she appeared to him on the road (*Opera*, p. 644).
Ficino's mother, Monna Sandra, had had dreams correctly presaging deaths
in the family (*Opera*, p. 615). Ficino himself inherited this prophetic gift;
he often cast successful horoscopes, successfully predicted both war and
plague in 1477, and once (a direct analogue to Strozza's experience) was
promised recovery from his own serious illness in a dream.

As Strozza cried in petition at the outset of his suffering, "Rise furies,
and this furie of my bane, / Assaile and conquer" (IV, i, 38–39), so Ficino
elaborated a system in which fury played a principal part. He described four
furores, those induced by poetry, mystery, prophecy, and love, concluding
that "no man possessed by *furor* is content with ordinary speech but breaks
forth into shouting and singing and chants. Wherefore any *furor*, either that
of prophecy, or of mysteries, or of love, since it leads to singing and poetry,
can rightly be said to find its completion in the poetic *furor*." Strozza's
invocation of the aid of the Furies seems pointed when we recall that at the
beginning of the play he had addressed the other prophetic character, Poggio,
as "my furious nephew." In Poggio, as in Strozza, the fury of prophetic
vision—as Ficino explains—makes him a true poet, possessor of the divine
afflatus. In the light of this insistence that true poets are furious seers, inspired
dreamers, we come to appreciate how fully Chapman has prepared the antithesis between the theatrical art futilely employed by the authors of the
masques and the grotesque dreams of furious Poggio. We now know, too,
why Strozza's reading of the poetic masque was not only more "poetic" but
more true than the masque itself. The carnal boar metamorphosed into Diana,
the broom-man philosopher who "passion sweepes from thought," were
obscured promises (made only partially "peruiall" through the veiled prophecy of their Herculean allusions), types of Strozza, the rapt physician who
verifies a dream of health snatched in angelic vision.

Medicine, however, permeates the play's last scenes in many other respects, reminding us of how the Renaissance critical debate on Aristotelian *katharsis* in art sought a grounding between the extremes of passion psychology and religious lustration. That Mendice should masquerade as Medice is more than a pun, as we see when the result of his machinations is the soul-healing paradox of the wounds suffered by both Strozza and Vincentio, and this medical focus is carried into yet another channel of action by the venomous disfigurement and miraculous restoration of Margaret's beauty.

In act IV it becomes apparent that the fundamental structure of *The Gentleman Usher* is the interaction between the mutually illuminating events involving Strozza and those involving Vincentio and Margaret. We have been reviewing Strozza's wounding and consequent translation through patience to a state of divine vision and prophecy. We have not noted, though, that in attributing his new-found patience to Cynanche, Strozza describes a "true wife" as one whose

> true woorth
> Makes a true husband thinke, his armes enfold
> (With her alone) a compleate worlde of gold.
> (IV, iii, 35–37)

In the immediately preceding scene, Margaret and Vincentio meet secretly while the others hunt. Fearing that Alphonso and Lasso intend to betroth Margaret to Alphonso and so frustrate the young lovers, they enact a rite of "natural marriage" before God. In this self-authorized ceremony under the eye of deity alone Margaret proposes an image of marriage to which Strozza's eulogy is an echo. She pledges that

> If you be sicke, I will be sicke, though well:
> If you be well, I will be well, though sicke:
> Your selfe alone my compleat world shall be,
> Euen from this houre, to all eternity.
> (IV, ii, 175–79)

A further analogy between the two actions is seen in the lovers' insistence that their marriage is valid because it accords with divine and natural law; they defy the laws of a society which is itself unnatural—as demonstrated by Alphonso's rivalry with his son or Mendice's success at court almost as clearly as by Poggio's report on the unnatural combat of dogs and horses. At the critical point in their tryst, Margaret queries rhetorically:

> may not we now
> Our contract make, and marie before heauen?
> Are not the lawes of God and Nature, more
> Than formall lawes of men?
>
> (IV, ii, 129–32)

This anti-Hobbesian view of man in a primitive state of nature recurs later in more titanic tones when Strozza defends his defense of the young couple against the Duke's mandate:

> A vertuous man is subject to no Prince,
> But to his soule and honour; which are lawes,
> That carrie Fire and Sword within themselues
> Neuer corrupted, never out of rule.
>
> (V, iv, 59–62)

For a moment early in the final act of the play Alphonso realizes that his command (disobeyed by Mendice in the event) for Vincentio not to be harmed is motivated by "Nature's" power in man (V, i, 162–65). When he is ultimately confronted by a wounded Vincentio, a disfigured Margaret, and Strozza as spokesman for natural man, the Duke recognizes his own lapse from natural sentiments and laments:

> O would to God, I could with present cure
> Of these vnnaturall wounds; and moning right
> Of this abused beautie, ioyne you both
> (As last I left you) in eternall nuptials.
>
> (V, iv, 84–87)

Thus calmed through the hard pedagogy of Strozza, Alphonso resigns the role of unnatural tyrant, and in the denouement drives Mendice from court and blesses the marriage of Vincentio and Margaret. We are perhaps justified in recalling Sandy's eulogy upon another virtuous winner: "*Yet* Hercules *better deserued a Deity then all the rest of the* Heroes: *who conquered nothing for himselfe: who ranged all ouer the world, not to oppresse it, but to free it from oppressors and by killing of Tyrants and Monsters preserued it in tranquillity.*" And "tranquillity" is just the word, because Strozza's analogy with Margaret and Vincentio must be completed, the moral bond with natural magic welded tight, by the establishment of "patience" within the patients as well as the physician.

It is clear that Vincentio and Margaret exhibited an initial impatience

in attempting to abrogate the fullness of providential time with a union
"now"—a term of temporal pressure repeated throughout their marriage
ritual. The impatience exhibited in this scene of star-crossed lovers is juxtaposed to the fury of *Strozza agonistes* in the preceding scene as an analogue,
but set in profounder perspective by the following scene, in which Strozza
has been translated to the certitude of patience through his own wife's efforts.
In short, act IV establishes the primacy of "natural" man over the contrived
tyrannies of society, only to bring this Rousseauistic attitude immediately
into question by underlining patience under providence; ripeness is all.

In act V we see the result of this crucial discrepancy between Strozza
and the lovers. In the opening scene, as we have noticed, Alphonso begins
to feel the tug of nature. But the machinery for filicide is already in motion,
and in the second scene we hear both Strozza's crescendo of poetry upon
patience and his visionary knowledge that Vincentio has been wounded in
body or soul—alternatives which can be coped with by the divinely contemplative healer. Strozza orders the Doctor to

> beare with you
> *Medcines* t'allay his danger: if by wounds,
> Beare pretious Balsome, or some soueraigne iuyce;
> If by fell poison, some choice *Antidote*,
> If by blacke witchcraft, our good spirits and prayers
> Shall exorcise the diuelish wrath of hell,
> Out of his princely bosome.
>
> (V, ii, 57–63)

The following scene reveals Margaret, believing Vincentio to be dead, in-
viting the willing connivance of Cortezza in her self-disfigurement. Encouraged by the hypocritically reticent aunt, the girl smears over her face a
violent acid. In destroying her own beauty Margaret is—albeit tempted by
a wicked agency—attempting that escape from the body and its passions
which Strozza has effected in becoming "nought else but soule." However,
she has done so in the wrong phase. She is God's subject *furens*, not *patiens*,
and therefore echoes the pre-visionary courtier Strozza, rather than Strozza
the seer made patient with providential promises. As the scene closes, Margaret's apostrophe uses a medical image to draw her furious grief, and
Alphonso's unnatural passion, into the aura of demonic magic which coun-
terpoints the spiritual magic of Strozza and his cures:

> Smart pretious ointment, smart, and to my braine
> Sweate they enuenom'd furie, make my eyes

Burne with thy sulphre, like the lakes of hell,
That feare of me may shiuer him to dust,
That eate his own childe with the jawes of lust.

(v, iii, 78–82)

The play's last scene is constructed around a sharp concentration of the movement by which Margaret, Vincentio, and Alphonso all run that course of conversion from *homo furens* to *homo patiens* for which Strozza has already been pattern and spokesman.

As Alphonso and Lasso exchange their first premonitions of the danger to Vincentio, the demonic Cortezza—who embodies fully the perverted lust of the aging which is only a passing, unnatural passion in Alphonso—rushes in to report Margaret's self-abuse; she is immediately followed upon stage by the disfigured and disheveled Margaret, who frantically accuses Alphonso of destroying her beauty, Vincentio's life, and the natural expectations of love, sealing her attack with a curse. Alphonso, staggering under this assault, then receives a messenger who reports Vincentio's dangerous wound. Before he has an opportunity to react to either discovery, Strozza, Cynanche, Poggio, and Doctor Benevenius appear on the one side and Mendice with his wounded son on the other. The stage is now a tableau of passion's slavery: Alphonso stands at bay, faced by the diabolic Cortezza and medicine-man Mendice and by the spiritual visionaries and physicians, and looks upon the dreadful results of his passion.

It is now that Strozza attacks the unnatural tyranny which could foster a filicide; Alphonso replies in imagery which recapitulates Strozza's own Herculean experience of physical suffering and spiritual transcendence:

How thicke and heavily my plagues descend!

Poure more rebuke vpon me worthie Lord,
For I have guilt and patience for them all.

(V, iv, 67–70)

His first generous thought in the state of patience is for the young lovers. Vincentio responds in a fashion that reveals how he, too, has passed into a spiritual transcendence of physical accidents, has learned Ficino's dictum that "every soul should retire from the pestilence of the body and withdraw into the mind, for then fortune will spend its force on the body and not pass into the soul":

since I make no doubt I shall suruiue
These fatall dangers; and your grace is pleasde,

To giue free course to my vnwounded loue;
T'is not this outward beauties ruthfull losse,
Can any thought discourage my desires:
And therefore, deare life, doe not wrong me so,
To thinke my loue the shadow of your beautie,
I wooe your vertues, which as I am sure
No accident can alter or empaire;
So, be you certaine nought can change my love.

(V, iv, 90–99)

Vincentio, too, can now say with Strozza, "the Iudiciall patience I embrace /
. . . Leaues me nought else but soule" (IV, iii, 48–51). And, in Margaret's
response, the circle of self-conquest is completed. She tenderly rejects his
offer, but rejects it because she has learned to await the fullness of time:

when the most needfull rights
Of Fate, and Nature, haue dissolu'd your life,
And that your loue must needs be all in soule,
Then will we meet againe: and then (dear Loue)
Loue me againe, for then will beautie be
Of no respect with loues eternitie.

(V, iv, 110–15)

All are now become *homines patientes*, and it remains only for a final act
of spiritual healing to complete the harmony. Doctor Benevenius, who, with
his pious chorus, has almost become Strozza's alter ego, steps forth upon
the moment of Margaret's patient acceptance of suffering. Petitioning
"Heauen, and Art," he applies to her face "an Elixar drawne through seuen
yeares fire" (V, iv, 124) which will restore her outward beauty in neoplatonic
harmony with her inward state. Then, "if heauen consent," he prophesies a
cure for Vincentio on the seventh day thereafter. Thus the spiritual healing
of the visionary Strozza has been re-enacted upon his friends down to the
smallest detail. Patience has re-created the bodies of all the protagonists
under the transcendent mark of spirit.

One may well question, though, why concinnity was not kept by
making Strozza the direct instrument of the later cures, as he was of his
own. The answer lies in the final hundred lines of the play, which seem at
first to confuse, if not abrogate, the thematic development toward harmony
in patience. Benevenius having restored the lovers' hopes, Mendice is brought
in for questioning, and Strozza attacks him so passionately that he must be
restrained by the Duke and Vincentio so that Mendice may confess and be

exiled rather than be killed on the spot. Strozza at this point repeatedly recalls the vision which has effected restoration through

> that good Angell,
> That by diuine relation spake in me,
> Fore-telling these foule dangers to your sonne,
> And without notice brought this reuerend man
> To rescue him from death.
>
> (V, iv, 199–203)

This same angel has assured Strozza that Mendice is a vile imposter, meriting death. "Which," says Strozza "will instantly appear, / And that I feele with some rare mircale" (213–14). Strozza's

> spirit propheticke
> Hath inward feeling of such sinnes in him,
> As aske the forfait of his life and soule
> (220–22)

and he knows "it is heauens justice / To plague his life and soule." Acting as justice's minister, Strozza now draws his sword, crying at Mendice, "and heer's heauens justice" (232–33), at which point he is restrained by the Duke. Under these pressures, Mendice confesses that he has been supported by gypsy sorcery and is driven into exile in limbo, crying, appropriately enough for the demonic agent he has been, "Ile runne and hide me from the sight of heauen" (277). Thus, at the close, the larger implications of the tragicomedy of *The Gentleman Usher* are made explicit in almost paradigmatic fashion: comedy emerges from the threat of tragedy, in the medieval sense of the two terms, as it always must in the divine creation because spiritual magic has exorcised the demonic.

This anger of Strozza's, then, has been an inspired anger. "My hand / Forbidden is from heauen to let him liue," Strozza cries (227–28). But both Strozza and heaven do permit Mendice to live, and the rationale for the patient man's anger must be sought in the announcement which precedes his wild entrance. Strozza, remarks a courtier, is "burning in zeale of friendship" (V, iv, 39). Zealous anger constitutes the final bond between Strozza and the tradition of exegetical commentary upon Hercules. Waith has shown the path by which Hercules' irascible nature is transmuted into a manifestation of the Christian concept of righteous indignation: "Thomas Aquinas uses this term, *ira per zelum*, for a praiseworthy anger which is in accordance with right reason. He quotes Gregory the Great as saying that *ira per zelum* troubles the eye of reason whereas sinful anger blinds it. It is important to remember that the terrible rage of Hercules, vanquishing monsters and chastising tyrants, or suffering in his poisoned robe, could have the meaning of that justifiable anger which is not opposed to reason and which the great man requires in his struggle with a corrupt world. So *The Gentlemen Usher* closes in comedy: Strozza's paradoxically angry patience drives the demonic physician from the court, and spiritual harmony is restored through the healing vision of more truly Herculean hero than the posing and defeated Bussy.

In a fashion he probably never dreamed, *The Gentleman Usher* verifies Guarini's contemporary assertion that tragicomedy alone provides *katharsis*. Here Chapman has shown that tragedy is a true lustration which purges man of passion; but also that man so purged transcends tragedy to take his role in the divine comedy of the creation. Strozza's prophetic dreams raise him to the world of the imagination (Ficino had seen that prophetic *furor* always ends in making a man a poet), and so he becomes the only true playwright and manipulator in a world of art, artifice, and deception. Mendice, the demonic, could not explicate the masque of lies which was the feeble theatrical invention of the passion-ridden Duke at the opening of the play. Strozza, dreaming prophet, opens by interpreting the masque in a sense which the others cannot seize upon, and closes the play as the instrumental voice of the greatest playwright, who raises the action from the theatrical spectacle of courtly intrigues to the spiritual theater of the soul in which God is both seer and seen.

EDWIN MUIR

"Royal Man":
Notes on the Tragedies of George Chapman

Chapman's virtues and faults are both excessive, and are combined in such a way that the faults seem to heighten the virtues, and the virtues to stiffen the faults. He erects his imperfections into principles, and keeps them erect by an act of will. When he succeeds he achieves an elevation beyond what seems possible, and when he fails, collapses into fantastic bathos. His mark is excess, itself a fault which he had seen splendidly displayed in Marlowe, the poet of his time whom he admired most. In Marlowe it is a quality of desire and imagination; in Chapman, of character and will. He is excessive on moral grounds, and because he believes that "royal man" should be excessive.

> Your mind, you say, kept in your flesh's bounds,
> Shows that man's will must ruled be by his power,
> When by true doctrine, you are taught to live
> Rather without the body, than within,
> And rather to your God still than yourself;
> To live to him, is to do all things fitting
> His image, in which, like himself, we live;
> To be his image, is to do those things
> That make us deathless, which by death is only;
> Doing those deeds that fit eternity;
> And those deeds are the perfecting the justice
> That makes the world last . . .

From *Essays on Literature and Society*. © 1949 by Edwin Muir, 1965 by The Hogarth Press, Ltd. Harvard University Press, 1965.

Chapman is not interested in human nature, or in practical morality, or in evil, but in the man of excessive virtue or spirit or pride. His tragedies show us one great figure and a crowd of nobodies who succeed somehow in destroying him. We do not believe in their power to do this until it is done, for the conflict is between a man of flesh and blood larger than life and puppets of cardboard. Yet the hero's death is real; so that we involuntarily think of it as self-inflicted or as brought about by some power outside the drama, the acts of the other characters being incapable of accounting for it. The death of Bussy D'Ambois and of Byron have, therefore, a sacrificial quality; we seem to be watching the pursuit and destruction of "royal man" by an invisible hunter. But we see them simultaneously merely as men who ignore the limitations of human life and are bound to destroy themselves; and their ostensible betrayers, the Montsurrys and La Fins—minuses whose very names seem unreal—can only look on and ratify the foregone verdict. These heroes really exist in another dimension from the rest of the characters, and have a different reality from the action in which they are involved. They wander about, like Chapman himself, enclosed in a dream of greatness and breathing the air of that dream.

It is in these remarkable figures that the dramatic interest resides, for they are conscious of another drama beyond the drama which is shown on the stage, and lift us up into it. In their great speeches they employ a language which is not meant for the other actors; they really talk to themselves, or address an imaginary audience outside the play. Chapman is not interested—except in one or two of his comedies—in character or even in action. He employs action merely to display the soul in one of those supreme crises where action itself seems to become irrelevant, since it has done all that it can do, has come to its end, and can be disregarded. He is concerned solely with the crisis as a thing in itself, for in the crisis the real drama of his heroes is born and they rise into their own world; he therefore tries to reach it without the wearisome labour of working towards it through a methodical arrangement of situations. We can feel his impatience to arrive at those places where the souls of his heroes can expand to their full range, places on the frontier-line between life and death, time and eternity, where all terms seem to become absolute. Consequently a situation which to other tragic figures would bring despair or resignation, merely evokes new potentialities in his heroes, as if it were the opportunity for which they had been waiting. In a sense, therefore, his tragic scenes transcend tragedy, or fail to reach it; for death is merely the final assurance of immortality to his heroes. They always possess this assurance; it is one of their distinguishing marks; but it grows stronger the nearer death comes. In their death the dimension of tragedy expands to include an extra one which is not quite compatible with it, for in dying they conduct us a little distance into their own immortality. They look into that, not backwards at their destruction, except in the elegiac mood in which one may grieve for something that has happened in the past to oneself, or to a friend, or to some legendary figure in a book. The tragedies end in this way because Chapman is concerned with the soul as he conceives it, and with hardly anything else.

This exclusive concern with the soul rather than with the way in which people behave makes him an erratic moralist. His judgments of conduct are sometimes strange and almost incomprehensible, the judgements of a man who is not interested in action, either on the stage or in the ordinary world. The action in a play is the prime means for bringing out the moral character of the actors and the moral significance of the situation. We do not come to know Bussy or Byron morally, as we know Macbeth and Hamlet, for the action has no real effect on them, since they live in a different world from the other characters, and are a law to themselves.

> There is no danger to a man that knows
> What life and death is; there's not any law
> Exceeds his knowledge; neither is it lawful
> That he should stoop to any other law.
> He goes before them, and commands them all,
> That to himself is a law rational.

In a play, which is a pattern of action and interaction, there must be an implicit standard of judgment applied to all the characters and running through the whole, otherwise its progress is confused and dislocated. Chapman's tragedies are full of such dislocations; sometimes we cannot even guess at the standard by which he judges the action; we find such monstrosities as the scene in the first act of *The Tragedy of Bussy D'Ambois*, where Bussy pays court to the Duchess of Guise in the fustian of a low actor, and insults the Duke so obscurely that one can scarcely make out what he means. It is a scene of fantastic vulgarity, yet it draws this splendid encomium on Bussy from the King's brother:

> His great heart will not down, 'tis like the sea,
> That partly by his own internal heat,
> Partly the stars' daily and nightly motion,
> Their heat and light, and partly of the place,
> The divers frames; but chiefly by the moon,
> Bristled with surges, never will be won,

> (No, not when th' hearts of all those powers are burst)
> To make retreat into his settled home,
> Till he be crowned with his own quiet foam.

There is no proportion between these lines and the conduct which inspires them; and there is little connection in *The Tragedy of Bussy D'Ambois* as a whole: here and there fine dramatic touches come and go, but leave the characters and the action as they were. When the end does come, after these fits and starts, it comes abruptly, we scarcely know how.

Chapman's figures therefore stick out of the play, or rather burst through it, making havoc of the dramatic machinery and fixing our eyes upon them amid the ruins. Once there, they speak unencumbered in Chapman's own voice, a voice habitually choked by a consciousness of things too great for ordinary utterance and requiring the explosive power of some portent to liberate it. These mouthpieces of Chapman are images of man in his original virtue; there is nothing else quite like them in English literature. The sources from which he might have derived them are obvious enough—his long familiarity with the Homeric heroes, his absorption in Roman history and Senecan tragedy, his knowledge of the lives of some of the Renaissance princes, who attempted so many things which had seemed unthinkable before, and are described by Burckhardt. But the image into which his imagination melted those various conceptions of "royal man" is striking and original. The French King, speaking of Bussy, gives the most complete idea of it:

> Cousin Guise, I wonder
> Your honour'd disposition brooks so ill
> A man so good, that only would uphold
> Man in his native noblesse, from whose fall
> All our dimensions rise; that in himself
> (Without the outward patches of our frailty,
> Riches and honour) knows he comprehends
> Worth with the greatest; kings had never borne
> Such boundless empire over other men,
> Had all maintain'd the spirit and state of D'Ambois;
> Nor had the full impartial hand of nature
> That all things gave in her original,
> Without these definite terms of mine and thine,
> Been turn'd unjustly to the hand of Fortune,
> Had all preserved her in her prime, like D'Ambois;
> No envy, no disjunction had dissolved

Or pluck'd one stick out of the golden faggot
In which the world of Saturn bound our lives,
Had all been held together with the nerves,
The genius, and th' ingenuous soul of D'Ambois.

The idea that if man had not fallen there would be no kings or subjects, no mine or thine, recurs in the tragedies, and evokes an image which cannot be described either as a new ideal of society or as a new state of being. Bussy D'Ambois and Byron are unfallen men among the fallen, but their virtues are not Adam's; they are not equipped with innocence, but with native noblesse, spirit and state, genius and an ingenuous soul, the virtues of the Renaissance. Bussy is like a cross between Adam and Achilles crossed again by something quite different, the Renaissance man stepping out of the Middle Ages into a new world. There is something legendary in this figure, out of which Chapman might have created the myth of his age if he had possessed greater dramatic power and a less erratic genius. The legendary quality appears more clearly in the description of Byron sitting his horse:

Your Majesty hath miss'd a royal sight:
The Duke Byron, on his brave beast Pastrana,
Who sits him like a full-sail'd argosy,
Danced with a lofty billow, and as snug
Plies to his bearer, both their motions mix'd;
And being consider'd in their site together
They do the best present the state of man
In his first royalty ruling, and of beasts
In their first loyalty serving; one commanding,
And no way being moved; the other serving,
And no way being compell'd; of all the sights
That ever my eyes witness'd; and they make
A doctrinal and witty hieroglyphic
Of a blest kingdom; to express and teach,
Kings to command as they could serve, and subjects
To serve as if they had power to command.

"A doctrinal and witty hieroglyphic of a blest kingdom": this is the hypothesis on which the real drama of Chapman's heroes is grounded, an action elevated above the ostensible action. This blest kingdom is not set in the past, a mere recollection of the Golden Age, nor in the future, a prophecy of a coming society, but rather in a perpetual present apprehended and to that degree lived in by the hero, the unfallen man. We accept this hero and his drama as real, perhaps because with one part of him man still lives in the world before the Fall, and with another in the world after it, since the Fall—assuming that it stands for anything in human experience—is not a historical event but something which is always happening. Chapman's heroes exist more largely in the world before the Fall than any other figures in tragedy; it is for this reason that they are so clearly conscious of their immortality; for this reason, too, perhaps, that they are so awkward and clumsy in the world of action: we could hardly expect adroitness and expedience from these men existing

> In all free-born powers of royal man.

It is not, then, the world in which they move, but the world we see through their eyes which gives Chapman's heroes their greatness. Their nature demands two things from that world created in their image: freedom and glory, but not power or love. In almost any page of the tragedies we find proofs of Chapman's possession by these qualities:

> Hot, shining, swift, light, and aspiring things
> Are of immortal and celestial nature. . . .
> To fear a violent good, abuseth goodness;
> 'Tis immortality to die aspiring,
> As if a man were taken quick to heaven;
> What will not hold perfection, let it burst. . . .
> I'll wear those golden spurs upon my heels,
> And kick at fate; be free, all worthy spirits,
> And stretch yourselves, for greatness and for height.

This aspiring life just touching the earth and perpetually mounting into the air is suggested finely in his descriptions of his heroes fighting:

> Like bonfires of contributory wood
> Every man's look show'd, fed with other's spirit.
>
> D'Ambois (that like a laurel put on fire
> Sparkled and spit). . . .
>
> And then like flame and powder they commixt
> So spritely, that I wish'd they had been spirits.
>
> He turn'd wild lightning in the lackeys' hands.
>
>   their saucy fingers
> Flew as too hot off, as he had been fire.

The battles then in two half-moons enclosed him,
In which he showed as if he were the light,
And they but the earth. . . .

These combats are not kindled and fed by merely human passion; they are like an explosion of the elements into speed and fire, impersonal, nonhuman, transmuting the fighting heroes into those

Hot, shining, swift, light, and aspiring things

which to Chapman were of immortal and celestial nature. In a well-known passage Clermont D'Ambois, Bussy's brother, says:

And know ye all (though far from all your aims,
Yet worth them all, and all men's endless studies)
That in this one thing, all the discipline
Of manners, and of manhood is contain'd;
A man to join himself with th' Universe,
In his main sway, and make (in all things fit)
One with that all, and go on, round as it.

Clermont is expounding a high philosophical idea; but there are more ways of joining oneself with the universe than those he lays down, and Chapman's heroes inevitably make for that junction, whether in battle or in speculation or in death. Bussy's last speech calls up a gigantic vision of his memory being taken into the keeping of universal nature:

The equal thought I bear of life and death
Shall make me faint on no side; I am up;
Here like a Roman statue I will stand
Till death hath made me marble; oh, my fame,
Live in despite of murder; take thy wings
And haste thee where the grey-eyed morn perfumes
Her rosy chariot with Sabaean spices,
Fly, where the evening from th' Iberian vales,
Takes on her swarthy shoulder Hecate,
Crowned with a grove of oaks; fly where men feel
The cunning axletree; and those that suffer
Beneath the chariot of the snowy Bear:
And tell them all that D'Ambois now is hasting
To the eternal dwellers . . .

There is no other last speech like that in Elizabethan drama. "Oh, my fame, live in despite of murder" recalls Hamlet's wish that his memory might be vindicated; but Hamlet does not confide it to the universe, but to Horatio, mortal like himself:

> If thou didst ever hold me in thy heart,
> Absent thee from felicity awhile,
> And in this harsh world draw thy breath in pain,
> To tell my story.

The difference is great, the difference between an imagination which penetrates deep into human life, and one which is concentrated upon a great idea. The essential thing about Chapman's heroes, as about Marlowe's, is that they are framed of the four elements, not that they are human beings obliged to live somehow with other human beings; they are nearer to earth, water, air and fire than to us as we know ourselves. Marlowe gives the concoction from which Chapman's heroes were drawn:

> Nature that fram'd us of four elements,
> Warring within our breasts for regiment,
> Doth teach us all to have aspiring minds.

For Marlowe's poetry, too, like Chapman's, is inspired by a philosophical idea of man, not by human life as the observer sees it. His idea at first seems to be much the same as Chapman's, but in reality is very different; for though like Chapman he is in love with freedom and glory, he is also in love with their rewards, with

> the ripest fruit of all
> That perfect bliss and sole felicity,
> The sweet fruition of an earthly crown.

Chapman's heroes have no ambition to achieve an earthly crown. They love freedom and glory disinterestedly as states of the soul, for their own and for the soul's sake. Their aspiring minds reach for a state in which freedom and glory are possessed purely, without admixture, as things in themselves. Bussy does not try to gain power over others, but merely to live after the pattern of "royal man." Byron is drawn into plots against his king, but his hostility is nothing more than that of a man who feels he is a king against another who merely is one. His plots bring him to the scaffold; they also precipitate his spiritual tragedy, for he can no longer enjoy freedom and glory in their purity after he has yielded to private ambition and envy. He is an unfallen man who yields to the persuasions of the fallen and becomes one of them, greater than them still, but no longer different from them. He loses his native noblesse by trying to win the noblesse of this world.

We do not come to know Bussy and Byron morally, for they are never affected by that action, never tested by it; but we do come to know what morality is—or what morality is to Chapman—through their mouths. That morality is a passionate, disinterested devotion to freedom and glory, the

> Doing those deeds that fit eternity.

Chapman carried his idea of freedom and glory to excess, no doubt, but excess was at the root of his virtues.

> Since I am free,
> (Offending no just law), let no law make
> By any wrong it does, my life her slave:
> When I am wrong'd, and that law fails to right me,
> Let me be king myself (as man was made),
> And do a justice that exceeds the law.

Chapman's conception of morality is partial: in concentrating on greatness it pays little attention to goodness. But it is disinterested; it rises above the very thought of expediency, and takes us into the region of absolute things.

L. G. SALINGAR

The Revenger's Tragedy
and the Morality Tradition

Tourneur's plays have too often been described as if they were texts for
illustration by an Aubrey Beardsley. They have suffered as a result. Symonds
read *The Revenger's Tragedy* as a melodrama with agreeable thrills and some
needless moralizing; and, on this reading, it was not difficult for William
Archer, applying the standards of naturalism, to make the play appear
ludicrous. Though Mr. Eliot has supplied a corrective by pointing out that
the characters are not to be taken as studies in individual iniquity, but as
figures in a pattern with a poetic life of its own, his essay on Tourneur again
misrepresents him. He is made "a highly sensitive adolescent with a gift for
words . . ."

> The cynicism, the loathing and disgust of humanity, expressed
> consummately in *The Revenger's Tragedy*, are immature in the
> respect that they exceed the object. Their objective equivalents
> are characters practicing the grossest vices; characters which seem
> merely to be spectres projected from the poet's inner world of
> nightmare, some horror beyond words. So the play is a document
> on humanity chiefly because it is a document on one human being,
> Tourneur; its motive is truly the death motive, for it is the
> loathing and horror of life itself.

This is the reading of the 'nineties again. Tourneur's poetry, however, unlike
the Romantic poetry of decadence, has a firm grasp on the outer world.
Cynicism, loathing, and disgust there are in *The Revenger's Tragedy*; but if
Tourneur were merely giving expression to a neurotic state of mind, he

From *Scrutiny* 6, no. 4 (March 1938). © 1961 by Cambridge University Press.

would hardly have written successful drama at all. The "object" of his disgust is not the behavior of his characters, singly or together, so much as the process they represent, the disintegration of a whole social order. It is this theme, particularized and brought to life by the verse, that shapes the pattern of the play; and it is developed with the coherence, the precise articulation, of a dramatist assured that his symbols are significant for his audience as much as for himself. Tourneur is writing in the contemporary Revenge convention; but behind the Revenge plays is another dramatic influence, working in harmony with Tourneur's narrowly traditionalist outlook, that of the Moralities. *The Revenger's Tragedy* is a logical development from the mediaeval drama.

The Moralities had been the staple of popular drama when Marlowe began writing, and their methods were absorbed into the blank verse narrative play. That they were absorbed, not abandoned, is clear from *Faustus*; and Mr. Knights has pointed out that their influence on Jonson and his contemporaries was considerable and varied. They offered the Elizabethans a group of stock situations, types, and themes which had been utilised for the representation of social and religious problems throughout the changes of a century; and the later drama could rely on their familiarity in presenting fairly complex situations simply and effectively on the stage. The Morality influence makes itself felt, under the Senecanism and the literary satire, through the conventions of the Revenge plays themselves, and in *The Revenger's Tragedy* most strongly of all. The characters in the Moralities are personified abstractions and moral or social types, representing the main forces making for or against the salvation of the individual and social stability; they have no dramatic functions outside the doctrinal scheme. The actions on the stage are symbolic, not realistic, and the incidents are related to each other logically, as parts of an allegory, or as illustrations of the argument. *The Revenger's Tragedy* is constructed on closely similar lines. Miss Bradbrook has analysed the narrative into "a series of peripeteia," representing "the contrasts between earthly and heavenly vengeance, and earthly and heavenly justice"—linked as the parts of an allegory rather than as a natural sequence of events. The characters are exclusively the instruments of this movement, and it is from this point of view that they explain themselves to the audience; their speeches reveal their world, rather than individual minds. The Duke and his court are simply monstrous embodiments of Lust, Pride, and Greed; Vendice and the other revengers, despite the intensely personal tone of their speeches, are portrayed in the same way. The characters' motives are generalized and conventional—Lussurioso, for example, is an extreme case of Pride and Lust—and many of the speeches are general satiric tirades, spoken in half-turn towards the audience. This is a narrower dramatic pattern than Marston's, and more like those of the Moralities; but Tourneur gains in dramatic coherence from the earlier examples. With Jonson, he was the last writer to apply them successfully.

"I see now," says Ambitioso in the underplot—the traditional comic underplot in which the Vices are confounded—"there's nothing sure in mortality, but mortality." The contrast between the skeleton and the specious overlay provided by wealth and sensuality is fundamental to Tourneur and the Morality-writers alike. When Pride, in Medwall's *Nature*, leads Man to debauchery, he prepares for him "a doublet of the new make":

> Under that a shirt as soft as silk,
> And as white as any milk
> To keep the carcase warm.

These lines might have provided Tourneur with his text. Medwall, however, writes with an equanimity, a sense of security in the values of Nature, that Tourneur has lost. His sense of decay, of the skull, is overpowering:

> Advance thee, O thou terror to fat folks,
> To have their costly three-piled flesh worn off
> As bare as this; for banquets, ease, and laughter
> Can make great men, as greatness goes by clay;
> But wise men little are more great than they.

The Stoical conclusion is feeble beside the savage intensity of the first lines. Death has triumphed, and the only course left open to Vendice is to convert a horrified recoil into a grim acceptance, turning the forces of death against themselves. Nevertheless, the fascination of physical decay has not corrupted Tourneur's satiric purpose; there is nothing mechanical in Vendice's wielding of the lash. The changes of tone in this first soliloquy with the skull imply an attitude active and controlled:

> When two heaven-pointed diamonds were set
> In those unsightly rings—then 'twas a face
> So far beyond the artificial shine
> Of any woman's bought complexion,
> That the uprightest man (if such there be
> That sin but seven times a day) broke custom,
> And made up eight with looking after her.
> O, she was able to ha' made a usurer's son
> Melt all his patrimony in a kiss;

And what his father fifty years told,
To have consumed, and yet his suit been cold.
But, O accursed palace!
Thee, when thou wert apparelled in thy flesh,
The old duke poisoned . . .
O, 'ware an old man hot and vicious!
'Age, as in gold, in lust is covetous.'

                                                    (I, i.)

The contrasts between life and death, between natural virtue and the effects
of lust and greed, are not merely presented—they are shown as a unified
process in Vendice's mind, a process which extends through the whole world
of the play. The imagery associated with the skull is concrete, exact, and
dramatically useful; Tourneur builds up a system of relationships between
images and situations which gains in cumulative effect—these lines, for
example, have a bearing on the ironic undertones of the scene where the
Duchess tempts Spurio, who is wearing her jewel in his ear ("had he cut
thee a right diamond . . ."), and, again, on the second appearance of the
skull, poisoned with cosmetics. The pun in the first line is flat, but not
extraneous; it emphasizes the way in which the symbols are to be taken—
the physical world is treated, in a peculiarly direct and consistent manner,
as emblematic of the moral order, man in relation to the divine will. This
moral order is rigidly identified with the traditional social hierarchy of ranks
and obligations; but the narrowness of Tourneur's outlook makes for concentration, and his poetic material is ranged and ordered by reference to the
experience of society as a whole. In this passage, the physical contrast between
the "diamonds" and their sockets, visible on the stage, prepares for, and
supports, the crude cynicism of the parenthesis, which marks the change of
tone. The complete degeneration of virtue is represented by placing the
"usurer's son" on the same footing of sensuality as "the uprightest man,"
the mock inflation overturning any protest from respectability. Here, however,
the tone changes again: the "patrimony," by implication the ill-gained result
of greed, is itself "melted" away, and, though virtue cannot be reinstated,
divine justice is vindicated in the rhyme. Vendice's tone mounts again as
he reverts to the palace; but the Duke, with the "infernal fires" burning in
his "spendthrift veins," has already been paralleled with the usurer's son—
the two types of social disintegration are juxtaposed throughout the play—
so that Vendice's exultant determination on revenge appears as part of an
inevitable cycle of feelings and events.

The trite "sentences" at the end of Tourneur's most passionate speeches are meant to enforce this sense of inevitability by lowering the tension and appealing to the commonplace. Tourneur himself calls them "conceits," and continually draws attention, in Marston's manner, to his virtuosity in using them. The resemblance to Marston, however, is only superficial; they are more closely akin to the popular moralists and the Morality writers. Vendice's emblem is an example: "A usuring father to be boiling in hell, and his son and heir with a whore dancing over him."

Again:

> O, you must note who 'tis should die,
> The duchess' son! she'll look to be a saver:
> "Judgment, in this age, is near kin to favour."
> (I, iv.)

> Could you not stick? See what confession doth!
> Who would not lie, when men are hanged for truth?
> (V, i.)

These popular aphorisms and tags of Seneca Englished gave Marston and Tourneur a large part of the raw material from which their more ambitious speeches are developed. But while Marston works up his material as a self-conscious litterateur, Tourneur adheres to the Morality mode. The language of the latter is plain and colloquial, but adequate, as a rule, to the simple didactic purpose; a speech to the audience from Lupton's *All for Money* is typical:

> Is not my grandfather Money think ye of great power
> That could save from hanging such abominable whore,
> That against all nature her own child did kill?
> And yonder poor knave that did steal for his need
> A few sort of rags, and not all worth a crown,
> Because he lacks money shall be hanged for that deed,
> You may see my Grandsire is a man of renown:
> It were meet when I named him that you all kneeled down.
> Nay, make it not so strange, for the best of you all,
> Do love him so well, you will come at his call.

The audience is included in the framework of the play, the function of the speeches being to expound the theme to them from their own point of view. Marston's sophisticated railing has quite a different effect; it draws attention to itself:

PIETRO: Tell me; indeed I heard thee rail—
MENDOZA: At women, true; why, what cold phlegm could choose,
    Knowing a lord so honest, virtuous,
    So boundless loving, bounteous, fair-shaped, sweet,
    To be contemn's, abused, defamed, made cuckold!
Heart, I hate all women for't; sweet sheets, wax lights, antique
bedposts, cambric smocks, villanous curtains, arras pictures, oiled
hinges, and all the tongue-tied lascivious witnesses of great
creatres' wantonness.

(The Malcontent, I, vii.)

The lively phrasing here is at odds with the ostensible moral purpose—it is
true that Mendoza is gulling Pietro, having cuckolded him himself, but his
speech is in the same style as the Malcontent's own speeches;—the literary
exhibitionism accompanies a confusion of dramatic motives. Tourneur's railing is more surely realized; it is presented in the older and simpler dramatic
mode:

VENDICE: Now 'tis full sea abed over the world:
    There's juggling of all sides; some that were maids
    E'en at sunset, are now perhaps i' the toll-book.
    This woman in immodest thin apparel
    Lets in her friend by water; here a dame
    Cunning nails leather hinges to a door,
    To avoid proclamation.
    Now cuckolds are coining apace, apace, apace, apace!
    And careful sisters spin that thread in the night
    That does maintain them and their bawds i' the day.
HIPPOLITO: You flow well, brother.
VENDICE: Pooh! I'm shallow yet;
    Too sparing and too modest; shall I tell thee?
    If every trick were told that's dealt by night,
    There are few here that would not blush outright.

The direct appeal to the audience, as M. C. Bradbrook remarks, is bathetic;
but it is significant of the condition of success for the first speech, Tourneur's
single-minded attitude towards subject and audience together. The shaping
influence is that of the Moralities, transmitted directly through Jonson.

It was this influence which enabled him to use the Revenge conventions
so successfully. His main preoccupations appear in his first work, *The Transformed Metamorphosis*, clumsily set forth in the form of a vision. The insti-

tutions of church and state, and even the objects of the physical world, are
perverted from their original and proper functions; Pan, for example, the
church, has become a "hellish ill o're-mask'd with holiness"—"Pan with
gold is metamorphosed." The Prologue describes the poet's bewilderment
at the Cimmerian darkness in which he finds himself:

> Are not the lights that Jupiter appointed
> To grace the heav'ns, and to direct the sight,
> Still in that function, which them first anointed,
> Is not the world directed by their light?
> And is not rest, the exercise of night?
> Why is the sky so pitchy then at noon,
> As though the day were govern'd by the Moon?

This has the naivety, the misplacement of emotion, that finds its counterpart
in the cynicism of *The Revenger's Tragedy*. The conceits are painstakingly
clumsy because Tourneur is genuinely bewildered; he treats them as if they
were literal statements of fact. It is evident, however, that they are not
affectations of style, as with many of his contemporaries, but organic parts
of his thought. The symbolism of the poem reappears in the play, in the
pervasive imagery of metamorphosis, falsification, and moral camouflage. It
has been thoroughly assimilated to the rhythms of dramatic speech:

> Last revelling night,
> When torch-light made an artificial noon
> About the court, some courtiers in the masque,
> Putting on better faces than their own,
> Being full of fraud and flattery
>
> (I, iv.)

> Ha, what news here? is the day out o' the socket,
> That it is noon at midnight? the court up?
>
> (II, iv.)

The details are worked out in relation to a central group of metaphors,
repeated, on the level of action, in the disguises and deceptions which
compose the plot. Here again, the method is derived from the Moralities.

These disguises and deceptions are symbolic, not naturalistic—an occasion is even created for making Castiza herself appear in a falso character.
Vendice is disguised three times—when, as Piato, he enters "the world"
and becomes "a man o' the time," a court pander; a second time, then he
appears as a fantastic "character" of himself, a melancholy, litigious scholar;

and finally, as a masquer. The disguises are distinguished from the disguiser; what Vendice does in his assumed roles affects his character as Vendice, but the relationship is circumscribed and conventional; no provision is made to render it plausible, realistically, that Vendice would or could have sustained his roles. When he tempts his sister, he is not Vendice in disguise, he is Vendice-become-Piato; Piato and Vendice are sharply distinguished. Nevertheless, Vendice suffers from what Piato has to do; and the separate roles, moreover, are complementary to each other. At first, Vendice is the honest malcontent, the nobleman wronged and depressed by poverty; then he becomes a member of the society that has wronged him. He is sardonically aware of himself in his role, as if necessity, not policy, had changed him, just as it threatens to change his mother—(this is the way in which Flamineo and Bosola fuse the roles of villain and critic). He is morally involved in his actions as Piato; and when he appears in the conventional fatal masque, he s justly the victim as well as the instrument of heavenly vengeance. The second disguise is a caricature of his original position. Thus the different roles are not linked together by reference to circumstantial probability, but by reference to the dramatic and social functions of the original character, as with Edgar in *Lear*. The disguisings are related symbols of a transformation within the moral and social order.

Symbolic disguising with a similar dramatic purpose was a stock convention of the Moralities; sometimes there is a change of dress, sometimes only of name. This was not merely a convention of the stage; it embodied popular beliefs about the methods of the Deceiver—"the devil hath power To assume a pleasing shape." Thus, in Medwall's *Nature*, Pride and Covetise beguile Man under the names of Worship and Worldly Policy, the other Deadly Sins being disguised in the same way. Moreover, the disguisers, besides their attributes as moral types, are usually given, more specifically than any other figures in the play, the attributes of a particular social class. Man, in *Nature*, is a noble, but he is made representative of humanity in general; it is emphasized, on the other hand, that Pride is a knight, and the Deadly Sins only appear as officers of the household. In the later Moralities, social themes, as distinct from theological, become more prominent; and the moral role of the disguisers is often completely merged into their role as the agents of social change. In the Marian play, *Respublica*, for example, the Reformation is engineered by the profiteer Avarice, disguised as Policy; and the characters with aliases in *The Tyde Taryeth No Man* are the broker, Hurtful Help, who operates under the deceptive title of Help, and his accomplices.

The disguisers are contrasted with the other characters in that the latter represent the permanent and unequivocal moral standards which maintain social stability. Even in the middle-class Moralities of the sixteenth century, the disguisers—and the vices in general—frequently stand for "usury" in its various forms; the other characters, for its opponents and victims. Traditional ethics under the Tudors subsume social and economic questions directly under moral categories; the system rests on the belief that the social order has been established by Nature in accordance with the divine will. This is expounded by Nature herself at the beginning of Medwall's play:

> Th' almighty God that made each creature,
> As well in heaven as other place earthly,
> By His wise ordinance hath purveyed me, Nature,
> To be as minister, under Him immediately,
> For th' enchesoun (*the reason*) that I should, perpetually,
> His creatures in such degree maintain
> As it hath pleased His grace for them to ordain.

This is the ethic of a society predominantly agricultural, in which "everything . . . seemed to be the gift of nature, the obvious way of life, and thus the result of the Divine ordering, whether as a good gift or as a penalty." In order to enjoy the divine bounty, to maintain each individual in the sufficiency appropriate to the station in which he was born, it was necessary to observe the conditions on which it was given; and the satisfaction of the profit-motive, of "greed," or, equally, the wasteful gratification of selfish pleasure, whether on the part of knight, burgher, or peasant, interfered with this primary necessity. They were "against nature," contrary to the obvious expression of the divine will. Opportunities for personal aggrandisement, by means of capital investment, organizing ability, or technical innovation, were, relatively, too few and unimportant, before the sixteenth century, seriously to disturb this traditional order; and it seemed evident that they could only be taken at someone else's expense. By the end of the century, as commercial enterprise, money power, and new industrial techniques began to dominate economic life, they seemed to involve a change in the whole relationship between man and nature, between the individual and his vocation. To conservative minds, it meant the substitution of appearance for realities.

Hence, while the Elizabethans applied the Morality conventions of disguise to a variety of new purposes, the earlier associations were not lost. The tradition of dramatic allegory, with disguising as an essential part, was also maintained by the court masque; and *Cynthia's Revels*, in particular, with its satire on the social climbers and rootless adventurers infesting the court, is avowedly a combination of masque and Morality. "The night is come," says one of the Children in the Induction, explaining the plot, "and Cynthia intends to come forth . . . All the courtiers must provide for revels; they conclude upon a masque, the device of which is . . . that each of these Vices, being to appear before Cynthia, would seem to be other than indeed they are; and therefore assume the most neighbouring Virtues as a masquing habit." Here Jonson turns the popular ethic against the courtly, the Morality against the masque; for it was the convention of the masques that the courtiers who came to dance as virtues or deities were in fact the incarnations of the qualities they assumed; the masque itself was a social institution, representing the court as the magnificent embodiment of the virtues by right of which it claimed to govern. *The Malcontent, Women Beware Women*, and *The Revenger's Tragedy* make ironic use of this function of disguisings in the masque. In Tourneur's case, especially, the masque, as a symbol of courtly riot, is treated from the point of view of the Morality. The courtiers in the masque described by Antonio are Morality Vices—

> Putting on better faces than their own
> Being full of fraud and flattery;

and,—throughout the play, descriptions of revels form the nucleus of the satire, leading up to the fatal masque at the end. They are associated with the references to bastardy and prostitution, and to "patrimonies washed a-pieces," and with the images of cosmetics and of justice "gilt o'er" with favour. Against the "forgetful feasts" is set the image of the skeleton. The corruption of the court by wealth and luxury, and its violation of the moral order which justifies high rank, is set beside the effects of usury, both alike overthrowing the standards of Nature. Virtue and honour, on the other hand, are identified, as in Castiza's first soliloquy, with the norms of the traditional manorial order, which Tourneur makes to stand for social norms in general. Several of his metaphors are taken from the payment of rents—vengeance, for example, is a "quit-rent."

Professor Knights' description of the structure of a Shakespearean play, then, is peculiarly appropriate to *The Revenger's Tragedy* also: it is "an expanded metaphor, by means of which the original vision has been projected into forms roughly correspondent with actuality, conforming thereto . . . according to the demands of its nature." The central metaphors, and the technique of presentation, are the products of mediaeval ways of thought, as they had taken shape on the stage in the conventions of the Moralities. With his narrow and hypersensitive mentality, his imperviousness to the psychological make-up of individuals, and his intense preoccupation with ethics, Tourneur could not have written successful drama except by means of their example.

The total impression created by the development of his plot, by the figures of the lecherous old Duke and his court, by the imagery and rhythms of the verse, is that of a hectic excitement, a perverse and over-ripe vitality on the verge of decay; the themes of the danse macabre, suggested in *Hamlet* and *The Malcontent*, dominate *The Revenger's Tragedy*. But the satire is not hysterical; Tourneur maintains an alert sardonic irony which makes its objects grotesque as well as disgusting. The sense of proportion expressed in the style is not that of the Revenge plays; it comes from the Moralities, and from Jonson. Jonson's influence is most apparent in the scene where Vendice tempts his mother and sister; the subject is from *The Malcontent*, the style from Volpone:

> VENDICE: Would I be poor, dejected, scorned of greatness,
>   Swept from the palace, and see others' daughters
>   Spring with the dew o' the court, having mine own
>   So much desired and loved by the duke's son?
>   No, I would raise my state upon her breast;
>   And call her eyes my tenants; I would count
>   My yearly maintenance upon her cheeks;
>   Take coach upon her lip; and all her parts
>   Should keep men after men, and I would ride
>   In pleasure upon pleasure . . .

> VENDICE: How blessed are you! you have happiness alone;
>   Others must fall to thousands, you to one,
>   Sufficient in himself to make your forehead
>   Dazzle the world with jewel, and petitionary people
>   Start at your presence . . .

These passages are not mere echoes of Jonsonian phrasing: they have the energetic hyperbole and the finely measured scorn of Jonson's best manner. The scene continues with a passage of brilliant extravaganza:

> VENDICE: O, think upon the pleasures of the palace!
>   Secured ease and state! the stirring meats,
>   Ready to move out of the dishes, that e'en now
>   Quicken when they are eaten!
>   Banquets abroad by torchlight! music! sports!
>   Bareheaded vassals, that had ne'er the fortune

> To keep on their own hats, but let horns wear 'em!
> Nine coaches waiting—hurry, hurry, hurry—
> CASTIZA: Ay, to the devil,
> VENDICE: Ay, to the devil! (*Aside*) To the duke, by my faith.
> GRATIANA: Ay, to the duke: daughter, you'd scorn to think
>   o' the devil, an you were there once.
>
> (II, i.)

The excitement of these passages is hardly the product of a nightmare vision. On the contrary, it is controlled and directed by a sense of the crude realities underlying the court's fantastic behaviour. The source and character of Tourneur's grotesquerie is indicated, again, by Spurio's soliloquy:

> Faith, if the truth were known, I was begot
> After some gluttonous dinner; some stirring dish
> Was my first father, when deep healths went round,
> And ladies cheeks were painted red with wine,
> Their tongues, as short and nimble as their heels,
> Uttering words sweet and thick; and when they rose,
> Were merrily disposed to fall again.
>
> (I, ii)

The nervous and sinister tones of the mockery are balanced by the "primitive" realism.

Nevertheless, Tourneur does not escape from his cycle of decay; there is nothing in the play, in its scheme of moral and social values, to compensate for Vendice's fall. In the process of commercial development, which had brought new hopes and possibilities to the middle classes, Tourneur saw only that the court had been uprooted from the people and the soil, while the old-fashioned gentry were left to their honour, their poverty, and their discontent. As, throughout the sixteenth century, landlord and ploughman alike had been submitted to a growing dependence on money, and their customary incomes had proved inadequate to meet rising costs and a rising standard of living, the stability of the old hierarchy had broken down. Many of the nobility and gentry were forced to give up their "hospitality" or to sell their estates; and their successors and survivors, knowing, with Burghley, that "gentility is nothing else but ancient riches," had acted accordingly. The nobility themselves had become enclosers, joint-stock-holders, company-promoters, monopolists; the court, at the turn of the century, was the happy-hunting-ground for adventurers and profiteers. Until the end of Elizabeth's reign, this commercialization of the nobility was in harmony with the main economic and political needs of the middle classes: but when the latter had outgrown their royal tutelage, the powers of the court became obstructive; and when titles were sold and honours conferred on irresponsible favourites, it became clear that the system of court privileges opened the way to the machiavellian and the sycophant. The fount of honour was poisoned at the source. While "the disproportion between honour and means" became more glaring, large numbers of the lesser gentry, deprived of the security of the old order, found themselves landless men, dependent on an uncertain or an insufficient patronage, men without "vocations." Tourneur's Vendice is one of the dramatic spokesmen of these malcontents. His independence belongs to the past; the present is contaminated by the values of "gold." On the basis of this contrast, which is extended to society as a whole, Tourneur's poetry formulates an exceptionally coherent response to the life of his time. But the business of buying and selling, the accumulation of wealth without social responsibility, which has hoisted sensuality to its evil eminence in his court, is accepted as normative and final; it becomes a process by which the values of Nature and the impulses which go to maintaining a civilized life are inevitably decomposed into their opposites. This conception forms the organizing principle in Vendice's second speech to the skull, where the complex themes and symbols of the whole play are concentrated into a single magnificent passage.

The irony of this speech is reinforced by the dramatic situation: "all the betrayed women are in a sense represented by the poisoned skull of Vendice's mistress—not only she herself, but Antonio's wife, Castiza, who would have been betrayed, and the imaginary "country lady" whom the Duke thought he was about to seduce." Similarly, "yon fellow" is the imaginary profligate turned highwayman, the approaching Duke, and the Duchess's youngest son, who has already appeared under judgment for rape, and is ironically despatched in the next scene. Thus the skull becomes the fitting symbol, as it is the final result, of the process represented by the action and the imagery, by which solid realities are exchanged for treacherous appearances. The metaphor of "exchange" is important: Vendice's irony turns, in this speech, on the ambiguities of the word "for," referring both to equivalence in exchange and to purpose or result. In the first lines, a complex group of relationships are associated in the image contrasting the "labours" of the worm—physically present in "expend" and "undo"—with a silken bedizement of the lady for whom they are undertaken, a contrast which appears, at the same time, as one between the silk and the skeleton it covers; it is for the skull that the labours are ultimately intended. The "silkworm" is also the worm of the grave; it suggests, too, the poor weaver,

"undone" for the sake of the wealthy—the contrast between rich and poor
is made explicit in the next speech;—and the colours of the silk and of the
gold which is paid for it are made flat and wan by the suggested comparison
with her "yellow" face. The speech is developed round a further series of
exchanges:

> Does the silkworm expend her yellow labours
> For thee? for thee does she undo herself?
> Are lordships sold to maintain ladyships
> For the poor benefit of a bewitching minute?
> Why does yon fellow falsify highways
> And put his life between the judge's lips,
> To refine such a thing, keeps horse and men
> To beat their valours for her?
> Surely we're all mad people, and they
> Whom we think are, are not; we mistake those,
> 'Tis we are mad in sense, they but in clothes.
>
> (III, v.)

In the third and fourth lines, the process of commercial exchange is again
ironically invoked; the social stability implied by "lordships" and "maintained" is undermined in the colloquial sarcasm of "ladyships," and the
"bewitching minute" of lust is a "poor benefit" to exchange for an inherited
estate—"poor," too, in the sense that procreation is made futile. "Bewitching" recalls the earlier scene in which it was suggested that Gratiana's attempt
to prostitute her daughter was due to diabolic possession; it detaches Vendice
from the dissolution he contemplates and yet implies that it is inescapable.
"Yon fellow" implicates the Duke and his stepson as well as the broken
gallant, so that "falsify" attaches to the royal justice itself together with the
royal highway. There is also a suppressed pun on counterfeit coinage, which,
with the corrosive impression of "falsify," is carried on in the next lines: by
his emphasis on the root senses of the verbs ("maintain," "falsify," "refine"),
Tourneur sets up a characteristic tension between the imagined activities
and the ideal relationships to which they ought to conform. In the old
dispensation—as in Medwall's play—Nature had appointed Reason to govern
Sensuality; here, Reason has been overturned. It takes its revenge, against
the irrationality of the "bewitching minute," in the contrast between the
life and the moment of sentence. The judgment is also the Last Judgment.
As before, the mounting rhythm then returns, after a pause, to the slow,
heavy syllables referring to the skull, the final cause, it is suggested, as it

is the final stage, of the whole movement—"to refine such a thing." The phrase, coming at this point, implies both that the overlay of "refinement" on her "ladyship" is as futile, and as deathly, as the poisoned cosmetic on the skull, and that this comparison actually clarified a state of affairs present wherever bones are clothed with flesh. The next phrase again catches in its puns the self-destruction of a powerful stimulus; "keeps" relates it to "maintains," four lines above; "beat their valours" refers primarily to the fierce courage of the highwaymen, but "beats" also means "abates," and "valors" are "values"—once again the purchase of death for life. Thus the perversion of the impulses making for life finds its culminating expression in the image of violent action, and the activity is simultaneously nullified by means of the puns. The last three lines generalize what has already been revealed to the senses. Just as the great lady of the first lines has dissolved into her "ladyship," so all seeming realities have been reduced to the skull; so that to murder the Duke with the poisoned skull is a fully appropriate revenge.

Tourneur's symbols, then, are organized by applying to the contemporary world the standards of the mediaeval social tradition, as it had survived through the sixteenth century. But *The Revenger's Tragedy*, with its alternation between finely wrought passages of high mental and nervous tension and passages of clumsy sententious generalization, represents an emotional equilibrium which Tourneur evidently could not maintain. He had profited by the example of Jonson, who had remodelled the Morality drama, with its barely delineated types and its sparse, loosely connected incidents, into something more solid and closely-knit; but Jonson's mind was the more elastic, more confident of the permanent validity of his standards, more independent and detached. His dramatic structures allow of a varied interplay of motives and experiences; Tourneur's do not. In *The Revenger's Tragedy* he succeeded in directing the response to his situation by presenting Morality figures who express, or arouse, acute and powerful, but narrowly restricted emotions. When, instead of dealing with types, he tried to examine individual motives, and to argue out the reasons for his judgments, he failed. By comparison with the earlier play, *The Atheist's Tragedy* is abstract and forced. The best passages, such as the description of Charlemont's supposed death at Ostend, are set speeches, almost independent of their dramatic contexts; the symbolism is mechanical, the poetic theorising lame and unconvincing. Charlemont, who, unlike Vendice, leaves his revenge to heaven, is an uninteresting paragon; and D'Amville's villainy and Castabella's innocence are so natively paraded that Tourneur defeats his purpose—if Castiza's shrill chastity were emphasized in the same way, so that the puppet became a person, she would be nauseating. Charlemont and his father have some of the virtues Tourneur attributed to Vere and Salisbury; but when he comes to offer his positive values, they are formal and, dramatically, lifeless.

With Jonson and *The Revenger's Tragedy*, the influence of the mediaeval tradition virtually came to an end. None of the Stuart dramatists whose main work came later—with the partial exception of Massinger, in his comedies—attempted to revive it; the trend of dramatic writing was towards semi- or pseudo-naturalism. Webster fumbled with the Revenge conventions in the effort to develop something relatively new to the stage—to excite varied or conflicting sympathies for individuals at odds with their surroundings. His picture of society resembles Tourneur's; but the Morality elements, which had represented for the latter the dramatic equivalents for a central core of judgments and feelings, have disappeared; and Webster, unable to come to rest on any attitude, from which to value his people, more stable or more penetrating than a pose of stoical bravado, could not write coherent drama at all. Where they are not simply melodrama, his plays depend on exploiting immediate sensations, disjointed from their dramatic contexts; and this applies not only to his stagecraft, but to his verse, which works by analogous means, and which gains, as Tourneur's loses, from quotation in short passages. His plays, with their unrealized "sense of tragic issues" in the individual, point towards a dramatic reorientation, a development from Shakespeare, which they do not themselves achieve. After Shakespeare, the only dramatist to achieve such a reorientation was Middleton.

B. J. LAYMAN

Tourneur's Artificial Noon:
The Design of The Revenger's Tragedy

The characters of *The Revenger's Tragedy* have "nimble and desperate tongues," and their brains "swell with strange invention." An interpreter of the play must try to avoid their example. But a glance at the fast-growing body of Tourneur criticism, much of it contentious, will show that the task is not easy. "I'll unmask you," the Revenger exclaims to his "bony lady" (III.v.48); and critics cannot resist the infection of his terrible and masterly fervor. Almost unanimous in their agreement with T. S. Eliot's pronouncement that Cyril Tourneur is "a great English poet," they have proceeded to explain this greatness in ways that often cancel out. Does, for instance, his play succeed by realizing a state of mind, or a state of affairs? Eliot himself ascribes its poetic power to the success with which it projects Tourneur's private cynicism, a "loathing and disgust of humanity" which Eliot calls "immature." But L. G. Salingar is no less sure that the play projects instead, by way of a maturely intelligent handling of "the Morality tradition," a disintegrating social order. Disagreement has been loudest over the kind of moral sense, if any, that Tourneur makes; and my quarrel is with those, now I believe a majority, who would offer us a master of "ethical design," pursuing with doctrinal orthodoxy a "firm moral scheme." I have in mind, besides Salingar, such interesting students of the play as Inga-Stina Ekeblad, R. A. Foakes, Peter Lisca, Peter B. Murray, and John Peter. I agree with these writers that Tourneur does indeed obtrude upon us morality of a kind— shown most clearly, perhaps, in the resoundingly unproblematical doomsday vocabulary which he makes one of his trademarks. The seven deadly sins are

From *Modern Language Quarterly* 34, no. 1 (March 1973). © 1973 by the University of Washington Press.

insistently *named*, and there is no need for nice discrimination: a nest of dukes is a nest of dukes. I agree also that this "indignant morality" is not the mere pose "under which he tries to dissemble his gloating appetite for horrors," as William Archer scornfully declared. Nevertheless, I disagree with these apologists' utilitarian postulates about the kind of play Tourneur wrote; and in the discussion that follows I hope to show why.

Any search for the essential design and economy of the play should begin and end with its climactic and greatest scene, and with that moment of the hero-villain's exclaiming, "I'll unmask you." Vindice playing pander has escorted a bashful "country lady" to the trysting place of his enemy the old Duke, there to have her "kiss his lips to death" (III.v.105). As audience we are meant to be as deceived, momentarily, as is the brother Hippolito by this disguised lady and by Vindice's mock-courteous conversation with her. Since the inducements to sin with which he regales her are the same he used earlier to mesmerize his own mother and revolt his sister, this latest conquest is in keeping with the paradoxical role he has made for himself already, very fully, in the play. He is "that strange-composed fellow" (I.i.96) who, while he perceives more completely than anyone else the abounding depravity of "this present minute" (I.iii.26) and appoints himself its scourge, also makes of himself its most infectious exponent. Hippolito's words capture the exact irony: "This our age swims within him" (I.iii.24). Vertiginously he combines the extremes of his chaste sister and corrupted mother.

And this is the creature who in "a throng of happy apprehensions" (III.v.30) has lured the masked lady, the depraved Duke, and us into a "darken'd, blushless angle . . . Wherein 'tis night at noon" (III.v.14–19). An essential part of the design that rouses in him such transports—"O sweet, delectable, rare, happy, ravishing!" (III.v.1)—is that it should afford climactic outlet for *all* his widely conflicting drives. It enables him, by wagging at us his minatory death's-head, to exhibit the wages of sin with irreproachable élan. At the same time, his "I'll unmask you" is the shameless *coup de théâtre* of an exhibitionist—a show-off whose naïve vanity (" 'twas somewhat witty carried, though we say it" [V.iii.97]) is in fact his eventual undoing. His vindictive design is also "witty" in some of the more biting Elizabethan senses of the word. That the country lady who receives his fevered attentions should stand revealed as the long-dead Gloriana, "la gloriosa donna della sua mente"; that this chaste victim of "palsy-lust" should retaliate with lips poisoned like those of a prostitute; that the incorruptibility which her lover venerates should propel him into acting as her pander—these and similar ironies strike us with their superb deftness. Staying within the Italianate decorum of the play, we might say of this design that it enables him simultaneously to unleash the righteous fury of a Savonarola, the virtuosic cruelty of a Cesare Borgia, and the self-regarding, defamatory satire of an Aretino.

Yet, as those who would offer us a play solidly grounded in the traditional pieties see it, Tourneur has ironically distanced himself from all save the Savonarola in Vindice; and they go on to discuss, often very illuminatingly, the Elizabethan conventions of "Revenge Tragedy, Satiric Comedy, and Morality" which he has successfully exploited. Foremost with them is the "ethical design" which he has imposed upon all his wit, theatricality, and seeming morbidity. But no matter how skillfully done, their trick of aligning the dramatist with the good Vindice while divorcing him from the bad must seem, to me at least, special pleading. I see Vindice's unmasking act as supplying the capstone of an imperfect yet formidable structure of interacting imagery and incident in the play at large. A single elaborately ironical conceit is enacted with insistency no less than manic; and while this paradigm may leave us in no doubt that Tourneur was against sin, it draws us back to Eliot's much-discredited suggestion that he was against life as well. The power of his metaphorical "night at noon" derives not from the distinctness of the two realms, as his apologists would insist, but from their horrible oneness.

The fixity of Vindice-Tourneur's imagination is announced in the opening speech of the play, where Vindice apostrophizes first the old Duke and his obscene clan, then the skull of Gloriana which he holds, and lastly "Vengeance, thou murder's quit-rent" (I.i.39). The sequence in which he discharges his inflamed feelings puts the play as a labyrinth of revenge and retribution instantly before us, with characteristically jarring shifts of tone and attitude.

> Duke; royal lecher; go, grey'-hair'd adultery;
> And thou his son, as impious steep'd as he;
> And thou his bastard, true-begot in evil;
> And thou his duchess, that will do with devil.
> Four excellent characters—
>
> (I.i.1–5)

In the verve of these oxymora, the practiced hyperbole, is heard at once Vindice's public voice as satirist. But the vituperation, having come to a sudden halt, plunges forward in a new vein of private anguish:

> O, that marrowless age
> Would stuff the hollow bones with damn'd desires,
> And 'stead of heat, kindle infernal fires

> Within the spendthrift veins of a dry duke,
> A parch'd and juiceless luxur. O God!—one
> That has scarce blood enough to live upon,
> And he to riot it like a son and heir?
> O, the thought of that
> Turns my abused heart-strings into fret.
>
> (I.i.5–13)

Convincingly tormented and inward as this may be, its indebtedness is painfully clear. In whom except Hamlet has lust in those past the age provoked such nausea? Tourneur's images, nevertheless, are his own and take their place in a developing pattern that is certainly not Shakespeare's. Hamlet addressing poor Yorick had exclaimed, "Here hung those lips I have kissed I know not how oft!" and then had ordered the jester to get him to my lady's chamber. The sardonic point is like Tourneur's, the implementation totally different: we cannot imagine Hamlet carting about and declaiming to the skull of Ophelia:

> Thou sallow picture of my poison'd love,
> My study's ornament, thou shell of death,
> Once the bright face of my betrothed lady,
> When life and beauty naturally fill'd out
> These ragged imperfections,
> When two heaven-pointed diamonds were set
> In those unsightly rings—then 'twas a face
> So far beyond the artificial shine
> Of any woman's bought complexion,
> That the uprightest man (if such there be
> That sin but seven times a day) broke custom,
> And made up eight with looking after her.
> O, she was able to ha' made a usurer's son
> Melt all his patrimony in a kiss,
> And what his father fifty years told,
> To have consum'd, and yet his suit been cold.
>
> (I.i.14–29)

"Sine aliqua dementia nullus Phoebus," Marston had boasted of his *Malcontent*. Vindice begins the congested and unhinged final stretch of his speech by celebrating the virtue and beauty of his poisoned love with hyperbole designed, it would seem, to counterpoint and illuminate that with which he execrated the dry Duke: his animus makes sense as that of a bereaved true lover. Yet how swiftly he is sidetracked! The artificial shine of bought complexions, introduced overtly to extend the praise of Gloriana's bright face, triggers instead seven lines of cynical jesting and raillery, culminating in the incisive vignette of usurer and son. He then remembers the matter in hand, a skull, as suddenly as he had forgotten it.

> But O, accursed palace!
> Thee when thou wert apparel'd in thy flesh
> The old duke poison'd,
> Because thy purer part would not consent
> Unto his palsy-lust; for old men lustful
> Do show like young men, angry, eager, violent,
> Outbid like their limited performances.
> O 'ware an old man hot and vicious:
> *Age, as in gold, in lust is covetous.*
>
> (I.i.30–38)

Yet even as he narrates the lurid circumstances of his private grief, sententiousness draws him from the "old duke" to "old men lustful," and at last to "Age" itself. The most astonishing of such oscillations concludes the speech:

> Vengeance, thou murder's quit-rent, and whereby
> Thou show'st thyself tenant to Tragedy,
> O, keep thy day, hour, minute, I beseech,
> For those thou hast determin'd!—hum, who e'er knew
> Murder unpaid? Faith, give Revenge her due,
> Sh' has kept touch hitherto—be merry, merry,
> Advance thee, O thou terror to fat folks,
> To have their costly three-pil'd flesh worn off
> As bare as this—for banquets, ease and laughter,
> Can make great men, as greatness goes by clay;
> But wise men little are more great than they.
>
> (I.i.39–49)

For five and a half lines the wronged lover vows with heavy-breathing melodrama to pay murder with murder and beseeches the skull, now become Vengeance itself, to "keep thy day, hour, minute." But the private revenger, at the very top of his bent, loses himself in the greater rapture of "O thou terror to fat folks"!

Granting that the Hamlet echoes are indeed telltale and that Vindice with his antic disposition is a not unprecedented amalgam of Revenger,

Satirist, and Preacher, we should resist letting this knowledge explain away the dramatic and ethical ambiguities of the role as Tourneur has developed it. Observe the single phrase, "My study's ornament." While within the garish context of love and revenge it is appropriately bizarre, providing better than any ghost the motive and the cue for passion, its idiom at the same time evokes St. Jerome and his powerfully anonymous *memento mori*. Vindice, if he had so wished, could not have prevented the skull of his beloved from swelling into symbol; but the eagerness with which he appoints himself custodian of this object both particular and universal bears careful watching. It helps explain how he can become as involved in the doom of fat folks as in paying off murder; its larger effect, however, both now and hereafter, is to subvert rather than uphold any system of ethical norms.

The raggedness of Vindice's ethics is matched by the obsessed state of his imagination. He may seem merely the typical satirist or malcontent in venting his spleen so indiscriminately; observed more closely, however, his exertions of sensibility appear in their purely Tourneurian character. All the parts of the speech are knit together by the motif of a huge disinheritance, and by a suggestion of the suddenness with which this doom occurs. The Duke's veins are spendthrift, and he riots it in a savagely ironic imitation of that self-despoiling appetite which satire cynically attributes to every "son and heir." Since he is dry and parched, the fires of lust will make fast work of him—just as the son's patrimony, fifty years a-growing, melts in a single kiss. Fat folks, meanwhile, shudder "To have their costly three-pil'd flesh worn off"; and Gloriana's diamonds are lost forever.

Yet we see that the goods of life which are to vanish so swiftly may be the positive goodnesses of Gloriana or the ugly products of lust, greed, and pride—jesting Death, as in the *danse macabre*, has no care. Thus Vindice, with a like impartiality, can shift or desert his moral stance. The life which Tourneur projects arranges itself in legible patterns to a degree that is phantasmagoric; evenhanded justice, however, is merely one of Death's "vizards," a passing appearance assumed by the ghastly absolute. And since Vindice, plunging with black exhilaration from one to another of its domains, is the panegyrist of this absolute, it follows that he should betray a profound uncertainty about positive values. Gloriana's centrality is again seen. Her former beauty and natural perfections are celebrated, yet Vindice's allegiance seems less to what she has been than to the bare and unconditioned object he grasps in his hand. The flesh in which she was appareled figures uneasily in a surrounding poetry where vileness is all.

Vindice's description of Gloriana balances that of the Duke in a detailed play of comparison and contrast. Whereas marrowless age has stuffed his "hollow bones with damn'd desires," "life and beauty naturally fill'd out [her now] ragged imperfections." The fires of lust kindled in his spendthrift veins are set over against her "bright face" and against those "heaven-pointed diamonds," her eyes. The latter image, by equating her virtue and beauty, stresses the contrast between the Duke and his victim as both physical and spiritual. We *see*, however, not her brightness but her very sallow picture, the immemorial death's-head. Her diamonds are gone, and only their sets, "those unsightly rings," remain to be fingered. The punning "unsightly" best conveys Gloriana's duality, her co-presence *in morte* and *in vita*, and the seeming strife of attitude in Vindice. Dispossessed of their treasure, these hideous sockets resemble the hollow bones of the Duke who murdered her. Unnatural vice has triumphed over natural virtue, and living foulness found its own image (now become a universal symbol of impending doom) in the beautiful thing it has destroyed. The structure of ironies is as devastating, and as ethically uncentered, as that of the unmasking scene itself.

Vindice has been taught by his study's ornament an appropriate contempt of the world but a very inappropriate pride as well. Emulating "that eternal eye that sees through flesh and all," he sees—to borrow from Donne's *Anatomie of the World*—"How witty's ruin, how importunate / Upon mankind!" (99–100). As we have observed, this sudden, witty ruin occurs in his imagination typically as a "disheiring": "I have seen patrimonies washed a-pieces, fruit-fields turned into bastards, and, in a world of acres, not so much dust due to the heir 'twas left to, as would well gravel a petition" (I.iii.50–53). Here, grafted with poignant virtuosity onto the contemporaneously satirical, is the lost patrimony of all mankind. And here, for the moment, Vindice's seeing might appear unmarred by either pride or moral contradictions. Yet Lussurioso hearing these lines exclaims, "Fine villain!" because he assumes that the nature of this fellow who knows "I' th' world strange lust" (I.iii.56) and is so "deeply fathom'd into all estates" (I.iii.75) must be subdued to what it works in. Just before, Vindice has obscenely jested, calling himself "a bone-setter . . . A bawd, my lord; one that sets bones together" (I.iii.43–45). And we have seen with what driving excitement he does indeed set bones together, with his imagery in the opening speech, and actually in the assignation episode. A disinherited son himself, he should know that witty ruin does not need his own strange inventions. They swell his brain nevertheless.

In the sharpening focus of Vindice's self-address to Vengeance—"O, keep thy day, hour, minute"—is to be found the essence of what he perceives, and of what he conspires to force upon his victim's sight:

> If he but wink, not brooking the foul object,
> Let our two other hands tear up his lids,
> And make his eyes, like comets, shine through blood.
>   (III.v.202–4)

The motif of minute, sometimes changed to hour, noon, or midnight, recurs in the play with unmistakable salience no less than twenty times, sixteen of these in scenes leading to the assignation and three more in that scene itself. This minute bears a necessary relation to the drossy age of the play's setting, but is obviously not the same. The latter—"this immodest season" (I.iii.11), "this luxurious day wherein we breathe" (I.iii.110)—merely exploits satirically the Jacobean Italy of lust and treachery which both dramatist and audience had by heart. The real signature of the play is to be found in Hippolito's speech treacherously recommending his brother to Lussurioso:

> My lord, after long search, wary inquiries,
> And politic siftings, I made choice of yon fellow,
> Whom I guess rare for many deep employments;
> This our age swims within him, and if time
> Had so much hair, I should take him for time,
> He is so near kin to this present minute.
>   (I.iii.21–26)

Subtly the lines wrench a personification of Time to represent first the age or times, and then, climactically, a solitary instant. And what may seem mere hyberbole is helped by its matrix of image and incident to resonate with eschatology: in accepting the skull as his co-protagonist, Vindice becomes, indeed, a doomsday laureate. The present minute he is nearest kin to is not, however, simply the moment of damnation, but that moment realized *to the exclusion of all else.*

His assassination of the Duke thus asks to be appreciated aesthetically and metaphysically. It is what Webster would have called Vindice's crowning "night-piece" by virtue of what he is able to "crowd" into its "minute" (III.v.123). When, "like a slobbering Dutchman" (III.v.165), the Duke rapaciously kisses his country lady, Vindice stands ready with a torch, "that his affrighted eyeballs / May start into those hollows" (III.v.148–49), Gloriana's unsightly rings whose diamonds the old debauchee had stolen. So that none of the surreal propriety of the killing sight may be lost, the Revenger adds not merely himself—" 'Tis I, 'tis Vindice, 'tis I" (III.v.168)— but also the complementary spectacle of exactly timed retribution afforded by Spurio and the Duchess, come to cuckold the Duke in his own trysting place. "Begot in impudent wine and lust" (I.ii.192), "By one false minute disinherited" (I.ii.168), the Bastard repays his maker in kind; and "one incestuous kiss picks open hell" (I.ii.175). In sum, Tourneur's imagination realizes and defines, and is defined by, "the poor benefit of a bewitching minute" (III.v.75).

This obsessive patterning might be considered moral in so far as it shows justice commending "th' ingredience of our poison'd chalice / To our own lips." But morality needs the dimension of time for its unfolding; and when time for Macbeth comes to signify nothing, he feels tied to a stake, animal rather than human. Within the metaphor and metaphysics of *The Revenger's Tragedy* time has little place, and the revenger and his victims appear tied to the same stake. Nothing is problematical, all is ordained, conforming with monotonous regularity to the coinage of Vindice's brain. If the undoing of the Duke is, as Inga-Stina Ekeblad would call it, an "exemplum horrendum" (p. 489), it figures in a strangely unorthodox homiletics. The Duke's virtual existence in the play is at best a quasi-temporal one. As he lurches with malice and cunning toward the inestimable benefit of a bewitching minute, we see only the conjunction of lust-swollen veins and hollow bones; and as he thinks himself most its master, we see that moment flash upon him the blinding fact of his perpetual enslavement. He can register nothing in dying except to gasp, "I cannot brook..." (III.v.222). The schema is self-determining—as perfect as it is inflexible.

A vision or fiction of conduct as mechanically contrived and of human nature as reduced to a few spastic gestures may be made to work very well for farce or satire, but it is hard to imagine it as working well for tragedy. This is especially so when the contrivances are as ironic and intricately interlocked as those which—to use again one of Tourneur's own most insistent words—swell his world. Picking up the plot at almost any point— the trial scene of the Youngest Son, for instance—we encounter their profusion. True to type, the Son is guilty of rape, having "fed the ravenous vulture of his lust" in a "vicious minute," an "artificial noon" (I.iv.27–44). Brought to trial, he thinks himself invulnerable, parades his insolence before his judges, and shrugs off Lussurioso's hypocritical warning, "O, do not jest thy doom... play not with thy death" (I.ii.49–53). Whereupon the Duke proceeds to play with death in his own gratuitously cruel way, refusing to interfere with the pronouncing of judgment until only a single word is suspended between the boy and his doom. What "his wither'd grace" (I.ii.97) does not know is that in contriving this emblematic predicament for the Son he has helped do the same for himself, since by his act he hardens his already contemptuous Duchess's resolve to "kill him in his forehead"

(I.ii.108). The younger doom-jester, looking for release "E'en every minute" (III.iv.37), will go his death in a farcical scene where the word "trick" is repeated nine times; and the older has in store Gloriana's pretty hanging lip, her grin that flashes through his perfumed mist.

My quarrel, however, is not with Tourneur's right to his theme of "Why this is hell!" nor with any seriocomic decorum per se. A good Calvinist, viewing all sin as a fall out of freedom into necessity, might well find such a decorum ideal; and the joke of the slave of passion who dreams himself an architect of fortune can certainly bear repeating. I wish merely to stress both the aesthetically and the ethically disturbing consequences of Tourneur's having channeled the power of his intelligence and imagination into a reiterated definition of that convulsive moment when the time-ridden destroy themselves; to argue that this obsessive patterning is ultimately *undramatic* if drama is taken to imply conflicts and their resolution in time; and to insist, lastly, that it represents a very harrowing rigidification of consciousness.

Shakespeare is the giant of an epoch whose drama in its largest sense was the drama of consciousness—attested to no less by Montaigne at one extreme, inexhaustibly essaying himself alone, than by Bacon at the other, pleading for "broken knowledge" and contending against his Idols. A distinguishing mark of its greatest works—those of Michelangelo, Shakespeare, Cervantes, and Racine—is that they *cannot* be described as Ernst Robert Curtius described *The Divine Comedy*: "perfect superposition of Dante's within upon the cosmic without, and mutual interpenetration of the two; congruence of soul and world." They must be described instead in such a way that soul and world, the within and the without, are held together only by an inquiring, open, and unresolved dialectic. Curtius's words, on the other hand, might very well be taken to describe *The Revenger's Tragedy*; and that is part of the charge I would bring against Tourneur—he is a Dante *très manqué*, whose responsiveness to his experience, while sporadically moving and brilliant, is ultimately self-entangling and self-nullifying. In what other play of its period, one may wonder, is subject installed so patently at the expense of object? The Duke, Lussurioso, Spurio, and the Duchess cross the stage in abstract silence, visible only that they may be absorbed into Vindice's poetry (half diatribe, half dithyramb) of "this present minute," no more real than fat folks or the usurer's son, and decidedly less real than the presiding skull. The Depraved, the Skull, the Revenger, and the versification itself, hectically contracting and expanding, all are of a piece—"Savage, extreme, rude, cruel, not to trust"—bearing witness to that sinewy thread their maker's brain lets fall through every part. What Gide called the "state of dialogue" is not to be found in the play. The skull is the agent in a realm

where no effective counteragent exists; and while Vindice addresses his beloved volubly, the very soul and secret of her responding eloquence is,
inevitably, her grinning silence.

Those critics who would reinforce their view of Tourneur's moral health-
fulness by praising his "firm grasp of the outer world" have some admittedly
very striking passages on which to base their claims. Here, for instance, is
Vindice as he sets the "golden spurs" to his mother that "Will put her to
a false gallop in a trice" (II.ii.45–46):

> No, I would raise my state upon her breast,
> And call her eyes my tenants; I would count
> My yearly maintenance upon her cheeks,
> Take coach upon her lip, and all her parts
> Should keep men after men, and I would ride
> In pleasure upon pleasure.
>
>   (II.i.95–100)

It may be conceded that these rhapsodic confoundings of daughter and ducats
are the product of a vigilant intelligence which in its apprehension of the
sordid "triumph of the economic virtues" fully deserves the kind of admiration L. C. Knights has promoted for Jonson's sorties anticipating Tawney.
We may admire too the nice consistency of Tourneur's having adjusted his
disinheritance theme to this particular recurrence of a world upside down,
"fruit-fields turned into bastards." His witty corrupting of words, in its
mirroring of the bastardizing of natural relationships and feelings, makes
skepticism regarding the solidity of his insights impossible. Yet, for all its
seemingly moral "hold upon an outer reality," the speech is less a slice of
life than of the Vindice we have come to look for; and its wonderful rhetoric
abounds in every kind of control except that of aesthetic distance. As satire
its success in debauching the mother should be the exact measure of its
success in invigorating us; but it is too Vindicean to manifest any such purity
of purpose. The mother's greed is treated as a sensual thing, excited by
sensual things; and the son's voice speeds as always along its predestined
course toward its own "false gallop" of "men after men," "pleasure upon
pleasure." The passage thus embodies that very tumescence of sin which it
execrates, and we have once more the spectacle of a hectic morality "reeling
toward hell"—or at least toward the terrible inertness of that nasty joke
which in all its forms is always the same: noon is midnight, pleasure is pain,
"doing" undoes, and life is death.

Tourneur's apologists might, however, point to other passages whose
moral purposiveness is less easy to impugn. One of Vindice's favorite stunts

as satirist is to deplore the improvidence of virtue. Assuming his Piato
disguise, he casts off "fool-bashfulness, / That maid in the old time, whose
flush of grace / Would never suffer her to get good clothes" (I.iii.12–14). He
prevails upon Gratiana to "chide away that foolish country-girl / Keeps company with your daughter, chastity" (II.i.82–83), and asks, "Who'd sit at
home in a neglected room, / Dealing her short-liv'd beauty to the pictures, /
That are as useless as old men" (II.i.213–15), perorating, "All thrives but
chastity, she lies a-cold" (II.i.227). The ease with which we construe such
passages, distinguishing between false values and true, is obvious. That maid
in the old time, though she may lie a-cold, thrives upon grace and shares
with Castiza the saving folly of shunning the good clothes which are to be
had only by transposing "all her parts" into commodities. Tourneur's entente
with his reader is proclaimed very loudly indeed, as it is also, more subtly,
in another of Vindice's *accelerando* passages:

> Now 'tis full sea abed over the world;
> There's juggling of all sides. Some that were maids
> E'en at sunset are now perhaps i' th' toll-book.
> This woman in immodest thin apparel
> Lets in her friend by water; here a dame
> Cunning, nails leather hinges to a door,
> To avoid proclamation; now cuckolds are
> A-coining, apace, apace, apace, apace;
> And careful sisters spin that thread i' th' night
> That does maintain them and their bawds i' th' day.
>
> (II.ii.136–45)

"You flow well, brother," says the servile Hippolito, truthfully; and Vindice
complacently rejoins, "Puh, I'm shallow yet." But he flows well only when
he is enclosed, as here, within the "luxurious circle" of his imagination.
The water he navigates is just large enough to serve the cunning of a woman
in immodest thin apparel. Tourneur does not, however, allow the speech to
end with the orgastic onomatopoeia of line 143. "Careful sisters," their
anxious industry colored by "apace, apace," labor into the night, spinning
the thread that maintains them—and their bawds. Perhaps by evoking "The
spinsters and the knitters in the sun, / And the free maids that weave their
thread with bones," his flickering irony "dallies with the innocence of love /
Like the old age"—only to make blacker the artificial night of the new age,
in which toiling harlots present the exigencies of *se maintenir* and the Graces
vanish to become the Fates. The lines might well have helped set a standard
for the author of *The Waste Land*.

The "concrete, compressive and suggestive power" (Ekeblad) of their imagery surpasses that of the simpler cognate passages which I have quoted, but is surpassed by another, standing near the heart of the unmasking scene. The careful sisters' labors are as "yellow" as those by which the silkworm undoes herself:

> And now methinks I could e'en chide myself
> For doting on her beauty, though her death
> Shall be reveng'd after no common action.
> Does the silk-worm expend her yellow labours
> For thee? for thee does she undo herself?
> Are lordships sold to maintain ladyships
> For the poor benefit of a bewitching minute?
> Why does yon fellow falsify high-ways,
> And put his life between the judge's lips,
> To refine such a thing? keeps horse and men
> To beat their valours for her?
>
> (III.v.69–79)

"Undo" is eerily perfect, like the "come to dust" of Shakespeare's chimney sweepers. The analogues of the play which it reaches out to and conjoins are again absolutely antithetical—rural honesty and courtly shame, old health and new disease—so that again a sense of the terrible dislocations of modernity is very strong. Yet surely here, as suggested much earlier in this study, the quicksands of Tourneur's entente reveal themselves with a climactic finality. Vindice, custodian of the skull as in the beginning, has "fitted" *us* no less than the old Duke with his "quaint piece of beauty (III.v.52–53). Gloriana, not Castiza, presides as the maid whose flush of grace would not suffer her to get good clothes or even to retain her apparel of flesh. In death as in life she "has somewhat a grave look about her"; and all in vain the silkworm expends her yellow labors. "Here's an eye . . . A pretty hanging lip . . . a cheek keeps her colour" (III.v.54–60). Eyes, lips, and cheeks, all that with Castiza had seemed part of the natural goodness of creation, are apostrophized now in their *real* being as portions of a killing horror. Gloriana's beauty was as real as beauty can be—not real enough.

The contempt-merging-with-wonder of "For thee? for thee . . . ?" does not lessen as Vindice sweeps on:

> Does every proud and self-affecting dame
> Camphor her face for this? and grieve her maker
> In sinful baths of milk, when many an infant starves

> For her superfluous outside—all for this?
> Who now bids twenty pounds a night, prepares
> Music, perfumes and sweetmeats? All are hush'd;
> Thou mayst lie chaste now.
>
> (III.v.84–90)

Like another crazed moralist and would-be revenger, Vindice has made his awed encounter with a looped and windowed raggedness that owes the worm no silk: both he and Lear have been vouchsafed a terrible vision of "the thing itself." What Lear sees, however, is a wretch answering with his uncovered body the extremity of the skies, and he welcomes the physic of a like exposure. How different Vindice's gloating is:

> Here's a cheek keeps her colour, let the wind
> Go whistle;
> Spout rain, we fear thee not; be hot or cold,
> All's one with us.
>
> (III.v.60–63)

All flesh, unaccommodated or not, is as deceiving and fraudulent as the painting of the harlot; and ladies' "false forms" are mirrored and absolutized by the poisoned and poisonous "skull in tires." "Here's fine revolution, an we had the trick to see't," comments Hamlet. But Vindice's trick is to see no revolution at all. Horror of the skull is made to express and promote horror of the self-prostituting flesh. The only finally truthful function life can have is to figure death and the begetting of death; and thus the only finally real action of Tourneur's play is that of a reflexive verb, whose subject and object are the same.

Tourneur's apologists would offer us a moralist who, having masterfully drawn a landscape of depravity, masterfully shakes his death's-head to abash all whores and whoremongers, drunkards and epicures. But this, I have tried to show, is quite to miss "the quaintness of [his] malice." Gloriana, "robed in holiness," may *seem* to prepare us for the truth that will set us free. Fully unmasked, she has only her own nullity to bestow.

EUGENE M. WAITH

The Rhetoric of Tragicomedy:
The Poet as Orator

The pattern of tragicomedy which dominates the Beaumont and Fletcher plays imposes upon them a special language whose effect [discussed elsewhere] is above all emotional. There are, of course, speeches whose sole purpose is to convey information, and others which define a character or present an idea, but the most memorable and distinctive speeches are the tirades, the laments, the defenses of honor, which contain the very life of Fletcherian tragicomedy. Therefore, a study of the genre culminates logically in an examination of this emotional language. Since the comedies provide the least suitable material for such an examination, I shall not add to the comments already made on the language of Fletcher's comedy. Much of the language of the tragedies, however, is indistinguishable from the language of the tragicomedies. The examples to be considered come from these two sources.

The language of the poet was commonly described in the Renaissance in the terms of rhetorical analysis, for Aristotle's clear distinction between poetic and rhetoric had been lost. In Aristotle's scheme the function of the poet is to imitate an action, the function of the orator to persuade men of the truth; the poet's enterprise is imaginative, while the orator's is practical. Hence, as C. S. Baldwin makes clear, the play, presenting action, is the emblem of poetic, and the public address, exhorting to action, is the emblem of rhetoric. In Rome, in the last years of the republic and the beginning of the empire, rhetoric was so much in the ascendant that it largely took over the province of poetic. Horace's unsystematic art of poetry ascribes to the poet the didactic function of the orator and thus blurs the basic Aristotelian

From *The Pattern of Tragicomedy in Beaumont and Fletcher*. © 1952 by Yale University Press.

distinction. The most detailed studies of language are made by the rhetoricians Cicero and Quintilian, who also tend to confuse the functions of orator and poet. And in the declamation, popular and influential, in spite of the disapproval of the best rhetoricians, poetic is incorporated in rhetoric, for the imaginative presentation of a scene is one of the chief devices for scoring a point in a controversia. In the Renaissance Cicero and Quintilian were the great authorities on style, Horace was widely admired, and the declamation was a school exercise. It is not surprising that rhetoric dominated poetic.

To discuss poetic style from the point of view of rhetoric is to regard the poem as a means to elicit a certain response rather than to regard it, as we are more apt to do, as almost an end in itself—a living entity whose form gives unique expression to certain thoughts and feelings. Each method has its advantages. The Renaissance method is well suited to the study of dramatic poetry, especially when it is poetry of primarily emotional appeal, for this sort of poetry is good just to the extent that its creates its effect. Rhetorical analysis is singularly appropriate, as I hope to show, in examining the language of Fletcherian tragicomedy.

George Puttenham makes the connection between poet and orator explicit in his *Arte of English Poesie* when he says that "the Poets were also from the beginning the best perswaders, and their eloquence the first Rethoricke of the world . . . " He develops the comparison at greater length in a passage where he is discussing the use of rhetorical figures:

> Now if our presupposall be true, that the Poet is of all other the most auncient Orator, as he that by good & pleasant perswasions first reduced the wilde and beastly people into publicke societies and civilitie of life, insinuating unto them, under fictions with sweete and coloured speeches, many wholesome lessons and doctrines, then no doubt there is nothing so fitte for him, as to be furnished with all the figures that be *Rhetoricall*, and such as do most beautifie language with eloquence and sententiousnes. . . .
> So as if we should intreate our maker to play also the Orator, and whether it be to pleade, or to praise, or to advise, that in all three cases he may utter, and also perswade both copiously and vehemently.

This conception, shared by Puttenham with most of his contemporaries, that the office of the poet is to persuade men of the truth derives most directly from Roman rhetoric and underlies the familiar Renaissance doctrine of the dual function of poetry. In Sidney's words, which owe much to Horace:

Poesie therefore is an arte of imitation, for so *Aristotle* termeth it
in his word *Mimesis*, that is to say, a representing, counterfetting,
or figuring forth: to speake metaphorically, a speaking picture:
with this end, to teach and delight.

And that mooving is of a higher degree then teaching, it may
by this appeare, that it is wel nigh the cause and the effect of
teaching. For who will be taught if hee bee not mooved with
desire to be taught?

The importance of "moving" in relation to teaching is recognized by
Aristotle not in the *Poetics* but in the *Rhetoric*, where he shows that the orator
cannot depend on argument alone but through his knowledge of human
nature must make his point emotionally convincing. The Greek word for
persuasion, the accepted aim of rhetoric, was *psychagogia*, sometimes translated as "enchantment of the soul," a word which was used first of the
conjuring of the souls of the dead and then applied metaphorically to the
magic of words by which the mind may be directed. To effect this enchantment the mind must be transported, not merely reasoned with. Thus the
poet as a persuader, confronted with the same problems as the orator, finds
his task divided like the orator's into two parts, one of which is an appeal
to man's rational faculties, the other to his emotions.

In order to achieve these distinct objectives both poet and orator must
master certain appropriate variations of style, for Renaissance rhetoric (following in the steps of Cicero) taught that a given style is necessary to produce
a given effect upon an audience. As G. L. Hendrickson has pointed out,
Aristotle's division of rhetoric soon gave rise to a distinction between a
pragmatic style appropriate for argumentation and a more elaborate style
appropriate for an emotional appeal. Furthermore, since the nature of Aristotle's division is such that one style corresponds to proofs drawn from the
subject matter itself, while the other style corresponds to proofs extraneous
to the subject matter, it is easy to regard the elaborate style as consisting
in unessential ornament and to make a distinction between content and form.

It is possible to interpret Aristotle's division as threefold by emphasizing
his subdivision of the orator's second function into *ethos* (making his character
look right) and *pathos* (putting his hearers in the right frame of mind).
Following this lead, Cicero in *De oratore* and *Orator* assigns to the orator the
functions of teaching, pleasing, and moving (*docere, conciliare* or *delectare*, and
movere) and equates with these functions the plain style, the middle style,
and the grand style—the first clear, precise, and conversational in tone, the

second highly ornamented to please the ear, the third even more exuberantly
figurative to sway the passions by its vehemence. All the figures of rhetoric
are suitable for the middle and grand styles, and Cicero especially recom-
mends to his orator the practice of amplifying his theme. Thomas Wilson
expresses his understanding of Cicero as Follows:

> Exornation is a gorgious beautifying of the tongue with borrowed
> wordes, and change of sentence or speech with much varietie.
> First therefore (as *Tullie* saith) an oration is made to seme right
> excellent by the kind selfe, by the colour and juice of speech.
> There are three maner of stiles or inditings, the great or mightie
> kinde, when we use great wordes, or vehement figures.
>
> The small kinde, when wee moderate our heate by meaner
> wordes, and use not the most stirring sentences.
>
> The lowe ["lawe," 1585 edition] kinde, when we use no *Met-
> aphores* nor translated words, not yet use any amplifications, but
> goe plainly to worke, and speake altogether in common wordes.

The conviction that "moving is of a higher degree than teaching" and
the association of an elaborate style with the power to move partly explain
the emphasis which the Renaissance placed upon "copiousness" and upon
the figures of rhetoric with which the style can be embellished. All rhetoricians were convinced that the object of eloquence was to inculcate wisdom,
but, as it were in spite of themselves, they allowed the weight of their
criticism to fall upon the means of achieving this end. While believing that
the ideal orator must be not a specialist but a man of almost universal
learning, Cicero make such a point of the superiority of the grand style that
he gives ammunition to those who would make eloquence an end in itself.
His treatment of the Sophists, who are ordinarily accused of this perversion
of rhetoric, indicates his own position. In the *Orator*, far from condemning
them wholly, he merely points out their limitations—that they seek to
delight more than to persuade, that their style is more charming than
vigorous. The Sophists are the orators of the middle style, which is "fuller
and somewhat more robust than the simple style . . . but plainer than the
grandest style. . . . It is, as a matter of fact, a brilliant and florid, highly
coloured and polished style in which all the charms of language and thought
are intertwined." The grand style of oratory excels the Sophistic in being
yet more "copious" and more vehement. Thus Cicero and his followers
consciously or unconsciously separate content from form, isolate style, or
elocutio, which Wilson calls "that part of *Rhetorique*, the which above all

other is most beautifull," and encourage elaborateness as a means to persuasion.

Since poet and orator were so closely associated, rhetorical theory inevitably had a powerful effect on poetic style. Moody Prior has shown the fondness of the early writers of Elizabethan tragedy for a highly ornamented style in which patterns of sound play an important part. The imitation of Seneca, which encouraged this tendency, may itself have been partly due to the cultivation of a Ciceronian taste in rhetoric. In Seneca's plays, in any case, the Elizabethan dramatists found a declamatory style closely related to the Sophistic tradition recorded by the Elder Seneca for the benefit of his sons. The flowers of rhetoric bloom luxuriantly in Senecan tragedy. As Elizabethan tragedy developed, the formal and florid style of the early plays was superseded by a style less self-conscious and, as Moody Prior observes, more closely bound to the dramatic action. Although the style of Fletcherian tragicomedy is affected by this movement in that it often borrows the vocabulary of conversation, as Dryden noticed, and makes use of flexible and varied rhythms, it is characteristically elaborate and related more loosely to the poetic action than is the style of Shakespeare, Webster, Tourneur, or Jonson. The Beaumont and Fletcher plays provide more examples of Sophistic rhetoric than the plays of any of their contemporaries. In the poetry of these plays eloquence is more important than wisdom; virtuosity is cultivated at the expense of relevance. It may be that this style is the result of the reinforcement of current rhetorical theory by the influence of the declamatory style in satire and romance and, more directly, of the declamations of Seneca the Elder. But all questions of influence aside, it is apparent that such a style is peculiarly oratorical and that it is by Renaissance standards the proper choice for a sort of drama which seeks mainly to delight and to move, or, as we should say, in which there is a marked decrease in meaning and a proportionate increase in the relative importance of emotion.

Although the style of Fletcherian tragicomedy is typically elaborate, there are two reasons why it is not uniformly so. One is that the three styles distinguished by Cicero were thought not only to be conducive to three different effects but to be appropriate to three categories of speakers and of topics—the grand style for gods and princes and what concerns them (and hence for hymns, epics, and tragedies), the middle style for the "civiller and better sort" of citizens and their affairs (and hence for comedy), and the plain style for laborers of all kinds, including shepherds, and for "base and low matters" (and hence for pastoral and satire, although the Juvenalians, as we have seen, often soared above this level). The decorum of tragicomedy, which is the inheritor of tragedy, epic (via romance), comedy, pastoral, and satire, properly makes room for every style. The second reason for stylistic variation in the Beaumont and Fletcher tragicomedies is, of course, their multiple authorship. Much has been written about the styles of the three chief collaborators, Fletcher, Massinger, and Beaumont, which the verse tests have helped to distinguish. It is not of the first importance which dramatist was responsible for a given style, and in what I have to say I shall not be primarily concerned to prove that certain characteristics were Fletcher's and his only, or Massinger's or Beaumont's. Accepting in the main the distinctions already made, I shall illustrate what seem to me valid differences between the styles of the three chief authors, but I shall discuss them as variations of one style, as they would doubtless appear to be if nothing were known of the authorship of the plays. The differences I shall mention may properly be thought of as gradations of the tragicomic style.

The range of the style between the obviously elaborate and the seemingly plain can be seen by comparing the lament of Demetrius in *The Humorous Lieutenant* upon the supposed death of Celia with the speech which Arbaces makes in *A King and No King* when he first realizes that he is in love with his sister. Demetrius speaks as follows:

> O matchless sweetness, whither art thou vanished?
> O thou fair soul of all thy Sex, what Paradise
> Hast thou inrich'd and blest?
>
>   art thou dead *Celia*,
> Dead my poor wench? my joy, pluckt green with violence:
> O fair sweet flower, farewel; Come, thou destroyer
> Sorrow, thou melter of the soul, dwell with me;
> Dwell with me solitary thoughts, tears, cryings,
> Nothing that loves the day, love me, or seek me,
> Nothing that loves his own life haunt about me:
> And Love, I charge thee, never charm mine eyes more,
> Nor ne're betray a beauty to my curses:
> For I shall curse all now, hate all, forswear all,
> And all the brood of fruitful nature vex at,
> For she is gone that was all, and I nothing—
>
>   (IV, ii)

This is what we should call "rhetorical" language today, meaning that the style is showy and calls attention to itself by its wealth of ornament. With its balance and antithesis, its repetition and alliteration, it is "brilliant and florid" like the style which Cicero associates with the Sophists. The sound of the lines is vastly important.

Superficially very different is Arbaces' speech:

> Why should there be such musick in a voyce,
> And sin for me to hear it? All the world
> May take delight in this, and 'tis damnation
> For me to do so: You are fair and wise
> And vertuous I think, and he is blest
> That is so near you as your brother is;
> But you are nought to me but a disease;
> Continual torment without hope of ease;
> Such an ungodly sickness I have got,
> That he that undertakes my cure, must first
> O'rethrow Divinity, all moral Laws,
> And leave mankind as unconfin'd as beasts,
> Allowing 'em to do all actions
> As freely as they drink when they desire.
>
> (III)

In this passage patterns of sound are much less obvious than in Demetrius' lament: there is none of the repetition and very little of the alliteration which are so abundant in the other passage. The one conspicuous aural effect which is used here and not in the passage from *The Humorous Lieutenant* is rhyme, and that is used sparingly. Although the rhythm is a more regular iambic pentameter, relatively free of the extra syllables found in every line of Demetrius' lament, the pattern of five accents is less insistent on account of the greater number of run-on lines. The passage from *The Humorous Lieutenant* is typical of Fletcher's versification and the passage from *A King and No King* of Beaumont's. With regard to the relative importance of patterns of sound the two original partners represent opposite ends of the scale.

In vocabulary both passages are as simple as they are extravagant in sentiment, but Beaumont's passage begins, at least, on a conversational tone, while Fletcher's launches immediately into the formality of a set piece. In spite of the hyperbole in which Arbaces indulges, his speech conveys some impression of naturalness, while that of Demetrius appears to be flamboyant artifice from beginning to end. The difference, though it is one of degree, has a marked effect on the appeal which each passage makes.

The less formal rhetoric tends to produce a sharper delineation of character. For the emotional effect at which it aims, Fletcher's passage relies heavily upon its compelling rhythm, its verbal elaboration, and the formal tone which serves notice immediately that what follows is pitched in a high emotional key. Beaumont's passage, with its quieter tone and simpler diction, relies much more upon the depiction of an individual in a tragic plight. The definition of character is one of the means by which Arbaces' speech evokes pity; his lines are characteristic of him in this situation, whereas the lines of Demetrius might have been spoken by many others. They express the situation but not the man. The rhetorical means chosen to make this situation emotionally persuasive might equally well be applied to other situations as well as to other characters. Beaumont's more careful suiting of language to a particular character in a particular situation is comparable to the use of description as a rhetorical device in the Senecan declamations and elsewhere. The emotional effect is heightened by the clarity and immediacy of the representation. In this respect Beaumont's rhetoric is a good example of rhetoric in poetic—of rhetorical means closely related to poetic action. . . .

One of the best speeches in *The Maid's Tragedy* again shows Beaumont's style to advantage, while revealing a little more about its operation. Evadne has just come to Amintor holding the knife with which she has killed the King and proclaiming, "Joy to *Amintor!*" He replies:

> Those have most power to hurt us that we love,
> We lay our sleeping lives within their arms.
> Why, thou hast rais'd up mischief to his height,
> And found out one to out-name thy other faults;
> Thou hast no intermission of thy sins,
> But all thy life is a continual ill;
> Black is thy colour now, disease thy nature.
> Joy to *Amintor!* thou hast toucht a life,
> The very name of which had power to chain
> Up all my rage, and calm my wildest wrongs.
>
> (v)

The quiet, reflective tone of the first two lines is extraordinarily effective in the circumstances and makes a brilliant contrast to the bitter denunciation which follows. As in the speeches of Arbaces the diction is free of the more conspicuous patterns of sound. Here, however, the relative simplicity does not accompany a concentration upon the individual character. Although Amintor's nature is reflected in the speech, the pathos of his situation is rendered by other means—first by a generalization and then by a hyperbolic denunciation which makes Evadne the epitome of evil. In spite of the explicit statement of Amintor's characteristic respect for royalty, the speech is less personal than the speeches of Arbaces which I have quoted above. This moment in the drama is given the maximum of effectiveness by the familiar rhetorical means of amplification—by the sentious generalization and hyperbole—but the line could be applied with only the slightest changes to other situations in other plays.

Since the sentious utterance recommended by the experts in rhetoric is used by many dramatists who are quite unlike Beaumont or Fletcher, a brief comparison may be useful here. When Ferdinand is killed in the last scene of *The Duchess of Malfi* his dying breath is spent on a sentious couplet:

> Whether we fall by ambition, blood, or lust,
> Like Diamonds, we are cut with our owne dust.

This speech is effective not because of its aphoristic expression of a moral truth but because it applies so exactly to the principal characters of the play. Even the Duchess, though only slightly tainted by the encompassing evil, has destroyed herself by stooping to a deception of which she disapproves. At the same time her tragedy illustrates the superlative value of human nature and its resistance to all but its own corruption. The power of Ferdinand's aphorism, then, is seen in its sudden illumination of the compound tragedies in this play. Amintor's touching observation,

> Those have most power to hurt us that we love,
> We lay our sleeping lives within their arms,

has no such effect. It applies primarily to the relationship of the King and Evadne and hence seems to evoke pity for the murdered tyrant. The generalization has no direct bearing upon the denunciation which follows or upon Amintor's situation. The effectiveness of the lines depends upon generality rather than particularity. Vagueness is all. . . .

Although Beaumont's versification is usually easy to distinguish from Fletcher's, the styles of the two men are not so different with regard to rhetorical devices as they might seem from the first two examples I have quoted. Beaumont's poetry is usually less ornamented but far from plain. In tone it tends to be more conversational. Sometimes, but not often, it operates through a vivid realization of an individual in a unique situation. Most often some of the familiar rhetorical devices for amplification are used to make the character's plight moving, and the more indiscriminately these devices are used the less precisely the emotion evoked fits the given situation. There comes a point beyond which rhetoric is not simply a means of making the action of the play persuasive but rather the means of exciting emotions for which the action of the play provides an occasion. Where this is the case the emotion is more vague and the rhetoric more ornamental. The change could be illustrated by many more passages which extend all the way from the plainest style of Beaumont to the most elaborate style of Fletcher. The point I have described would be passed long before leaving Beaumont for Fletcher.

One more quotation from *Philaster* will show how the styles of the two men blend on occasion. Here the repetition and alliteration of Fletcher are combined in such a way with versification more characteristic of Beaumont that the passage has been attributed to both authors. It is an antifeminist tirade so general that it is unnecessary to give the occasion on which it is spoken by Philaster:

> Now you may take that little right I have
> To this poor Kingdom; give it to your Joy,
> For I have no joy in it. Some far place,
> Where never womankind durst set her foot,
> For bursting with her poisons, must I seek,
> And live to curse you;
> There dig a Cave, and preach to birds and beasts,
> What woman is, and help to save them from you.
> How heaven is in your eyes, but in your hearts,
> More hell than hell has; how your tongues like Scorpions,
> Both heal and poyson; how your thoughts are woven
> With thousand changes in one subtle webb,
> And worn so by you. How that foolish man,
> That reads the story of a womans face,
> And dies believing it, is lost for ever.
> How all the good you have, is but a shadow,
> I'th' morning with you, and at night behind you,
> Past and forgotten. How your vows are frosts,
> Fast for a night, and with the next sun gone.
> How you are, being taken all together,
> A meer confusion, and so dead a *Chaos*,
> That love cannot distinguish. These sad Texts
> Til my last hour, I am bound to utter of you.
> So farewel all my wo, all my delight.
>
> (III, i)

Again a comparison may help to show what is distinctive in Beaumont and Fletcher's use of common rhetorical devices. Shakespeare contrives for

Troilus a speech in which individual disillusionment is amplified and generalized:

> This she? No, this is Diomed's Cressida!
> If beauty have a soul, this is not she;
> If souls guide vows, if vows be sanctimonies,
> If sanctimony be the gods' delight,
> If there be rule in unity itself—
> This is not she. O madness of discourse,
> That cause sets up with and against itself!
> Bifold authority! where reason can revolt
> Without perdition, and loss assume all reason
> Without revolt: this is, and is not, Cressid!
> Within my soul there doth conduce a fight
> Of this strange nature, that a thing inseparate
> Divides more wider than the sky and earth;
> And yet the spacious breadth of this division
> Admits no orifex for a point as subtle
> As Ariachne's broken woof to enter.
>
> (*Troilus and Cressida*, v, ii, 137–52)

It is clearly a trick of rhetoric to develop to the point of logical absurdity the impossibility of Cressida's betrayal, yet all the rhetorical energy here is harnessed to accelerate the main movement of the play. The story of Troilus' fatal infatuation is seen against a background of ideal order described in the famous speech on "degree" given by Ulysses in one of the opening scenes. Inversions of moral values are directly related there to disturbances of the entire cosmic hierarchy:

> Frights, changes, horrors
> Divert and crack, rend and deracinate
> The unity and married calm of states
> Quite from their fixure!
>
> (I, iii, 98–101)

The statement "If there be rule in unity itself— / This is not she" makes explicit the connection of the hero's dilemma with the philosophical scheme of the play. It is a generalization which not only enhances the dramatic moment but reveals its place in the larger structure. The speech is furthermore perfectly suited to the character of Troilus, for the duplicity which it cries out against is the very fault to dismay one who is "as true as truth's simplicity / And simpler than the infancy of truth." Here, as in no play by Beaumont and Fletcher, the rhetorical elaboration is thoroughly integrated with the other elements of the drama.

Before discussing further the relation between elaborate style and emotional effect, we must consider another use of language in the Beaumont and Fletcher plays which at first appears to aim at an intellectual rather than an emotional effect. One of the best examples is the reply of Cleopatra in *The False One*, when her sister Arsino asks her whether she can "stand unmov'd" in the face of the present danger:

> Yes, *Arsino,*
> And with a Masculine Constancy deride
> Fortunes worst malice, as a Servant to
> My Vertues, not a Mistress; then we forsake
> The strong Fort of our selves, when we once yield,
> Or shrink at her assaults; I am still my self,
> And though disrob'd of Soveraignty, and ravish'd
> Of ceremonious duty, that attends it,
> Nay, grant they had slav'd my Body, my free mind
> Like to the Palm-tree walling fruitful *Nile,*
> Shall grow up straighter and enlarge it self
> 'Spight of the envious weight that loads it with:
> Think of thy Birth (Arsino) common burdens
> Fit common Shoulders; teach the multitude
> By suffering nobly what they fear to touch at;
> The greatness of thy mind does soar a pitch,
> Their dim eyes (darkened by their narrow souls)
> Cannot arrive at.
>
> (v, iv)

This passage resembles others I have quoted in its somewhat conversational tone and its freedom from conspicuous patterns of sound such as adorn Demetrius' lament and Philaster's denunciation of women. With regard to other forms of rhetorical ornament, Cleopatra's speech, without being flamboyant, contains many metaphors and one simile of epic formality ("Like to the Palm-tree . . . "). The rhetoricians usually referred to such figures as "tropes," since the words are "turned" from their ordinary, literal meaning; Puttenham, who makes a different sort of classification, considers metaphor and simile as "sensable figures," appealing chiefly to the mind, in contrast to the "auricular figures," which appeal chiefly to the ear. On the basis of this classification of figures Cleopatra's speech would seem to appeal more to the mind than those speeches which depend heavily on "auricular figures" such as alliteration.

This kind of distinction seems to be supported by another difference between Cleopatra's speech and those we have been considering. Not only are there many run-on lines, as in Beaumont's verse, but several lines are grouped together in a tightly cohesive unit. A more solid logical structure unites the passage "I am still my self . . . that loads it with" than unites any six-and-a-half lines previously quoted. It is necessary here to follow the logical connections: "Though disrob'd . . . and ravish'd . . . [and though] they have slav'd my Body, my free mind . . . shall grow up . . . 'Spite of the envious weight that [i.e, fortune's malice] loads it with." Though flexible, this blank verse does not flow freely. It has a distinctive toughness and density derived from its argumentative structure.

The kind of blank verse just described is typical of Massinger. As Maurice Chelli says, "ses personnages pensent et raisonment beaucoup. Ils s'efforcent constamment de prouver, de convaincre, par des arguments bons ou mauvais, sincères ou sophistiques . . . " Swinburne's criticism is also to the point: "The style of Massinger . . . is radically and essentially unlike the style of his rivals: it is more serviceable, more businesslike, more eloquently practical, and more rhetorically effusive—but never effusive beyond the bounds of effective rhetoric—than the style of any Shakespearean or of any Jonsonian dramatist." "Serviceable, businesslike, eloquently practical" well describe a style whose great virtue, as seen in Cleopatra's defense of personal integrity, is the persuasive definition of an idea—in this case an ideal of conduct. For the emphasis of the speech is not so much on the character of the speaker as on what is said.

It might be concluded from this line of analysis that while the poetry of Beaumont and of Fletcher aims to please and to move, Massinger's poetry aims to teach, but this distinction is not valid. One flaw in such an argument is suggested by Cicero's comment that the plain style, which aims to teach, should be very sparingly embellished with metaphor (Wilson countenances no metaphors in the "lowe kind" of style). Massinger's style, though "businesslike," is metaphorical and not truly plain. Swinburne also characterizes it as "rhetorically effusive." And when the effect of Cleopatra's speech is carefully studied, the arousing of emotion is seen to be an important factor. Within the framework of the play the speech is designed to bolster the courage of Arsinoe, who responds to Cleopatra with the assurance, "I am new created." In the audience the speech is clearly intended to arouse admiration for Cleopatra by setting forth the nobility of her ideal. Intellectual

and emotional appeals are combined here as Cicero believed they should be.
The prominence of reasoning (when the speech is compared with Fletcher's
poetry or Beaumont's) should not obscure the characteristics which make
Cleopatra's words moving.

Most of Massinger's speeches in the Beaumont and Fletcher plays do
not have this combination of wisdom and eloquence. More typical is the
following speech of Sophia in *The Bloody Brother:*

> Divide me first, or tear me limb by limb,
> And let them find as many several Graves
> As there are villages in *Normandy:*
> And 'tis less sin, than thus to weaken it.
> To hear it mention'd doth already make me
> Envy my dead Lord, and almost Blaspheme
> Those powers that heard my prayer for fruitfulness,
> And did not with my first birth close my womb:
> To me alone my second blessing proves
> My first of misery, for if that Heaven
> Which gave me *Rollo,* there had staid his bounty,
> And *Otto,* my dear *Otto,* ne're had been,
> Or being, had not been so worth my love,
> The stream of my affection had run constant
> In one fair current, all my hopes had been
> Laid up in one; and fruitful *Normandy*
> In this division had not lost her glories:
> For as 'tis now, 'tis a fair Diamond,
> Which being preserv'd intire, exceeds all value,
> But cut in pieces (though these pieces are
> Set in fine gold by the best work-mans cunning)
> Parts with all estimation: So this Dukedom,
> As 'tis yet whole, the neighbouring Kings may covet,
> But cannot compass; which divided, will
> Become the spoil of every barbarous foe
> That will invade it.
>
>   (I, i)

Again groups of line are held together by the logical structure of the sentences, and the process of reasoning is conspicuously used, as in the careful
analogy of the dukedom with a diamond. But the substance of what is said
is very slight when compared to what Cleopatra says. The whole paraphernalia
of logical argument is used to elaborate Sophia's appeal for unity. Her speech

is an example of amplification and, as such, is primarily addressed to the emotions, though making use of the process of reasoning. Rymer shows his awareness of the copious elaboration by his comment, already quoted, that the speech "seems to present a *well-breath'd* and *practis'd Scold,* who vents her passion and eases her mind by talking, and can weep and talk everlastingly." Like many of Massinger's speeches, this one is, within the framework of the play, an oration, designed to move other characters on the stage while it also appeals to the emotions of the audience. Sophia's advice is made persuasive by devices which are conspicuous in the Senecan declamations—by an appeal for pity and by an ingenious analogy. Ingenuity is, in fact, the most notable characteristic of the speech. The means of persuasion, so cleverly chosen, make their own separate appeal, in the hope that the audience may be as much pleased by the performance as moved with pity for Sophia. This is rhetoric in the Sophistic tradition. . . .

It remains to see how Massinger's rhetoric is related to that of Beaumont and Fletcher. Though it may not often be so intensely emotional as theirs, the main distinction to be made is that Massinger relies upon the structure of argument even when the emphasis of the speech is clearly emotional. Two roughly comparable speeches from *The Double Marriage* illustrate the difference. The first, by Fletcher, is Pandulpho's lament for his son and reproach to his daughter-in-law who is the unwitting murderess. The second, by Massinger, is the tirade in which Sesse expresses grief and rage at the behavior of his daughter Martia.

> O my Son,
> Nature turns to my heart again, my dear Son,
> Son of my age, would'st thou go out so quickly?
> So poorly take thy leave, and never see me?
> Was this a kind stroak daughter? could you love him?
> Honour his Father, and so deadly strike him?
> O wither'd timeless youth, are all thy promises,
> Thy goodly growth of Honors come to this?
> Do I halt still ith'world, and trouble nature,
> When her main pieces founder, and fail dayly?
>
> (v, i)

> Thou, I want a name,
> But which to stile thee: All articulate sounds
> That do express the mischief of vile woman,
> That are, or have been, or shall be, are weak
> To speak thee to the height. Witch, Parricide,

> For thou, in taking leave of modesty,
> Hast kild thy father, and his honor lost;
> He's but a walking shadow to torment thee.
> To leave, and rob thy father; then set free
> His foes, whose slavery he did prefer
> Above all treasure, was a strong defeazance
> To cut off, even the surest bonds of mercy.
> After all this, having given up thy self,
> Like to a sensual beast, a slave to lust,
> To play the whore, and then (high Heaven it racks me)
> To find out none to quench thy appetite,
> But the most cruel King, whom next to Hell,
> Thy father hated; and whose black imbraces
> Thou shouldst have fled from, as the whips of furies;
> What canst thou look for?
>
> (v, i)

Pandulpho's emotion is projected in the repetition of "son" and "so" and in such combinations as "founder and fail dayly." It is the patterns of sound which make the pathos compelling in spite of a phraseology which is otherwise undistinguished. The feelings of Sesse are given a logical formulation: no names are adequate for Martia, but metaphorically speaking she is a parricide, since she has utterly disgraced her father; to have left and robbed him and freed his enemies is enough to deprive her of any claim to mercy, but having, in addition to all this, made herself the mistress of her father's worst enemy, what treatment can she expect? Sesse presents the legal case against his daughter, appealing to the judgment of an imaginary arbiter and in effect appealing to the sympathy of the audience. . . .

There is a special sort of brilliance, however, in which Massinger excels and which has a direct bearing upon the problem of appraising the style of Fletcherian tragicomedy. In *The Queen of Corinth* occurs a sort of *débat* between the lovers Euphanes and Beliza on the question of whether Euphanes should feel indebted to Beliza for the financial assistance she has given him. She offers to prove

> That whereas you profess your self my debtor,
> That I am yours.
> EUPHANES: Your Ladyship then must use
> Some Sophistry I ne'r heard of.

BELIZA: By plain reasons,
    For look you, had you never sunk beneath
    Your wants, or if those wants had found supply
    From *Crates,* your unkind and covetous brother,
    Or any other man, I then had miss'd
    A subject upon which I worthily
    Might exercise my bounty: whereas now
    By having happy opportunity
    To furnish you before, and in your travels,
    With all conveniencies that you thought useful,
    That Gold which would have rusted in my
    Coffers
    Being thus imploy'd, has rendred me a partner
    In all your glorious actions. And whereas
    Had you not been, I should have dy'd a thing
    Scarce known, or soon forgotten: there's no
    Trophy
    In which *Euphanes* for his worth is mentioned,
    But there you have been careful to remember,
    That all the good you did came from *Beliza.*

               (I, ii)

Ingenuity of reasoning, which plays some part in Sophia's speech, is here the whole show. There is no question of evoking powerful feeling but simply of delighting the audience with the cleverness of the debater's points. The same effect is even more apparent in the preposterous denouement of this play, when Beliza pleads for the death of Theanor on the grounds that he has raped her, though she knows that in fact he has not done so but has twice raped Merione, supposing her, on the second occasion, to be Beliza. Merione has just demanded Theanor in marriage when Beliza declaims:

      Is that justice?
  Shall one that is to suffer for a Rape
  Be by a Rape defended? Look upon
  The publick enemy of chastity,
  This lustful Satyr, whose enrag'd desires
  The ruine of one wretched Virgins honor
  Would not suffice; and shall the wrack of two
  Be his protection? May be I was ravish'd
  For his lust only, thou for his defence;
  O fine evasion! shall with such a slight
  Your Justice be deluded? your Laws cheated?
  And he that for one fact deserv'd to die,

For sinning often, find impunity?
But that I know thee I would swear thou wert
A false Impostor, and suborn'd to this;
And it may be thou art *Merione:*
For hadst thou suffer'd truly what I have done,
Thou wouldst like me complain, and call for vengeance,
And our wrongs being equal, I alone
Should not desire revenge: But be it so,
If thou prevail, even he will punish it,
And foolish mercy shew'd to him undo thee,
Consider, fool, before it be too late,
What joys thou canst expect from such a Husband,
To whom thy first, and what's more, forc'd embraces,
Which men say heighten pleasure, were distastful.

                                                             (v, iv)

In estimating the effect of this speech, it must be remembered that the audience and several characters on the stage, including notably Merione, are well aware that the situation presupposed by Beliza is entirely hypothetical. Persuasion is out of the question. The pleasure an audience derives from the speech may come in part from the perpetration of a trick upon the villain Theanor but much more from the display of forensic ability. Beliza's far-fetched reasoning is calculated to amaze and entertain. Several of her arguments are taken directly from the amazing and entertaining sallies of the declaimers whom Seneca the Elder heard on the case of the two maidens raped in one night (*Controversiae* i. 5). In the play as in the school of declamation the real object is not to convince anyone of anything and not to move the passions violently but to provide a certain emotional thrill and to delight by means of virtuosity.

In Fletcherian tragicomedy the "reasoning" style associated with Massinger is effective in realizing a typical scene of conflict as a sharply pointed debate. If the scene is to be realized in terms of intense passions, Fletcher's verbal gymnastics or Beaumont's less obvious devices of amplification are more suitable. But these alternative methods, while distinct, are also similar in one respect, that they are all on the same side of the main dividing line between the various sorts of style. For Cicero and other classical rhetoricians, the low style, whose aim is to teach, is in a category by itself. Both the middle and grand styles make an emotional appeal, though they are assigned the respective aims of pleasing and moving. These aims cannot be kept wholly distinct and the means by which they are to be achieved admittedly overlap. The styles of Beaumont, Fletcher, and Massinger are similar, then, in that they all concentrate upon an emotional effect.

The implications of the analogy I have drawn between Massinger's style and Sophistic oratory point to a still closer similarity between his style and those of Beaumont and Fletcher. I have suggested that Beaumont and Fletcher are more intensely "moving," Massinger more "pleasing," but if we reconsider the emotional effects of Beaumont and Fletcher with the precedent of the Sophistic declaimers in mind, we realize that even the most stirring speeches of Arbaces, Amintor, Philaster, and Demetrius do not thoroughly engage the emotions. The response to this sort of rhetoric is double: the hearer is moved and aware of being moved. He admires the verbal technique at the same time that he responds to it. Such a response, though I have described it in a most un-Ciceronian fashion, seems to be what Cicero means by being "pleased" as opposed to being "moved" and "swayed." His description of Sophistic oratory, the origin of the middle style, applies to the styles of all three collaborators on the Beaumont and Fletcher plays and thus underlines their essential similarity. In the following passage Cicero arbitrarily reserves the word "oratorical" for the style of the practicing orator as opposed to the declaimer of the schools:

> More care must be taken to distinguish the oratorical style from the similar style of the Sophists mentioned above, who desire to use all the ornaments which the orator uses in forensic practice. But there is this difference, that, whereas their object is not to arouse the audience but to soothe it, not so much to persuade as to delight, they do it more openly than we and more frequently; they are on the look-out for ideas that are neatly put rather than reasonable; they frequently wander from the subject, they introduce mythology, they use far-fetched metaphors and arrange them as painters do colour combinations; they make their clauses balanced and of equal length, frequently ending with similar sounds.

In this description are compounded elements of the styles of Beaumont, Fletcher, and Massinger. It might well serve as a description of the style of Fletcherian tragicomedy.

From the comparisons already made it may be apparent that Fletcher's style represents a greater specialization than the styles of his collaborators. He concentrates narrowly upon certain devices of which repetition is the most conspicuous. Puttenham puts repetition first in his third category of figures, the "sententious" or "rhetorical" figures, which appeal both to the ear and to the mind: "And first of all others your figure that worketh by

iteration or repetition of one word or clause doth much alter and affect the
eare and also the mynde of the hearer, and therefore is counted a very brave
figure both with the Poets and rhetoriciens . . . " In Demetrius' lament the
bravery of this figure is emphatically courted with the repetition of "dead,"
"dwell with me," "nothing that loves," "all," and less important words and
phrases. The repetition of "all" in the last three lines not only is the most
insistent repetition in the passage but illustrates a habit of Fletcher's of
placing the repeated word first in an accented then in an unaccented position
in the line:

> For I shall curse all now, hate all, forswear all,
> And all the brood of fruitful nature vex at,
> For she is gone that was all, and I nothing—

In this way the emphasis resulting from repetition is counterpointed against
the regular pattern of emphasis and produces the effect of syncopation. The
excitement of this sort of repetition is brilliantly exploited in Evadne's words
as she stabs the King to death. In reply to his plea for pity she says:

> Hell take me then; this for my Lord *Amintor;*
> This for my noble brother: and this stroke
> For the most wrong'd of women.
>
> (v)

Both the first and the second "this" receive a strong accent through trochaic
substitution; the third is in a technically unaccented position, preceding the
strongly accented word which ends the line. Thus one is aware of the strain
between the insistent pattern of accents on the repeated word and the normal
pattern of accents in the iambic line. In the third instance the strain becomes
acute.

The frequent alliteration in Fletcher's verse (a figure which Puttenham
naturally describes as making little appeal to the mind and hence "auricular"
rather than "sensable") is one of the chief indications of the importance of
sound patterns in the total effect. When the end-stopped line, the third of
the most obvious characteristics of his verse, is added to the other two, it
becomes clear that a formal arrangement of sounds is the basis upon which
Fletcher builds. For the end stopping, especially when accompanied, as it
so often is in Fletcher, by feminine endings, breaks the rhythmical flow of
the verse into well-defined units. Thus, in spite of the irregularity of extra
syllables, the regular beat of the iambic pentameter line is emphasized by
incessant repetition:

> Out thou impudence,
> Thou ulcer of thy Sex; when I first saw thee,
> I drew into mine eyes mine own destruction,
> I pull'd into my heart that sudden poyson,
> That now consumes my dear content to cinders:
> I am not now *Demetrius,* thou hast chang'd me;
> Thou, woman, with thy thousand wiles hast chang'd
>   me;
> Thou Serpent with thy angel-eyes has slain me;
> And where, before I touch'd on this fair ruine,
> I was a man, and reason made, and mov'd me,
> Now one great lump of grief, I grow and wander.
>   (*The Humorous Lieutenant,* IV, viii)

The sound of such lines as these is their most formidable weapon for the assault upon the spectator's emotions. The patterns of repetition and alliteration are interwoven with the insistent pattern of the five-foot line, reinforced by frequent parallels of construction.

Neither Beaumont nor Massinger relies so heavily upon versification for the desired emotional effect. Specifically, neither of them uses so much repetition, so much alliteration, or so marked a rhythm. Fletcher's unfailing sense of rhythm, perhaps his greatest gift as a versifier, recalls Cicero's belief in the importance of rhythm to the orator. Although no exact comparison can be made, since Cicero is solely concerned with prose rhythms, his comments reveal the recognition in rhetorical theory of the profound effect which rhythm may have upon an audience. Together with repetition and alliteration, Fletcher's rhythm makes of his verse a sort of incantation—a short cut to that "enchantment of the soul" at which the orator aims.

Quite contrary to the point of view which I have been maintaining is the opinion of certain critics of Fletcher's verse that it is extraordinarily unrhetorical, "natural," and "conversational." It is true that Fletcher successfully imitates the vocabulary of conversation and its casual structure, and in scenes where the emotional tension is comparatively relaxed (such as those which primarily convey information or those which are devoted to light, satirical comedy) the characteristics I have been describing are much less in evidence. These are scenes for which a low style is appropriate. But whenever the tension increases, as it does in each important scene, the formal patterns of sound become prominent, and the effect is far from conversational. Even in some of the freest and most natural passages there is stricter adherence to the five accents of the line as a rhythmical unit than in the blank verse of many other poets. The following lines of Celia in *The Humorous Lieutenant,*

lightly satirical in tone, are decidedly irregular and yet are more obviously
patterned than the expository lines of Melantius in *The Maid's Tragedy* placed
after them:

> If I stay longer
> I shall number as many Lovers as *Lais* did;
> How they flock after me! upon my Conscience,
> I have had a dozen Horses given me this morning,
> I'le ev'n set up a Troop, and turn She-souldier,   5
> A good discreet wench now, that were not hidebound
> Might raise a fine estate here, and suddenly:
> For these warm things will give their Souls—I can go
>   no where
> Without a world of offerings to my Excellence:
> I am a Queen, a Goddesse, I know not what—   10
> And no constellation in all Heaven, but I out-shine it;
> And they have found out now I have no eyes
> Of mortal lights, but certain influences,
> Strange vertuous lightnings, humane nature starts at,
> And I can kill my twenty in a morning,   15
> With as much ease now—
> Ha! what are these? new projects?
> Where are my honourable Ladies? are you out too?
> Nay then I must buy the stock, send me good Carding:
> I hope the Princes hands be not in this sport;   20
> I have not seen him yet, cannot hear from him,
> And that troubles me: all these were recreations
> Had I but his sweet company to laugh with me:
> What fellow's that? another Apparition?
> This is the lovingst Age: I should know that face,   25
> Sure I have seen't before, not long since neither.
>
>   (IV, i)

> All joyes upon him, for he is my friend:
> Wonder not that I call a man so young my friend,
> His worth is great; valiant he is, and temperate,
> And one that never thinks his life his own,
> If his friend need it: when he was a boy,   5
> As oft as I return'd (as without boast)
> I brought home conquest, he would gaze upon me,
> And view me round, to find in what one limb
> The vertue lay to do those things he heard:

Then would he wish to see my Sword, and feel   10
The quickness of the edge, and in his hand
Weigh it; he oft would make me smile at this;
His youth did promise much, and his ripe years
Will see it all perform'd.

                                                        (I)

The two long lines (8 and 11) in Celia's soliloquy are the major irreg-
ularities; the two short lines (16 and 17) are in reality the halves of one line,
separated to emphasize the break in the train of thought. Most of the lines
are end stopped, and of the three which are not (6, 8, and 12) the first two
end with a slight hesitation produced by the final unaccented syllable. The
accumulation of phrases whose grammatical connection is loose suggests the
language of conversation but also aids in maintaining the line as a rhythmical
unit, for the short phrase ("and suddenly," "I know not what") is paired
with a longer one to fill out a line. Despite the extra syllables in almost
every line, the feeling of pentameter is stronger here than in Melantius'
speech, where the pauses are so distributed in the last seven lines that no
sense of the line as a unit remains. This variety is a much closer approximation
of normal conversational freedom than the irregularity of Fletcher, which is
more apparent than real.

It is not only in conversational speeches that Fletcher uses the device
of accumulating brief phrases to make up the line. In some of the more
extravagant speeches, such as the following of Zenocia's in *The Custom of the
Country,* this mannerism, accentuated by the device of repetition, is carried
to exasperating lengths:

                        Do not do this
        To save me, do not lose your self I charge you,
        I charge you by your love, that love [you] bear me;
        That love, that constant love you have twin'd to me,
        By all your promises, take heed you keep 'em,
        Now is your constant tryal.

                                                    (IV, i)

The structure of the lines here is not essentially different from that in Celia's
speech. In both a seemingly casual arrangement of words contributes to a
regular pattern of rhythm that cannot be called either natural or·
conversational. . . .

The best illustration of the curious charm of Fletcherian rhetoric may be Memnon's burlesque heroics in *The Mad Lover* as he contemplates cutting out his heart:

> 'Tis but to dye, Dogs do it, Ducks with dabling,
> Birds sing away their Souls, & Babies sleep 'em,
> Why do I talk of that is treble vantage?
> For in the other World she is bound to have me;
>
> There love is everlasting, ever young,
> Free from Diseases, ages, jealousies,
> Bawds, Beldames, Painters, Purgers: dye? 'tis nothing,
> Men drown themselves for joy to draw in Juleps
> When they are hot with Wine: In dreams we do it.
>
>   (II, i)

The pleasure which these lines give is partly due to the burlesque, but even more to the sheer manipulation of words. The effect is essentially similar to that of other passages we have considered, though the meaning here is comic rather than serious. It would be quite false to conclude that Fletcher's patterns of sound have an absolute value, divorced from the meaning of the words, for in that case we should not be aware of the differences between the speeches of Archas, Demetrius, and Memnon. In all these speeches, however, the patterns of sound produce an excitement which greatly intensifies the emotions described by the words. In Memnon's soliloquy even the burlesque of heroic feeling becomes strangely moving. To look for the source of these emotional effects in Fletcher's imagery is unrewarding, for there is comparatively little imagery in his language—almost none of the sort of metaphor by which Shakespeare, Chapman, or Tourneur achieves emotional intensity. In Fletcher the verbal texture—the sound of the words arranged in formal patterns—is what chiefly moves and pleases. This is Fletcher's version of Sophistic oratory.

The predominance of the oratorical effect in Fletcherian tragicomedy fits very well the taste of the time in which Beaumont and Fletcher wrote. The learned and licentious monarch from the north set the fashion for his court in more than one way and through the court influenced the upper strata of society in the city. The Jacobean court is known for its sensational intrigues and scandals, such as those which became public property during the trial of the murderers of Sir Thomas Overbury. Equally well known is the lavishness of the entertainment made possible when James I emancipated his court from the restrictions of Elizabethan thrift: it was the period of the elaborate masques of Jonson and Inigo Jones. As these masques clearly reveal, however, the king's pleasure-loving courtiers were accustomed to a liberal mixture of learning with their artistic distractions.

It is not surprising that an audience with such tastes should be captivated by the extravagant eloquence of Sophistic rhetoric. There is a slight flavor of bookishness in the exploitation of a tradition so firmly rooted in the schools— an appeal to the educated spectator. Furthermore, the legalistic character of many of the forensic debates in Beaumont and Fletcher doubtless had a special appeal to the age which saw the wrangles of Chief Justice Coke with the sovereign. Sensational situations abound, each one fully developed as the basis of an intense emotional experience. Yet at the same time the pattern of Fletcherian tragicomedy tends, as we have seen, to nullify the total meanings which either comedy or tragedy may have and to substitute for them a more rarefied aesthetic satisfaction in purely formal relationships. Here is a direct appeal to tastes both cultivated and jaded. The emphasis falls upon a rhetoric which is itself formal in its reliance upon conspicuous patterns of sound and which is the chief means of projecting the emotion of the dramatic moments. Both the extravagance and the formality of this style were aptly designed to appeal to the Jacobean audience.

Technique becomes a matter of special interest for such an audience. Concerned with the separate dramatic effects of which the play is composed and familiar with the various literary precedents, the sophisticated spectator eagerly awaits not only the emotional experience but a revelation of how it is achieved. He is prone to admire sheer artistic dexterity. Thus the Jacobeans were apt to be pleased by the imitation of the masterpieces of declamation recorded by Seneca the Elder, for the enjoyment of such performances comes from a lively appreciation of rhetorical skill. The dramas of the younger Seneca, written in the declamatory tradition, had, as is well known, an immense appeal to the Elizabethans, and a large measure of the ranting verse of Kyd and others is doubtless attributable to this influence, but the rhetoric of most Senecan plays did not long stay in fashion. It was far less durable than Seneca's bequest of sententiousness or of the Stoical concept of heroic personal integrity. By the time Beaumont and Fletcher began to write, the imitation of Seneca, though still popular, was no longer a fresh artistic enterprise, but the moment was propitious for exploiting the possibilities of the declamatory style. To turn from the tragedian to the rhetores was to expose a new facet of a familiar tradition and gratify the taste of an audience interested in technique and more eager for delight than instruction. Each age takes something different from the storehouse of the classics; Beaumont and Fletcher were clever enough to see what would suit the theatrical world of their time.

To push further the correspondences between Beaumont and Fletcher and the court of James I is to risk being unfaithful both to the plays and to the audience which admired them. Critics as widely separated by age and purpose as Coleridge and the contemporary historian Esmé Wingfield-Stratford have made much of the political absolutism of Beaumont and Fletcher, citing *The Maid's Tragedy* and *The Loyal Subject* as plays which pandered to the king's taste. But the playhouse audience was not composed entirely of people who agreed with James I, and one must grant the justice of G. C. Macaulay's comment: "Surely if these authors were such devoted royalists, and aimed so constantly at exhibiting their loyalty on the stage, it is strange and even unaccountable that so few sovereigns are represented in their plays as a sovereign would desire to be represented, and that so many are set up as objects of contempt and hatred." If Archas is honored for being loyal, Virolet in *The Double Marriage* is honored for rebelling. Though Amintor's worship of sovereignty is presented as a virtue, the king who contrives his martyrdom is presented as a "libidinous tyrant," like the kings in *The Double Marriage* and *A Wife for a Month*. The literary ancestry of the tyrant as a stock type must also dissuade one from the simplicity of the argument that the Beaumont and Fletcher plays presented political views to please the court of their times. The attitudes toward tyrants in the plays would not have been pleasing to absolutists, if taken seriously, but were doubtless so familiar to readers of satire, romance, or the declamations that they were taken for granted as literary stereotypes. Finally, as I hope I have shown, there is no continuous specific meaning in plays like *The Maid's Tragedy* or *The Loyal Subject*. The circumstances involving wicked monarchs and loyal subjects are used as are various other plot structures to create the situations in which honor eloquently defends itself against dishonor.

It is safest, then, to relate the great popularity of Beaumont and Fletcher not to the ideas expressed in their plays but to the artistic taste of the times. The scandals and escapades of James I's courtiers must have made the sensational episodes in the plays more easily acceptable, and the successful imitation of the "conversation of gentlemen" would have had a similar effect, but this sort of timeliness was not what chiefly endeared Beaumont and Fletcher to their own generation. Shirley, whose flattering estimate was prefixed to the First Folio, praises them for the perfection of their art. He does not hesitate to say that the plays were a liberal education for the well-bred young men of the time, worth more than formal schooling and foreign travel combined. His reason for thinking so is an essentially aesthetic one, for his point (similar to Dryden's a few years later) is that Beaumont and Fletcher present in the most persuasive form every variety of human passion:

You may here find passions raised to that excellent pitch and by such insinuating degrees that you shall not chuse but consent, & go along with them, finding your self at last grown insensibly the very same person you read, and then stand admiring the subtile Trackes of your engagement. Fall on a Scene of love and you will never believe the writers could have the least roome left in their soules for another passion, peruse a Scene of manly Rage, and you would sweare they cannot be exprest by the same hands, but both are so excellently wrought, you must confesse none, but the same hands, could worke them.

("To the Reader")

This is an admirable description of the experience of a spectator who enjoys not only his emotional response but the "subtile Trackes" of his "engagement"—the strategy of the rhetorician.

To an age more apt to admire understatement than exaggeration, to an age shy of dramatic poetry, to an age brought up on the notion that it is more artful to express strong emotion on the stage by the smallest visible gesture or the briefest outburst, the exuberant rhetoric of Beaumont and Fletcher has very little appeal. The conventions of realistic tragedy and comedy have led the modern theater audience to expect something totally unlike Fletcherian tragicomedy. In our times the attitudes necessary for an enjoyment of this kind of artistic achievement have become attached exclusively to other arts—to music, for example, and to painting. There the most dramatic contrasts, the boldest designs, the purest abstractions, the most powerful emotional stimuli are frankly acknowledged and admired. Only in ballet, in opera, and in the more recent "musical drama" do such techniques enter the theater. One may speculate that if a modern audience approached Beaumont and Fletcher with the expectations it has on going to the opera, it would find much to enjoy, for it would accept the contrivance of the play more readily and would await the more declamatory passages as eagerly as the famous arias, duets, or quartets of grand opera.

Shakespeare has survived the changes of dramatic taste because his was never so narrowly a triumph of technique as was the triumph of Beaumont and Fletcher. We may, and do, misinterpret Shakespeare because of unfamiliarity with the dramatic conventions of his time, but the poetic integrity of his best work transcends these conventions. The genius of Beaumont and Fletcher is much more special. It is embodied in a particular rhetoric and in a dramatic genre which is, in effect, the projection of that rhetoric in the theater. Because the theatrical projection is fully and brilliantly achieved,

Fletcherian tragicomedy may be enjoyed today, once it is recognized for what it is, as an extreme of dramatic formalism. Declamations were exercises in oratory which came to be valued in themselves as entertainment. In somewhat the same way these tragicomedies are superb examples of dramatic art—a series of hypothetical situations made compelling by sheer technical virtuosity. In the sharply delineated conflicts of Fletcherian tragicomedy is the basic design of all drama.

M. C. BRADBROOK

Thomas Middleton

Middleton's tragedies are as similar in their methods of construction as they are different from the plays already considered [elsewhere]. Rowley's name appears on the title page of *The Changeling*, but it is difficult to see the possibility of his sharing in the main plot, for its unity is of a kind which not even the most sympathetic collaboration could achieve.

The connection between the two plots of this play is, however, very carefully worked out. It is indicated even in the title, "The *Changeling*," which describes both Antonio, the innocent, and Beatrice-Joanna, the inconstant woman (a usual meaning—see *Anything for a Quiet Life*, II. i. 71, and *OED sub verb.*).

The construction of the play is masked by the greater naturalism of the treatment. Compared with the characters of earlier plays, Middleton's are fuller, more natural and human. Their motives and actions may be conventionally "Italianate" (they have vestigial remains of the Revenge code in the melancholy of Tomazo the revenger and the appearance of the ghost), but their feelings and responses are normal. Beatrice-Joanna's famous outburst, when the murderer demands possession of her as a reward:

> Why 'tis impossible thou canst be so wicked
> Or shelter such a cunning cruelty
> To make his death the murderer of my honour—
> (III. iv. 121ff)

is only the most obvious illustration of Middleton's interest in the way the

---

From *Themes and Conventions of Elizabethan Tragedy.* © 1935 by Cambridge University Press.

mind works. Deflores' brief plea to the man he has cuckolded, when he hears
Beatrice-Joanna crying out in futile anger:

> Let me go to her, sir—
> (v. iii. 112)

is so assured of his right to calm her that the husband can but send him in.

The construction of the play is, however, partly dependent on themes:
briefly it may be described as a study in the conflict of passion and judgment,
and of the transforming power of love. All the characters (save Alsemero)
are entirely at the mercy of their feelings, which are instinctive and uncon-
trollable. Judgement is blinded, so that the characters practise all kinds of
deception and self-deception to gain their ends. Love is "a tame madness,"
a kind of possession which seizes upon a man and "changes" him so that he
is no longer recognisable. In the main plot the themes are worked out
naturalistically; in the subplot the use of the madmen, and of more literal
transformations, as well as more farcical action, makes a kind of phantas-
magoria. The key words are *change, judgement* and *will* (in the sense of
instinctive desire, often of sensual desire, as in Shakespeare). The connection
between plot and subplot is summed up in the final scene where the structure
of themes is explained.

ALSEMERO. What an opacous body had that moon
　　　　That last changed on us! here is beauty changed
　　　　To ugly whoredom; here servant-obedience
　　　　To a master-sin, imperious murder;
　　　　I, a supposed husband, changed embraces
　　　　With wantonness—but that was paid before—
　　　　Your change is come too from an ignorant wrath
　　　　To knowing friendship. Are there any more on's?
ANTONIO. Yes sir I was changed too from a little ass as I was
　　　　to a great fool as I am: and had like to ha' been changed to the
　　　　gallows, but that you know my innocence always excuses me.
FRANCISCUS. I was changed from a little wit to be stark mad
　　　　Almost for the same purpose.
ISABELLA *(to her husband).* Your change is still behind.
　　　　But deserve best your transformation.

(v. iii. 199ff)

Transformation is a useful word to describe the character changes in the
play: people are changed in the eyes of others, and they are also changed
radically in themselves by the power of love.

The play opens with Alsemero falling in love. It was "in the Temple" which he instinctively feels to be an omen (the use of omens as what would now be called promptings of the unconscious mind plays a large part in the play). In any case he is already transformed; from an ardent traveller he becomes a loiterer, from a woman hater a courtier so that his friend cries:

> How now: the laws of the Medes are changed sure: salute a woman:
> he kisses too: wonderful!
>
> (I. i. 60)

This sense of shock and discovery is the same in kind (though not in intensity of course) as the "discoveries" of Beatrice-Joanna, of Isabella and of Alsemero.

The dialogue which follows states the main theme. Alsemero roundly declares his love, to which Beatrice-Joanna replies:

> Be better advised, sir:
> Our eyes are sentinels unto our *judgments*
> And should give certain *judgment* what they see;
> But they are rash sometimes and tell us wonders
> Of common things, which when our *judgments* find
> They can then check the eys and call them blind.
>
> (I. i. 73ff)

Alsemero has seen her twice, however, and this he considers amply sufficient for the co-operation of eyes and judgement.

Deflores is then introduced, and Beatrice-Joanna's instinctive hatred of him. "She knows no cause for't but a peevish *will*." Beatrice-Joanna and Alsemero have a long discussion on the idiosyncratic character of the will (compare *The Merchant of Venice*, IV i. 44–62) and its instinctive pre-critical judgements. Beatrice-Joanna's father then appears and a conversation, in which asides and equivocations are frequent, shows to what extent Beatrice-Joanna's "will" is already transforming her. She says:

> I shall *change* my saint, I fear me: I find
> A giddy turning in me—
>
> (I. i. 158–59)

an echo of Alsemero's "I keep the same church, same devotion" which points the contrast between them. Her father explains to Alsemero that she is betrothed to Alonzo de Piracquo: immediately his plans change, he must go away. The father will have her married at once, "I'll want my *will* else."

Beatrice-Joanna adds aside, "I shall want mine if you do it." Finally Deflores, remaining to soliloquise, reveals his plight as the same one:

> I know she hates me
> Yet cannot choose but love her: no matter,
> If but to vex her, I will haunt her still:
> Though I get nothing else, I'll have my will.
> (I. i. 237–40)

The second act opens with Beatrice-Joanna busily deluding her own judgment. Alsemero's friend has just arranged an assignation, and she catches at his discretion as a justification for herself.

> How wise is Alsemero in his friend,
> It is a sign he makes his choice with *judgment*:
> The I appear in nothing more approved
> Then making choice of him . . .
> (II. i. 6ff)

She loves "with intellectual eyesight" as Alsemero thought he did.

Instead of Alsemero, Deflores arrives. He describes his own infatuation coolly (he is well aware of his ugliness, so that only "intellectual eyesight" could ever endure him) yet he does not despair, and when Beatrice-Joanna turns on "this ominous ill-faced fellow" he endures her patiently. He has a certain self-knowledge which sets him above the others, if it does not give him self-mastery.

> Why am I not an ass to devise ways
> Thus to be railed at? I must see her still,
> I shall have a mad qualm within this hour again
> I know't.
> (II. i. 77ff)

When he is gone Beatrice-Joanna enlarges on the feeling of danger he inspires in her. The scene concludes with an interview with her unwelcome lover, Piracquo. He refuses to recognise her very plain dislike of him, since love has overpowered his judgement too. His brother comments on his incredulity:

> Why, this is love's tame *madness*,

a significant link with the subplot.

All this interweaving of self-deception and self-awareness is supported by dialogue of the greatest ease and naturalness. There is no sustained heroic pitch as in Tourneur or Webster; the climaxes of feeling are simply expressed, not in obviously rich and poetic language.

> I have within my eyes all my desire . . .
>
> > (II. ii. 8)

> Here was a course
> Found to bring sorrow on her way to death
> The tears would ne'er have dried till blood had
> > choked 'em.
>
> > (II. ii. 37–39)

The scene in which Deflores is given the commission to kill Piracquo is one of ironic comedy. Having seen her secret interview with Alsemero he has hopes for himself and when Beatrice-Joanna seems more friendly he is really deceived into thinking her judgment is changed.

> BEATRICE-JOANNA. You've pruned yourself, methinks: you were
> > not wont
> > To look so amorously.
> DEFLORES. Not I—
> > 'Tis the same phisnomy to a hair and pimple
> > Which she called scurvy scarce an hour ago.
> > How is this?
> BEATRICE-JOANNA. Come hither; nearer, man.
> DEFLORES. I'm up to the chin in heaven!
>
> > (II. ii. 74ff)

At first he coaxes her into speaking because he half believes she is in love with him. She is trying to get her request out naturally and he makes things easy by importuning her.

> BEATRICE-JOANNA. Oh my Deflores!
> DEFLORES. How this? she calls me hers?
> > Already, my Deflores—You were about
> > to sigh out somewhat, madam? . . .
> BEATRICE-JOANNA. Would creation—
> DEFLORES. *Ay well said, that's it.*
> BEATRICE-JOANNA. Had made me man.
> DEFLORES. Nay that's not it.
>
> > (II. ii. 97ff)

He may be ironical, but it is hardly likely. They part mutually deceived, Beatrice-Joanna rejoicing at being rid of him and he in having won her.

The murder is quickly done and the great discovery scene follows. Beatrice-Joanna is congratulating herself on her judgement

> So wisdom by degrees works out her freedom.
>
> (III. iv. 13)

Deflores is something more than complacent as he enters and shows her the severed finger of Piracquo. She is horrified, for she had not visualised the murder; Deflores the hired assassin was to stand between her and the dirty business of the stabbing. He is quite callous physically, and cannot understand her qualms at the sight of the ring—"the first token my father made me send him." When she tells him to keep the jewel, however, her coarseness is exposed in turn by his retort:

> 'Twill hardly buy a capcase for one's conscience though
> To keep it from the worm, as fine as 'tis.
>
> (III. iv. 45–46)

His anger rises as he realises her attitude toward himself. The barriers of her modesty, dignity and stupidity are not easily broken; she only thinks of him as a servant and at first actually appeals to him on those grounds.

> Think but upon the distance that creation
> Set 'twixt thy blood and mine and keep thee there.
>
> (III. iv. 131–32)

Deflores' reply suggests that she has become "transformed": she is no longer the woman she was, since her love has altered.

> 'Twas chang'd from thy first love, and that's a kind
> Of whoredom in the heart, and he's chang'd now
> To bring thy second on, thy Alsemero.
>
> (III. iv. 144–46)

She is "the deed's creature," and one with him. It will be seen that later both Beatrice-Joanna and Alsemero acknowledge her transformation.

Deflores' speeches have also a naturalistic interpretation. The pain of his disillusion can be felt behind his violence; it breaks out finally in an appeal to her pity, as direct as hers to him:

> I live in pain now: that shooting eye
> Will burn my heart to cinders.
>
> (III. iv. 152–53)

When she submits he drops to a tenderness heard again in the final scene. It is one of Middleton's most daring and most perfectly managed modulations of feeling:

> Come rise and shroud your blushes in my bosom:
> Silence is one of pleasure's best receipts:
> Thy peace is wrought for ever in this yielding.
>
> (III. iv. 167–9)

The last two acts are worked out in the same manner as the first three. Beatrice-Joanna makes the same mistake with Diaphanta as she did with Deflores. "'Tis a nice piece gold cannot purchase," and so she bribes her maid to take her place on the marriage night.

Diaphanta's lust nearly wrecks the plan, as Deflores' had done. He arrives and suggests an alarm of fire, but Beatrice-Joanna is as slow now as heretofore to see the point of his proposals.

> BEATRICE-JOANNA. How, fire, sir? that may endanger the whole
> house.
> DEFLORES. You talk of danger when your fame's on fire?
>
> (v. i. 33–34)

The trick of the "magic" glass of water by which Alsemero tests her virginity is not out of place, for it belongs with the "omens" and other irrational elements rather than with the naturalism of character and speech; it is also reinforced by the stronger suggestion of "magic" in the subplot.

Alsemero is the only character whose "will" does not overpower his judgement. Beatrice-Joanna fears his clear sight (IV. i. 1–17). He is contrasted with Piracquo who would not hear a word against his betrothed:

> Were she the sole glory of the earth,
> Had eyes that could shoot fire into Kings' breasts
> And touched, she sleeps not here.
>
> (IV. ii. 106–8)

The quarrel with Tomazo de Piracquo seems "ominous" to him; but his innocence relieves him. At the moment of discovery he remembers his early scruples:

> O the place itself e'er since
> Has crying been for vengeance! the Temple . . .
>
> (v. iii. 73–74)

Beatrice-Joanna now appears hideous to him, even physically hideous, and
in that is akin to Deflores. Her transformation is complete, through the
discovery of her deceit.

> The black mask
> That so continually was worn upon't
> Condemns the face for ugly ere't be seen
>
> (v. iii. 3–5)

> O thou art all deformed.
>
> (v. iii. 78)

Beatrice-Joanna miscalculates a third time: she confesses murder but
denies adultery, thinking Alsemero will pardon the greater crime, since it
was done for his sake. She knows him no better than Deflores or Diaphanta;
he rejects her with horror and it is left for Deflores' resolution to cut the
thread, by murder and suicide. Beatrice-Joanna recognises her transformation, at first indirectly: of the word "whore" she says:

> It blasts a beauty to *deformity*
> Upon whatsoever face that breath falls
> It strikes it ugly.
>
> (v. iii. 33–35)

Finally she recognises her union with Deflores, and the significance of her
first "will" to dislike him (v. iii. 157–60).

The revenge of Tomazo de Piracquo is also a matter of will. At first
he likes Deflores, but later he feels an inexplicable recoil from him.

The subplot is connected with the main plot chiefly by implication. It
acts as a kind of parallel or reflection in a different mode: their relationship
is precisely that of masque and antimasque, say the two halves of Jonson's
Masque of Queens. The direct links at the end have already been mentioned:
there is also a scene of parallel action, first noted by William Empson, in
which Isabella, the wife of the madhouse keeper, is detected with her lover
by a servant Lollio. He proceeds to exact the same price from Isabella that
Deflores did from Beatrice-Joanna:

> Come, sweet rogue: kiss me, my little Lacedemonian: let me
> feel how thy pulses beat: thou hast a thing about thee would do
> a man pleasure, I'll lay my hand on it.
>
> (III. iii. 247–50)

Her reply is an inversion of Beatrice-Joanna's. She threatens in turn:

> Be silent, mute,
> Mute as a statue, or his injunctions
> For me enjoying, shall be to cut thy throat,
> I'll do't, though for no other purpose.
>
> (III. iii 253–56)

Deflores enjoyed Beatrice-Joanna in return for cutting a throat.

Isabella has two lovers, who are disguised as a fool and a madman in order to gain access to her. Antonio, the fool, throws off his hideous disguise, which he calls a *deformity* (III. iii. 195) and appears as her lover suddenly:

> This shape of folly shrouds your dearest love,
> The truest servant to your powerful beauties,
> Whose *magic* had the force thus to *transform* me.
>
> (III iii. 127–29)

It is parallel to Deflores' appearance as the lover of Beatrice-Joanna. The quality of the surprise is similar (not, of course, the intensity). The other lover never actually encounters her, but sends a letter in which he says:

> Sweet Lady, having now cast off this counterfeit cover of a mad-man, I appear to your best *Judgment* a true and faithful lover of your beauty . . . (Love) shapes and transhapes, destroys and builds again . . .

In the same scene Isabella puts on the disguise of a madwoman to meet the fool; but she is only temporarily transformed. Her speeches are full of references to Dedalus and Icarus, which suggest the dangerous nature of their secret and the preciousness of the reward. But the fool does not recognise her, and so she returns to her former state, and is never actually unfaithful to her ridiculous husband.

The chorus of madmen depict the bestial element in man, rather as Caliban does, or the rout in *Comus*. At the climax of the subplot, when Isabella is hard pressed by Antonio, Lollio cries 'Cuckoo! cuckoo!' and there is the direction:

> *Madmen above, some as birds, others as beasts.*

Bullen and other editors rearrange this, but it clearly means that the madmen appear on the upper stage in the masquing habits which they are to wear at their entertainment at Beatrice-Joanna's wedding. They are a symbolic presentation of evil. Isabella explains:

> They act their fantasies in any shapes [i.e. costumes]
> Suiting their present thoughts.

Already they have been heard within crying at the game of barley-break:

> Catch there: catch the last couple in hell!
>   (III. iii. 173)

The old worn pun gains in horror when Deflores echoes it to Alsemero in the final scene:

> I coupled with your mate
> At barley-break: now we are left in hell.
>   (v. iii. 165–66)

Vermandero adds, "It circumscribes us here," thinking of the actual chalk ring.

The supernatural element in the main plot is veiled: it depends on the omens and the "magic" effects of Alsemero's chemistry. The subplot is fantastic and pictorial. The masque of madmen, ostensibly prepared for the wedding, is actually given in rehearsal before Isabella at the end of act IV. She is summoned to it:

> Away then, and guide them in, Lollio:
> Entreat your mistress to see this sight.

The importance of this masque can be gauged by the comparison with that in Ford's *The Lover's Melancholy* (III. iii). Here the doctor Corax has a masque of melancholy men to cure the melancholy of the Prince. The different types of the disease are taken from Burton, and each is symbolically dressed. For instance, Lycanthropia has "his face whited, with black shag hair, and long nails and with a piece of raw meat." The wanton melancholy is "a Sea-Nymph big-bellied, singing and dancing," the point of this being of course that *mermaid* was slang for prostitute.

The Prince remaining unmoved, Corax adds:

> One only kind of Melancholy
> Is left untouched: 'twas not in art
> To personate the shadow of that fancy:
> 'Tis named love-melancholy . . .
> Love is the tyrant of the heart: it darkens
> Reason, confounds discretion: deaf to counsel
> It runs a headlong course to desperate madness.

The Prince, like Claudius in *Hamlet*, breaks off the revels abruptly. The significance of this passage with its symbolic treatment of madmen and the connection between love and madness involved in the symbolism is perhaps all the stronger for there being no trace of any direct influence of Middleton.

Throughout the scenes of the subplot of *The Changeling*, riddling games and tableaux keep up the bizarre horror.

> Here's a fool behind a knave, that's I: and between us two
> fools there is a knave, that's my master: 'tis but we three, that's
> all.
> We three, we three, cousin.
>
>   (I. ii. 202ff)

This is the husband posed between Lollio, his servant, and Antonio, his "patient," both of whom are deceiving him at the moment when they so firmly assert that he is the knave and they the fools. So Isabella is posed between her husband and her two lovers throughout the play. So Beatrice-Joanna is posed between her husband and her two lovers, Piracquo and Deflores, in the one scene where the supernatural is allowed to intrude overtly into the main plot, and the silent ghost of Alonzo appears to Deflores and Beatrice-Joanna as they plot the second murder, that of the waiting woman Diaphanta. Yet even here the tone is kept quiet. To Deflores the ghost is only a "mist of conscience," while Beatrice-Joanna does not even see it clearly enough to recognise it: it felt an "ill thing" that left a shivering sweat upon her. So firmly does each half of the play retain its own proper atmosphere, and yet so closely are they interwoven with each other. . . .

It is not absolutely necessary to grasp the scheme of imagery or even the themes, in order to appreciate the play. [It is] not completely dependent upon this scheme in the way in which the plays of Tourneur are: a great deal can be got from [it] on the level of narrative-and-character alone. But it is difficult to grasp the connection of plots and subplots in any other way, without which Middleton must seem to combine an exceptional power of construction and a wanton disregard of its elementary principles in the most curious way. It remains true, however, that the stress which should fall upon themes and imagery is much lighter in Middleton's plays than in those of most of his contemporaries. This is not to say that Middleton's language is less poetic or less important than that of the other poets, but that he also relies upon action and characterisation in a way which no one else did (except Shakespeare). His language too gains its effect by different methods from those of the majority of the Elizabethans; he does not rely upon explicit statement or direct speech but upon implication; nor upon a gorgeous and elaborate vocabulary, but upon a pregnant simplicity which is perhaps more difficult to achieve, and is certainly found more seldom.

MICHAEL NEILL

Massinger's Patriarchy: The Social Vision of A New Way to Pay Old Debts

An Houshold is as it were a little Commonwealth, by the good government whereof, Gods glorie may be advantced, and the commonwealth which standeth of severall families benefited.

> —JOHN DOD and ROBERT CLEAVER,
> *A Godly Forme of Household Government*

Like *The Merchant of Venice*, with which it is often compared, *A New Way* is about the pangs of transition to a capitalistic, cash-nexus society; and like Shakespeare, Massinger takes a fundamentally conservative attitude toward that process, asserting the primacy of communal bonds over legal bondage, of social obligation over commercial debt, of love over the law. *The Merchant*, however, founds its critique of bourgeois values upon a familiar Christian mythos—the opposition of the Old Law and the New— and in a reassuring comic paradox neutralizes its new man, the Machiavellian capitalist, by making him a representative of the Old Law, rendered obsolete by the sacrifice of Christ. The Jew-Devil Shylock "stands for" Law, Portia for Sacrifice. Though Sir Giles Overreach is sometimes made to appear like yet another diabolic incarnation from the Moralities, and though Massinger invokes scriptural analogues for his judgment of prodigal Welborne and the false servant Marrall, *A New Way* has no such thorough mythic foundation. Instead it appeals to a whole set of normative social assumptions which, although they were customarily justified by the Scriptures, are in fact peculiar to Massinger's own epoch. Because they belong, in Peter Laslett's phrase, to

From *Renaissance Drama*. © 1979 by Northwestern University Press.

"the world we have lost," they can make *A New Way* seem a less universal comedy than its predecessor; but they also make it considerably more vivid as a document of historical attitudes. Massinger brings alive, as perhaps none of his contemporaries can, the ingrained social beliefs that were to make Sir Robert Filmer's writings the handbook of a generation of Royalist gentry.

In the last big speech of the play, Welborne reminds us of the double nature of the "debts" that must be paid before the social order can be reestablished:

> there is something else
> Beside the repossession of my land,
> And payment of my debts, that I must practise.
> I had a reputation, but 'twas lost
> In my loose courses; and till I redeem it
> Some noble way, I am but half made up.
>
> (V.i.390–395)

The "making up" of his "worshipful" self is dependent on the "making up" of a moral obligation more powerful than any merely financial debt. The method of redemption he proposes is that of "service"—service to his king, fittingly discharged through his immediate social superior, Lord Lovell (II. 396–400). The idea of service is a crucial one in the play: and one which is pointedly taken up in the epilogue, where Massinger playfully sees himself as the servant of the audience, seeking his freedom by the "manumission" of their applause (II. 403–4). He elaborates the conceit in his dedicatory epistle, by way of graceful compliment to the Earl of Caernarvon, whose protection he seeks to earn "in my service," recalling that "I was born a devoted servant, to the thrice noble family of your incomparable Lady," and hopefully subscribing himself "Your Honour's true servant." Massinger, though he came of minor gentry, was born into service in the sense that his father was steward to the household of Henry Herbert, Earl of Pembroke; and the dedication invites us to read *A New Way* as a tribute to the ideals he imbibed at Wilton—as itself a new way to pay a personal debt of honor.

Even the element of topical satire in the play can be seen to accord with this complimentary purpose, since, as Patricia Thomson has pointed out, Mompesson, as Buckingham's protégé, was a natural enemy of the Herberts. But Overreach's villainy, of course, touches only tangentially on Mompesson's malpractice. Mompesson is important to the dramatist's imagination less as a venal monopolist than as the hideous type of an alarming social tendency.

A contemporary comment on Mompesson, cited by L. C. Knights, may help to make this point clearer:

> Sir Giles Mompesson had fortune enough in the country to make him happy, if that sphere could have contained him, but the vulgar and universal error of satiety with present enjoyments, made him too big for a rustical condition, and when he came at court he was too little for that, so that some novelty must be taken up to set him in *aequilibrio* to the place he was in, no matter what it was, let it be never so pestilent and mischievous to others, he cared not, so he found benefit by it.

Mompesson's crime amounted to a double violation of that principle of service on which the order of society was founded: he had betrayed the obligations of that office in which the king had placed him, and he had attempted to rise above that position in society to which God had called him. Overreach is an incarnation of that anarchic impulse which seemed to fuel Mompesson's corrupt ambition. In his brutal assault on the bonds of a society felt to subsist on an intricate hierarchical network of communal service and mutual obligation, he is the nightmare projection of emergent capitalism, the monstrous herald of that new social order whose perfection Marx was to describe:

> The bourgeoisie, wherever it has got the upper hand, has put an end to all feudal, patriarchal, idyllic relations. It has pitilessly torn asunder the motley feudal ties that bound man to his *natural superiors*, and has left remaining no other nexus between man and man than naked self-interest, than callous *cash payment*. . . .
>
> The bourgeoisie has stripped of its halo every occupation hitherto honoured and looked up to. . . . It has converted the physician, the lawyer, the priest, the poet, the man of science, into its paid wage-labourers.
>
> The bourgeoisie has torn away from the family its sentimental veil, and has reduced the family relation to a mere money-relation.

Overreach's household includes Marrall, Will-do, and Greedy—lawyer, priest, and justice—among its paid wage-laborers; and "family" for him— as his relations with his nephew, and ultimately with his daughter too, illustrate—simply denotes a nexus of money relationships: when Welborne has lost his money they are no longer kin.

In contrast to the vast and ruthlessly impersonal machine conceived by Marx, the social order imagined by most of Massinger's contemporaries was that of a large family ruled by a father-sovereign: each family was itself a commonwealth (a paternal monarchy) and the state a family of such petty commonwealths. The relationship was not merely one of analogy: for it was from the first family that the state itself had grown. The hierarchic order of society was thus a natural part of the divinely ordained scheme of things. Whatever the philosophic limitations of such patriarchalist thought, it took immense strength, as Gordon Schochet has shown, from its close correspondence to the practical socialization of the vast majority of seventeenth-century Englishmen for whom the family, or household, was the focus of most activity: "some form of paternal authority was the only kind of status relationship with which most of these people were familiar. . . . childhood was not something which was eventually outgrown; rather, it was enlarged to include the whole of one life." . . .

For the lesser members of the domestic commonwealth "social identity was altogether vicarious. The family was represented to the larger community by its head . . . and those whom he commanded were 'subsumed' in his social life." Constrictive as such a family looks from our point of view, it provided its members with a sense of secure identity, and gave to society at large a comfortably human scale whose threatened loss was understandably painful. Massinger's play is in some sense about this threat: and the horror it evokes in the dramatist helps to explain the titanic stature of Overreach. If Sir Giles's colossal ambition seems somehow too large for the world of social comedy that is because, in Massinger's imagination, he represents those forces whose insurgence menaces the very possibility of such a world, of an order that is in any familiar sense "social" at all. In the imagery of religious outrage with which this usurper is condemned, Massinger is appealing, like Dod and Cleaver before him, to the hallowed sanctions of patriarchalist ideology.

The very popularity of such treatises as Dod and Cleaver's in a period when traditional organic models of political organization were subject to an increasingly critical scrutiny is a testimony to the social insecurities that Massinger's play attempts to soothe. But patriarchalist writing itself reflects the pressures of Puritan dissent and the contractual theories with which such dissent was frequently associated. Michael Walzer has argued that the domestic commonwealth imagined by the Puritans Dod and Cleaver already has many features in common with the conjugal family that was to replace the traditional patriarchy. Their conception of the father's role is to some extent a legalistic one which emphasizes "office" and "duties" at the expense of the natural bonds of affection. Thus it tends to downgrade the historical bonding of kinship, and for the mutual obligations of parent and child, master and servant, to substitute the absolute authority of a father confirmed in office by a divinely ordained contract. In this autocratic commonwealth the nice distinctions of hierarchy which are native to the true patriarchal family are at a discount: where a household can be so simply divided into "The Governors" and "Those that must be ruled," even the basic distinction between children and servants is blurred. Overreach's autocratic tyranny, in which daughter and servants alike are treated as legally contracted agents of the master's will, and where the bonds of legal debt take the place of kinship as the principal links in the social chain, is as much an embodiment of a familial as of a commercial "new way." Though the connection may be one that the dramatist himself has not fully grasped, *A New Way to Pay Old Debts* is in some sense a play about religion and the rise of capitalism; and it is a reflection of Massinger's bitter conservatism that an atheistic iconoclast should come to epitomize the Puritan Household Governor.

In accord with his social menace, Sir Giles Overreach is presented as no common, petty miser—which even Shylock finally is—but a figure of heroic stature. He is a commercial and domestic Tamburlaine, whose *virtuà* invites the admiration of Lady Alworth's servants even as they denounce him for his griping extortion:

> FURNACE. To have a usurer that starves himself,
>   And wears a cloak of one-and-twenty years
>   On a suit of fourteen groats, bought of the hangman,
>   To grow rich, and then purchase, is too common:
>   But this Sir Giles feeds high, keeps many servants,
>   Who must at his command do any outrage;
>   Rich in his habit; vast in his expenses;
>   Yet he to admiration still increases
>   In wealth, and lordships.
>   (II.ii. 106–114)

The glamor of his conspicuous consumption links him with Jonsonian anti-heroes like Volpone, whose energetic delight in stratagem he explicitly echoes:

>   I enjoy more true delight
> In my arrival to my wealth, these dark
> And crooked ways, than you shall e'er take pleasure
> In spending what my industry hath compass'd.
>   (IV.i. 135–138)

But he is something larger and more terrifying than Jonson's vulpine magnifico: both "a lion, and a fox" (V.i.25), as Lady Alworth sees him—a figure who embodies the martial aspect of the Machiavellian tyrant as well as his political cunning. It is in heroic terms that we are repeatedly asked to see his diabolic prowess—by Order, for instance:

> He frights men out of their estates,
> And breaks through all law-nets, made to curb ill men,
> As they were cobwebs. No man dares reprove him.
> Such a spirit to dare, and power to do, were never
> Lodg'd so unluckily.
>
> (II.ii. 114–118)

—by Lord Lovell:

> I, that have liv'd a soldier,
> And stood the enemy's violent charge undaunted
> To hear this blasphemous beast am bath'd all over
> In a cold sweat: yet like a mountain he,
> Confirm'd in atheistical assertions,
> Is no more shaken, than Olympus is
> When angry Boreas loads his double head
> With sudden drifts of snow.
>
> (IV.i.150–157)

—and not least in his own vaunting hyberbole:

> LOVELL. Are you not frighted with the imprecations,
>   And curses, of whole families made wretched
>   By your sinister practices?
>
> OVERREACH. Yes, as rocks are
>   When foamy billows split themselves against
>   Their flinty ribs; or as the moon is mov'd,
>   When wolves with hunger pin'd, howl at her brightness.
>   I am of solid temper, and like these
>   Steer on a constant course: with mine own sword
>   If call'd into the field, I can make that right,
>   Which fearful enemies murmur'd at as wrong.
>
>   Nay, when my ears are pierc'd with widows' cries,
>   And undone orphans wash with tears my threshold;
>   I only think what 'tis to have my daughter
>   Right honourable.
>
> (IV.i.111–129)

"To have my daughter / Right honourable": the reiterated phrase becomes a kind of transformed bathos, like Tamburlaine's "sweet fruition of an earthly crown," Overreach's equivalent of riding in triumph through Persepolis. While at one extreme such language may link him with the mock-heroic bombast of Greedy, that "monarch . . . of the boil'd, the roast, the bak'd" (III.ii.20–21) and pillager of Furnace's pastry fortifications (I.ii.25–47), at the other it invites comparison with Lovell's heroic enterprise in the Low Countries; and the power struggle in which Sir Giles is engaged is, the play suggests, of equal moment to that undertaken by his noble adversary. For Overreach is a "blasphemous beast" not merely by virtue of those "atheistical assertions" which horrify Lovell, but through his titanic struggle to subvert an order of society decreed by God himself.

Massinger builds his social argument on the contrasted arrangement of four households or families. Temporarily excluded from this society is the déclassé Welborne, once a "lord of acres," who has prodigally squandered his estates and thus forfeited those titles ("Master Welborne," "your worship") which defined his proper place in the social order. The principal intrigue in the play is devoted to the restoration of this outcast to the power and privileges which belong to his gentlemanly rank and more specifically to his position as master of a great household.

Plain Timothy Tapwell and Froth, his wife, belong to that overwhelming majority who are not "free of the society of England," who have no natural powers beyond the compass of their own household. From Welborne's point of view, Tapwell, as his former under-butler, is still a "slave," a "drudge," a servant still bound to his master by the patronage Welborne has given him (I.i.17–28). Tapwell, on the other hand, sees himself very differently. Having acquired "a little stock" and "a small cottage" through frugal opportunism, he has duly "humbled" himself to marry Froth, and set up as an alehouse keeper, his own man (I.i.59–61). From this base he has risen to the point where he is "thought worthy to be scavenger;" and from the humble post of parish rubbish-collector he confidently expects to climb to even more exalted office:

> to be overseer of the poor;
> Which if I do, on your petition Welborne,
> I may allow you thirteen pence a quarter,
> And you shall thank *my worship*.
> (I.i.68–71; italics added)

Tapwell, in fact, is a find of low-life Overreach, his desire to become "worshipful" echoing Sir Giles's passion to have his daughter made "right honourable." He will have Welborne his petitioner as Sir Giles will have Margaret attended by whole trains of "errant knights" and Lady Downfalnes. For both men "office" denotes not the large Ciceronian concept but a narrow, functionally determined accession of personal power and prestige. Like Sir Giles, too, Tapwell professes a view of society which denies all traditional sanctions: it acknowledges no past, only a pragmatically organized present and a future of untrammeled aspiration. Welborne's appeals to ancient right and to the debts imposed by past generosity are equally vacuous to a man like Tapwell—there is no chronicle of honor or register of benefits in his commonwealth:

> WELBORNE. Is not thy house, and all thou hast my gift?
> TAPWELL. I find it not in chalk, and Timothy Tapwell
>   Does keep no other register.
>
>   What I *was* sir, it skills not;
>   What you *are* is apparent.
>   (I.i. 24–30; italics added)

His chalk register of debt is the equivalent of Sir Giles's parchment deeds; and both are presented, like Shylock's bond, as the emblems of a social vision which seeks to make the narrow scruple of commercial law the sole principle of human organization. For Tapwell, his fellow office-man, the constable, is the great Prince of this legalistic realm:

> There dwells, and within call, if it please your worship,
> A potent monarch, call'd the constable,
> That does command a citadel, call'd the stocks'
> Whose guards are certain files of rusty billmen.
>   (I.i. 12–15)

This sarcastic degradation of heroic language anticipates, in its heavy way, the cynical wit of the pun with which Sir Giles will deflate the pretensions of "errant" knighthood (II.i. 79).

Tapwell can detail the story of that "man of worship, / Old Sir John Welborne, justice of peace, and *quorum*" and even recall the magnanimity of his housekeeping, but the whole report is swept away in a single contemptuous phrase: "but he dying" (I.i. 30–37). Sir Giles (who has the current J.P., a jumped-up tailor's son, in his pocket) roundly confesses to Lovell, "I do contemn report myself, / As a mere sound" (IV.i.91–92). He is equally contemptuous of the obligations of friendship and the duties of office:

> 'tis enough I keep
> Greedy at my devotion: so he serve
> My purposes, let him hang, or damn, I care not.
> Friendship is but a word.
>
> (II.i.19–22)

And "Words," he insists, "are no substances" (III.ii.128)—they are empty ceremonious "forms" which disguise the fact that society is merely an arrangement of services rendered for cash. Given Overreach's philosophy, his desire to "Have all men sellers, / And I the only purchaser" (II.i.32–33) is nothing less than the longing for absolute tyranny. Dod and Cleaver's prescription for wise domestic government includes a warning against borrowing and usury: "Salomon saith, *The borrower is servant to the lender:* that is, beholding to him, and in his danger." The chain of debt created by Overreach's lending is one which seeks to override the traditional obligations of society, and to replace the patriarchal hierarchy with a vicious commercial autarchy, governed by himself, the unfettered master of an anti-family of slaves. His own household, where officers of church and state are already thrown together in indiscriminate bondage with children and servants, is the model for this new tyranny, where the issue of his inveterate opponents, the "true gentry," will be forced "To kneel to mine, as bond-slaves (II.i.81–89).

Set against the conspicuous consumption and cash-nexus relationships of Sir Giles's household is the ideal of liberal housekeeping embodied in the households of Welborne's dead father, of Lord Lovell, and most immediately of Lady Alworth. If the anarchic individualism and all-engrossing ambition of Sir Giles are emblematized in the names of Marrall and Greedy, the values of traditional society are suggested by those of the Alworth servants, Order and Watchall. Order, in particular, seldom misses an opportunity for sententious observation on the morality of true service and the hierarchical decorum for which he stands:

> Sir, it is her will,
> Which we that are her servants ought to serve it,
> And not dispute.
>
> (I.iii.4–6)

> Set all things right, or as my name is Order,
> And by this staff of office that commands you;
> This chain, and double ruff, symbols of power;
> Whoever misses in his function,
> For one whole week makes forfeiture of his breakfast,

> And privilege in the wine-cellar.
> (I.ii.1–6)

The sturdy sense of place which informs Order's humor in this last speech contrasts with the ludicrously exaggerated deference of Marrall who addresses even Lady Alworth's waiting-man as "your worship" (II.ii.132), and whose groveling before the reborn prodigal shows Massinger's gift for satiric farce at its best:

> MARRAL. Then in my judgement sir, my simple judgement,
> (Still with your worship's favour) I could wish you
> A better habit, for this cannot be
> But much distasteful to the noble lady
> (I say no more) that loves you, for this morning
> To me (and I am but a swine to her)
> Before the' assurance of her wealth perfum'd you,
> You savour'd not of amber.
> WELBORNE. I do now then?
> MARRALL. This your batoon hath got a touch of it.
> [Kisses the end of his cudgel]
>
> (II.iii.20–28)

The caricature of courtly style with its self-deprecating parentheses and tactful circumlocutions culminates in a perfect frenzy of servility. Marrall explicitly seeks a "place" in return for his vassalage, "the lease of glebe land [fittingly] called Knave's-Acre." But for him service is merely enslavement, place merely hire and salary. Like Greedy, devastated by the prospect of losing "my dumpling . . . And butter'd toasts, and woodcocks" (III.ii.307–308), Marall finds his "worship" only too readily dispensable.

True service on the other hand, because of its function in a scheme of mutual obligation, implies self-respect, a solid conviction of one's own worth. Spelled out in this way the opposition may seem too pat; but it is given dramatic life in the easy condescension and unforced kindness that characterizes relationships in the Alworth household—in the indulgence with which the mistress treats the choleric outbursts of her cook, Furnace, the dignity of his office wounded by her failure to eat (I.ii); and in the comically touching affection between the servants and "Our late young master" (I.ii and II.ii). The language in which young Alworth acknowledges their "service"—

> Your courtesies overwhelm me; I much grieve
> To part from such true friends, and yet find comfort.
> (II.ii.27–28)

—gracefully echoes the terms of his conversation with his own master, Lord
Lovell, and with his stepmother, and so places the relations of the domestic
"family" in living continuum with the more intimate connections of
kinship. . . .

The ending of the play vindicates, as it is bound to do, the traditional
bonds of service, housekeeping, and the patriarchal family. Marriage unites
the ideal households of the true gentry and establishes young Alworth as
master of his own; while Welborne, his financial and moral debts discharged,
sets out to redeem his honor under Lord Lovell in "service" to the supreme
patriarchy, "my king, and country" (V.i.398–99). The subverters of patriarchal order, on the other hand, are made to feel the hopeless isolation of
their position. Marall, the epitome of perverted service and false friendship,
is somewhat smugly dismissed by Welborne to take his own place, stripped
of office, among the masterless outcasts of this society:

> You are a rascal, he that dares be false
> To a master, though unjust, will ne'er be true
> To any other: look not for reward,
> Or favour from me,
>
>   I will take order
> Your practice shall be silenc'd.
>   (V.i.338–44)

If "This is the haven / False servants still arrive at" (II.349–50), the fate of
false masters is even more desperate. Overreach, who hurls from the stage
seeking "servants / And friends to second me" (II.312–13), finds only revolted
slaves. Forced to confront the ironic truth of his own aphorism, "Friendship
is but a word," he is left to the maniacal self-assertion of despair:

> Why, is not the whole world
> Included in my self? to what use then
> Are friends, and servants? say there were a squadron
> Of pikes, lin'd through with shot, when I am mounted,
> Upon my injuries, shall I fear to charge 'em?
>
>   no, spite of fate,
> I will be forc'd to hell like to myself.
>   (V.i.355–71)

If this speech seems to recall *Richard III*, the echo is fitting and perhaps
deliberate, since Overreach has come to embody that same anarchic principle

of self-love that Shakespeare incarnates in Richard of Gloucester. The forms
and bonds of communal society, which for Overreach were vacuous nothings,
prove immutably solid, while his own omnipotent bond becomes literally
"nothing," "void" (II. 289, 323), showing (through Marrall's ingenuity)
"neither wax, nor words" (I. 186). By the same token the chronicles of
honor, which in Overreach's eyes were so much historical dust, prove in-
destructible, while his own "deed" turns to dust before his eyes:

> What prodigy is this, what subtle devil
> Hath raz'd out the inscription, the wax
> Turn'd into dust! the rest of my deeds whole,
> As when they were deliver'd! and this only
> Made nothing.
>
> (V.i.190–94)

. . . Overreach's repudiation of society leaves him to the punishment of his
own consuming egotism, "myself alone," without servants, friends, or even
kin—a man without a family.

The last irony of his situation, of course, is that he has been a man trying
to make a family, a dynasty of "right honourable" descendants. For all his
bitter scorn for the "forms" of the hereditary order, for the hollowness of
"word," "name," and "title," Sir Giles is nevertheless mesmerized by these
same forms. The obsession renders him incapable of living consistently by
his ruthlessly economic analysis of society. The unrecognized paradox of his
desire to have his daughter made "right honourable" is what finally blinds
him to Lovell's stratagem and lures him into a pit of his own digging. He
is ultimately destroyed by the same monstrous fury of self-contradiction
which drives him to threaten honorable revenge against the man he hopes
his daughter will seduce:

> Do I wear a sword for fashion? or is this arm
> Shrunk up? or wither'd? does there live a man
> Of that large list I have encounter'd with,
> Can truly say I e'er gave inch of ground,
> Not purchas'd with his blood, that did oppose me?
> Forsake thee when the thing is done? he dares not.
> Give me but proof, he has enjoy'd thy person,
> Though all his captains, echoes to his will,
> Stood arm'd by his side to justify the wrong,
> And he himself in the head of his bold troop,
> Spite of his lordship, and his colonelship,

> Or the judge's favour, I will make him render
> A bloody and a strict accompt, and force him
> By marrying thee, to cure thy wounded honour.
>   (III.ii.140–53)

Marall's intervention ("Sir, the man of honour's come," I. 154) points up the absurd irony: the gestures, the rhetoric are those of the code he is seeking to subvert; they acknowledge debts and accounts of a kind he professes not to countenance; and they are echoed with savage pathos in the berserk frenzy of his final speech:

> I'll through the battalia, and that routed,
> I'll fall to execution.
> [*Flourishing his sword unsheathed*]
>   Ha! A am feeble:
> Some undone widow sits upon mine arm,
> And takes away the use of't; and my sword
> Glu'd to my scabbard, with wrong'd orphans' tears,
> Will not be drawn.
>   (V.i.360–65)

The disproportion between the ranting heroics of Overreach's defiance and the domestic ordinariness of the situations which provide it is not an arbitrary comic device: it is the expression of that fatal confusion of purpose on which his life is wrecked. Sir Giles is an instinctive revolutionary whose vision is fatally constricted by the values of the society against which he is in revolt.

But the confusion is not his alone: it also infects his maker. For all the consistency with which Massinger attempts to construct his patriarchal arguments, ambiguities remain in his own stance. Some of these appear in the characterization of his villain: the sense of unbalance which has worried critics of the play has much to do with the overplus of energy and dramatic life in Sir Giles—as though a part of Massinger identified with his violent iconoclasm. And something of the same subversive impulse may be felt in the treatment of Marrall. The psychological penetration with which Massinger uncovers the source of his peculiarly vicious symbiosis of envy and subservience surely springs from the dramatist's own early experience among the upper servants of a great household. The hysterical fury with which Marrall announces his own revolt reveals a sense of deep violation that helps to account for the other revolutionary currents in the play:

OVERREACH. Mine own varlet
    Rebel against me
MARRALL. Yes, and uncause you too.
    The idiot; the patch; the slave; the booby;
    The property fit only to be beaten
    For your morning exercise; your football, or
    Th' unprofitable lump of flesh; your drudge
    Can now anatomize you, and lay open
    All your black plots; and level with the earth
    Your hill of pride; and with these gabions guarded,
    Unload my great artillery, and shake,
    Nay pulverize the walls you think defend you.
                       (V.i.213–223)

Yet the levelers of the play can make no common cause: Marrall's revolt is merely against Sir Giles, and both are simply individualist anarchs. It was not until Congreve brought the two together in the character of the Double-Dealer, Maskwell, who combines something of Overreach's iconoclastic energy with Marrall's humiliated bitterness, that the English stage could produce a genuinely revolutionary comedy. Congreve, significantly, came from a social background very similar to Massinger's; but he wrote with two revolutions behind him—and even Maskwell had to be destroyed in the end.

A further uneasy ambiguity involves the problem of Overreach's own patriarchial authority; and this may be partly a function of Massinger's attempt to combine Jonsonian satire with a romantic comedy more immediately appealing to the Phoenix audience. The conventions of satire require that Marrall be thoroughly punished for his revolt; the conventions of comic romance require that Margaret be rewarded for hers. Massinger the conservative satirist is forced to argue that even the worst masters deserve to be obeyed, even while Massinger the romancer is vindicating the overthrow of tyrannical fathers. A sincere patriarchalist can hardly have it both ways, since the authority of fathers and masters is one and indivisible. But both ways are the way Massinger likes to have it: in *The Roman Actor,* for instance, a similar dilemma is resolved by a pious, but fundamentally evasive, appeal to legitimacy. The First Tribune acknowledges that Domitian was a tyrant who deserved his end, but warns his assassins that

            he was our prince,
    However wicked; and, in you, 'tis murder,
    Which whosoe'er succeeds him will revenge.
                 (*Roman Actor,* V.ii. 77–79)

Moralists like Dod and Cleaver had insisted on the limits to patriarchial authority, especially in the matter of forced marriages:

> This is a most unnaturall and cruell part, for parents to sell their children for gaine and lucre, and to marrie them when they list, without the good liking of their children, and so bring them into bondage . . . especially in this matter of greatest moment and value of all other worldly things whatsoever, let them . . . beware they turn not their fatherly jurisdiction and governement, into a tyrannicall soureness and waywardnesse, letting their will go for a law . . . the rule of parents over their children, ought to resemble the government of good Princes toward their subjects: that is to say, it must bee milde, gentle, and easie to be borne.

But children are granted no right of revolt against such bondage—"whatsoever they doe to their fathers and mothers . . . they doe it to God"—and those who marry without their parents' consent incur "the curse of God." Batty similarly insists that even foolish and crabbed parents must be obeyed, and inveighs against the impiety of "private spousages and secret contractes . . . enterprised and taken in hand without the consent of Parentes." Most patriarchial writing, however, admits an escape clause, and it is one which Massinger gratefully seizes upon. The child's final duty, after all, is to his Father in Heaven; and thus resistance become possible to parents or magistrates who command "wicked and ungodly things." "Wee must obey God rather than man," says Batty: "Honour thou thy father, so that he doth not separate thee from thy true father." From the moment Sir Giles orders Margaret to prostitute herself to Lovell, and she identifies the projected match as founded on "devilish doctrine" (III.ii.122), from the moment too at which Lovell, in confirmation, castigates the blasphemer's "atheistical assertions" (IV.i.154), we are meant to see that Overreach's government undermines the very foundations of patriarchal authority. No longer to be regarded as a natural father, he has become simply what Alworth called him, "Mammon in Sir Giles Overreach" (III.i.83).

The invocation of this Morality abstraction exactly anticipates the device by which Massinger seeks to bolster the uncertain ordering of his conclusion. That stroke of divine vengeance which suddenly paralyzes Overreach's sword arm—reminiscent of the astonishing coup by which D'Amville is made to dash out his own brains in the denouement of *The Atheist's Tragedy*—invites us to review the whole action in theological terms:

>   Here is a precedent to teach wicked men
>   That when they leave religion, and turn atheists
>   Their own abilities leave them.
>
> (V.i.379–81)

In the light of this comfortable moralization a quasi-allegorical scheme begins to emerge by which the whole conclusion is seen to hang on three familiar parables. Most obviously Welborne's redemption from his life of prodigal abandon recalls the forgiveness accorded to another repentant prodigal in Christ's parable. Hungry and in rags in the opening scene, Welborne is the very image of the starving prodigal in Luke; Lady Alworth kills the fatted calf in the feasting which marks his readmission to the patriarchal society, while Sir Giles, that "scourge of prodigals" is ironically cozened into sharing the biblical father's role:

> But the father said to his servants, Bring forth the best robe, and put *it* on him; and put a ring on his hand, and shoes on *his* feet.
>
> (Luke 15:22)

Overreach similarly commands Marrall

>   go to my nephew;
>   See all his debts discharg'd, and help his worship
>   To fit on his rich suit.
>
> (IV.i.33–35)

"This my son was dead, and is alive again; he was lost and is found" (Luke 15:24); and Overreach, however hypocritically, acknowledges a similar resurrection of the nephew whose kinship he has once denied. At the same time the envy and astonishment of the elder brother at the restoration of his wastrel sibling is echoed in the baffled indignation of both Marrall and Overreach at Welborne's sudden elevation. Finally, Welborne's offer of "service" to Lovell and his king at the end of the play is a transposition of the prodigal's penitence:

> I will arise and go to my father, and say unto him, Father, I have sinned against heaven, and before thee, And am no more worthy to be called thy son: make me as one of thy hired servants.
>
> (Luke 15:18–19)

The identification of "Mammon in Sir Giles Overreach" links the fable in turn to the parable which immediately follows the Prodigal Son in Luke— the Unjust Steward, a parable about the payment of debts and the morality of true service, which precisely anticipates the play's judgment of Marrall:

If therefore ye have not been faithful in the unrighteous mammon,
who will commit to your trust the true *riches?*
And if ye have not been faithful in that which is another man's,
who shall give you that which is your own?
No servant can serve two masters: for either he will hate the one,
and love the other; or else he will hold to the one, and despise
the other. Ye cannot serve God and mammon.

(Luke 16:11–13)

"I must grant / " Lady Alworth has reflected, as though with this passage in mind, "Riches well got to be a useful servant, / But a bad master" (IV.i.187–89). Sir Giles's own fate more loosely paraphrases the last of the parables in this series, that of Dives and Lazarus. The Overreach described by Furnace who "feeds high, keeps many servants . . . [is] rich in his habit; vast in his expenses" (II.ii.110–12) recalls that "rich man, which was clothed in purple and fine linen, and fared sumptuously every day" (Luke 16:19), spurning the beggar Welborne as Dives spurns the beggar Lazarus; and his desperate fate at the end of the play is equally suggestive. As Sir Giles is carried off to "some dark room" in Bedlam, his daughter reaches out to him—"O my dear father!" (V.i.378)—but between them, as between Dives and Lazarus, "There is a great gulf fixed:" Overreach, tormented by "furies, with steel whips / To scourge my ulcerous soul" (II. 368–69) is already in hell.

In the end this invocation of a theological scheme is a kind of cheat designed to silence the awkward questions the play has raised. Who, finally, are the innovators in this social upheaval; the old gentry who contrive a deceitful "new ways" to pay their "old debts," or Overreach, the proponent of contract and statute law? In *The Merchant of Venice* such questions are preempted by the triumphant appeal from Old Law to New which is implicit in the play's whole mythic structure: the Jonsonian realism of Massinger's satire forbids so nearly consistent a solution. Furthermore, the play's very conservatism has a revolutionary potential: Overreach, in many ways, is less a usurper than a legitimate patriarch who has tyrannically abused his powers and who accordingly is deposed. In the light of this we may remember that Coleridge thought Massinger "a decided whig," and that some dozen years after *A New Way* the dramatist's views on Charles's personal rule were to attract the indignation and censorship of the king himself. Overreach's deposition, though carried out in the name of the old hierarchic order, has awkward contractual implications—implications of a kind which would be spelled out in the trial and execution of the royal patriarch, Charles I.

Outwardly, however, the social vision of the play remains impeccably

conservative: once again the rigid and indiscriminate operation of law—the
new way—is mitigated by the equity of communal obligation—the old
debts. The patriarchal hierarchy is conceived not simply as a ladder of
authority, but also as a family circle—a circle bound by Seneca's decorum
of giving, receiving, and returning. The symbol for that bonding, here as
in *The Merchant*, is the ring. The ring with which Overreach unwittingly
secures his daughter's marriage to young Alworth completes with benign
irony a Senecan circle of obligation, by returning to Alworth the lands
unjustly taken from his father. Another such circle, broken by the ingratitude
of Tapwell and the unkindness of Overreach, is knit up in the restoration
of Welborne—a restoration brought about through Lady Alworth's acknowl-
edgment of obligations and determination to "redeem" what's past (I.iii.118–
19). In the last analysis the play's "new way" (for all its witty duplicity) is
an old way, the way of a vanishing society—new only by virtue of its
unsatisfactory appeal to New Testament values against the Old (ironically
epitomized in the "new man" Overreach). However harmonious the circles
contrived in this old new way, they cannot, even in comic fantasy, contain
those turbulent spirits whose rise would break the circle forever. Whatever
was restored in 1660, it did not include an intact patriarchal ideology. The
literature of the Restoration from *Aureng-Zebe* to *Abasalom and Achitophel,*
from *Venice Preserved* to *Love for Love,* is full of failing patriarchs, enfeebled,
corrupt, and ridiculous by turns. It contemplates a world where, in Otway's
words, "the foundation's lost of common good" and that "dissolves all former
bonds of service."

R. J. KAUFMANN

Ford's Tragic Perspective

Ford has not been altogether fortunate in his critics. They have been attentive, but perhaps Ford, like children, would have fared the better for a little healthy neglect. His reputation has been refracted into a grotesque pattern of distorted and partial images, largely, one supposes, because there is much distracting foreign matter in his canon, many invitations to irrelevancy in his historical position. As the last of the great Elizabethan tragic writers on the one hand and as the somewhat bookish exploiter of these great predecessors' visions on the other, he is set either too high or too low by standards quite external to his manifest performance. It is time we accord Ford his proper status as a minor classic writer on the scale of Emily Brontë, E. M. Forster, Hawthorne, and Scott Fitzgerald—writers typically obsessive in theme, deeply constrained personally, and nervously unresponsive to all save their main concerns. Such writers share in consequence a tendency to self-parody which is the underside of their splendid local intensities. The critic of great minor writing is obliged to enjoin his readers to observe decorum, not to ask too much of these writers, lest in so doing they miss the exquisite psychological disclosures which are the hallmark of such art.

It is one's initial sensitivity to the obsessive quality of Ford's art which provokes resistance to T. S. Eliot's accusation that Ford's plays are marred by the "the absence of purpose" and that, more particularly, *'Tis Pity She's a Whore* "may be called meaningless" since the "characters of the greatest intensity" are not seriously related to "an action or a struggle for harmony in the soul of the poet." In this essay I am attempting to show the insufficiency

From *Texas Studies in Literature and Language* 1, no. 4 (Winter 1960). © 1960 by the University of Texas Press.

of this judgment. Ford struggles purposively with humanity's genius for self-deprivation, with its puzzling aspiration to be the architect of its own unhappiness. He does this with the kind of persistence that argues "an action of the soul."

Recent years have been fruitful in the kind of cruel experience which makes Ford's anxious world imaginatively accessible—specifically, our acquaintance with the plays of the modern French theater has taught us to read him better. The sophisticated fairy tales of Anouilh, the geometry of neat but not portentous spiritual encounter in Giraudoux, the studies in the lonely and gifted man's search for a sufficient identity as we find it in Sartre's *Flies* and Camus' *Caligula*—all variously can instruct us in the tonal qualities and special intellectual mode of Ford's plays. Ford, too, is the type of intellectual who is humanly restive under the tyranny of mind and yet artistically dependent upon its more rigid formulations. Hence the neatly logical surface *and* the sense of inchoate emotion in these plays. All such playwrights share an insight into the self-defining quality of individual human action. If the root of existential thought is the conviction that each man "makes himself" through a qualifying series of choices, then Ford is as surely and as interestingly an existentialist as Sartre. But there is, I think, a more direct route to the analysis of Ford's tragic perspective.

In this essay I follow a set of interrelated themes through three plays: *The Queene, Love's Sacrifice,* and *'Tis Pity She's a Whore.* My narrower aim is to show Ford discovering more and more adequate means to project and analyze the central psychological motive which animates his protagonists. It will be initially sufficient to call this quality *jealousy,* though thereby we merely apply a label of convenience to a complex set of mental actions which Ford gradually explores. More broadly, I hope to reveal the special meaning of tragic jealousy for Ford, through examination of his key obsessive themes. The themes of *misalliance,* of the psychology of *vows,* of *counterfeiting,* all relate to Ford's heightened awareness of the *arbitrary* in human life. In fact it is as a student of the arbitrary that I see Ford and will seek to present him.

The core situation in Ford is one of misalliance, of natures subtly mismatched and progressively at odds with themselves and with received social sanctions. This central situation applies to external misalliance, as to marriages of persons of different social derivation in *Love's Sacrifice,* to unnatural extensions of social bonds, as in the incestuous love of *'Tis Pity,* and to the sad mismatching of youth and age in *The Broken Heart.* It can also apply without distention to the misalliance of the inner and the outer self in a single character. It is the most special quality of the Fordian hero that he "calls" himself to a role that his residual nature (conscience and shaping habits) will not permit him to fulfill. The protagonist misidentifies himself through a too arbitrary choice, disregards too much in himself, and tragedy results. It is this troubled contest between overt resolve and inner need, between what we demand and what we are free to accept, that makes for the tension of tragic experience.

Ford does not write simply about "problems," as his critics seem to wish; he slowly learns to write about irreducible *situations* in which the qualities of the participants necessarily harden into tragic contours *through* their relations with each other. It is just this concession that Ford implicitly exacts of us as his readers: that the human entanglements he writes about are precisely *not* problems, and the minute we literal-mindedly seek solutions, we collapse the delicately achieved balance of his plays. Ford is like Henry James in this. As a writer of terminal tragedy, he starts with the assumption of the good breeding and dignity of defeat. He denies us any vulgar "escape" from disaster (which is, after all, what a solution is). This preference for the noble identity secured in defeat Ford shares with the late Stoics and with the modern existentialist writers of the literature of extreme situations. The Sartre of *The Flies* would recognize a brother in the Ford of *'Tis Pity*.

Once this combined necessity for dignity in defeat and for triumph over misalliance in the self through the costly beauty of the kept vow is accepted, there is a marvellous, subdued consistency to Ford's plays. Only through constructive exertions of the protagonist's will is tragedy then possible. In effect, we watch Ford's heroes counterfeit an adequate heroic stature through equating of the self with an arbitrary vow, and, since these choices are never prudent or circumspect, rich opportunities are thereby earned for a death of dramatic intensity. The key phrase to Ford could well be Juliet's "If aught else fails myself have power to die." A powerful and personally organized death is the resolution of the soul's misalliance in Ford. But such deaths are no more perfect in their isolation than are the people who contrive them—there is the costly imperfection of jealousy which guarantees that the most stoical tragedy is still a social experience. We can watch Ford's insight and technical mastery grow together as he learns to organize adequately complex dramatic statements of these themes from the unformed but promising *The Queene*, through the halfway house of *Love's Sacrifice* to proper fullness in *'Tis Pity She's a Whore*.

II

The Queene is an imaginatively amphibious play, for if in its language it is halfway onto the cool strand of Ford's detached and attentive mature manner, it is also washed by the billowing falsities of Fletcher's tragicomic trickery. It bears no date. It seems to me clearly the sort of work a dramatist writes who is just discovering his proper personal themes but has yet to work free of the prevailing "correct" way to dramatize them. It is the test of Caroline originality to be able to transcend the facilities of Fletcher.

The Queene is a sort of sophisticated, theatrical fairy tale that does not quite maintain itself. Ford, whose interest in the type of gifted man still ludicrously open to flattery (and hence a candidate for $\bar{A}t\bar{e}$ is lifelong) has here in the central masculine role, Alphonso, an imperfectly convincing combination of Chapman's Byron and Shakespeare's King Ferdinand of Navarre, with a special vice of jealous misogyny. It is this seemingly paradoxical latter quality that will interest us, for I agree with Oliver that the play is a kind of preliminary attempt at the central action of Love's Sacrifice, "each of the plays treating a husband's baseless suspicion of the chastity of his wife." Ford being of analytical mind, he only slowly learned to do what a more spontaneously gifted writer does directly. He did not seem to work from a central core of fable. His plays have the quality always of being built up from separately conceived parts. This fact is useful to us in The Queene, for here we find in disjunction elements that mature reflection will fuse. I hardly want to do more than enumerate them, for Ford barely does more than that with them himself.

We will need the bones of the plot. It is double and rests, typically for Ford, on the Queen's unqualified love for the vain, intolerant, woman-hater and political revolutionary, Alphonso, whom she repeals from execution at the outset in order to place him on the throne as King. This is paralleled by the equally unreasoning love of Velasco, the heroic military commander, for a widow. Both infatuated characters are made violently unhappy by their passion. Both are laid under the most arbitrary injunctions by their loved ones. The Queen is asked, immediately after the wedding, to establish separate households and to forego the privileges of marital love until Alphonso is satisfied of her purity and fidelity. Velasco is ordered to surrender his valiancy and to earn the title of coward, before his love will be acceptable. These could be dismissed as the rather arch postulates of sophisticated theater from Euripides to Anouilh, but such generic leveling obscures the peculiar tone of this play. We can see that Ford, the young man from the provinces, the puritan of Christes Bloodie Sweat, will always be an imperfect recruit to this sort of unanchored moral world. He will not be able to forget that the capricious love-game rests on an ennui which "is a metaphysical emotion" stemming from an unappeasable sense of inner emptiness. This emptiness provokes of sense of unworthiness which is the seedbed for jealousy and sterile manipulation of others whose regard or love must always seem ulterior to one who cannot value himself. An analytical anthology of key assertions in the play will make this clearer.

Critics have made the sense of honor a key emotion in Ford. Perhaps— but as Velasco says, "Ide rather loose my honor then my faith," and later, "passions at their best are but sly traytors / To ruin honour" (2728–30). It can be put almost syllogistically, this basic logic of Ford's world: Passion is able to dominate all men; Honor (reputation) is a frequent casualty of such passion; therefore, to cling to honor alone is unavailing. However, the logic of extreme situations is to join forces with the passions you cannot overcome. If you have an undeniable attraction, the intelligent recourse, then, is to place not only your love but your converted virtue there. This means narrowing your sense of honor or self-esteem deliberately, for the pleasing of the loved object. Hence the arrogant indifference to the rest of the world of a Giovanni, an Orgilus, even a Perkin Warbeck. I am as certain as one can be of anything conjectural that Ford thrilled to Othello's "My life upon her faith," and that slowly he learned that this statement contains one of the most profound ironies in Shakespeare's masterpiece of irony, for it can be better read "Her life upon my faith." The faith being defective in a Giovanni as it is in an Othello, desperate tragedy results.

The main action of *The Queene* is the unconvincing homeopathic cure of Alphonso, who is "most addicted to this pestilence of jealousy," (3593) but not before Alphonso has mindlessly conjured up visions of adultery and has sent his Queen towards the scaffold to answer for it. He even praises her beauty as she is being prepared for execution, till one of the lesser characters anticipates the reader: "Heer's a medley love / That kills in Curtesie" (3425–26). His real reason for having his Queen killed (as opposed to his public reasons) forms one of those psychic outcroppings which are the real basis for our insights in literature as well as in life:

> had she bin still
> As she was, mine, we might have liv'd too happily
> For eithers comfort
>
> (3372–76)

This Calvinistic sentiment is, I think, a revealing one. Ford's characters are terrified by the threat of happiness which saps identity. They are forever controlling themselves, narrowing their characters down to monomaniacal attachments and pursuits which in turn they find more demanding than they can sustain. When we return to what we started from—Alphonso as a violent misogynist whose jealousy is stifling—we can see the full curve of the key theme. The Fordian hero fears women too much to have the faith in them which alone can save him. In *The Queene* we are far from the rarely subtilized jealousy and imperfect faith of a Giovanni, but the very inchoate quality of this earlier play provides a family of critical clues.

III

In *Love's Sacrifice,* we ask at once whether the title speaks of the sacrifices made *to* love or the very sacrifice *of* love itself through needless entertainment of passions destructively incompatible with it. It is this richer meaning that Ford pursued here, and only realized in later works. The grounds for believing the former are readily indicated. Clear cases can be made for all three characters in the triangle: the wronged husband Caraffa, the Duke, who has condescended to marry beneath him; his superficially errant Duchess, Bianca; and the troubled true lover, true friend, Fernando. Bianca is carried past herself into a real desire for Fernando, a desire which his courtly scruple and loyalty to the bonds of friendship will not permit him to gratify. Trapped in a relationship which cannot mature, she eagerly incites her shocked husband to murder her when he discovers and misinterprets this unperfected liaison. She asks to be and succeeds in becoming a sacrifice to her awakened sense of a love she is unable to obtain. Her problem is routine. Ford's handling of her development is sketchy, but promising. What in effect he shows us is that her character is decent but thin, lacking in the deeper compunctions we call nobility, and hence her undernourished sense of abstract honor would not alone have been sufficient to prevent adultery once she had put herself regularly in the way of temptation. It is one of Ford's distinctions that he understands the emotional process of the essentially feminine mind—the sluggish but impressive logic of radical emotion. We can say then at the outset that Bianca is a somewhat conventional self-elected martyr for love— her *sacrifice* is the standard romantic one of a now useless life *to* an unobtainable ideal of love.

Fernando, her lover, is at once passionate and scrupulous. His finer self is aroused by Bianca's confession of helplessness against her need for his love; he voluntarily imposes upon himself a restraint whereby he renounces ready physical gratification in the interests of her supposed welfare. We could say that he is able to sublimate his passion through the agency of his excited sense of honor. What he turns to in this renunciation is the rather melodramatic compensatory pleasure of a grand death, in which he can speak scornful words of the Duke's failure to have trust in the perfection of Fernando's talent of friendship. There is something priggish about Fernando, and a good bit of as yet undeveloped Fordian *hybris*. Or, better, there is

something close to $\bar{A}t\bar{e}$—to tragic infatuation with one's own sufficiency.
There is a nice distinction here: the man fraught with *hybris* believes himself
invulnerable to the gods; the man seized with $\bar{A}t\bar{e}$ thinks he already *possesses*
a full vision of himself and of the consequent interpretation that must be
put on his actions by all observers. *Hybris* teaches one to say, "Nothing can
happen to me." $\bar{A}t\bar{e}$ persuades one to think, "Since I know what I am doing,
no one else can misunderstand." Ford understood what confers significance
in the world of events. Others do shape notions; we are misunderstood. His
tragedies are mainly ones of $\bar{A}t\bar{e}$, of misguided and passionate attempts to
deny not only the right of the world to judge (the tenet of romantic individualism), but the very ability of the world to assign values where the ego
of the protagonist has established prior claims. The strange silences which
attend the movements of Ford's heroes have been remarked by critics. They
are silent because their private reasons are sufficient; the world's claims are
thus not opposed and equal, but negligible and incommensurate. Fernando
courts martyrdom in his own gently contemptuous fashion, refusing the
moral canons of "life-hugging slaves." He is a sacrifice to a somewhat abstracted notion of love, one not perfectly separable from chillier Stoic notions
of self-consistency.

The Duke sacrifices himself at the end of the play, largely because he
must preserve his precarious dignity. He cuts a poor figure throughout, and
his final theatrical self-execution before the dead "lovers'" tomb (in which
he then assigns himself a place—a troublesome *ménage à trois* in perpetuity)
is self-described as performed

> for Bianca's love
> Caraffa, in revenge of wrongs to her,
> Thus on her altar sacrificed his life.
>   (V,iii)

Were it not for the fact that, as Robert Ornstein has most interestingly
pointed out, we tend to accept as true the self-evaluations spoken by stage
characters not manifestly villainous and hypocritical, we would not find
much in this remark at all. The simple, sub-theatrical fact is that the Duke
has thoroughly botched everything, has displayed no hint of understanding
or love or character. We find his final act gratuitous, his joining the dead
lovers (whose relationship possesses at least a shred of validity) an intrusion.

Why does the play seem so centerless? Why do its well-phrased passions
seems so stagey and false? I think the answer lies not in putative ethical
confusion in the play which "preserves in the separate fates of the main
protagonists a consistent ethical scheme." Rather, it lies in the disastrously

wrong point of view from which Ford chooses to "narrate" or project his play. It has been noted by earlier critics that the play resembles *Othello*. I point out now that it is a very oblique *Othello,* and that the uselessly novel obliquity of Ford's vision is what subtracts from tragic concentration and spoils his dramatic scheme. Let me briefly indicate how this off-center view of the action affects the play.

What Ford omits in imitating Shakespeare's great play on the theme of misalliance is precisely the indispensable feature—the massive centrality of Othello himself. Shakespeare puts us squarely behind Othello, whose mighty figure steadily gains control over our imagination. By something very close to expressionist techniques, the latter part of the play becomes for us more and more a vision of the world as Othello mistakenly sees it; we are swept up and hurried to his dreadful, misconceived, and yet inevitable destiny. We are very precisely *with* Othello as he chooses and acts. Anyone who doubts this must not have felt the shocked recall to reality that Emilia's knock at the death-chamber door constitutes, nor noted how strange the intrusion of commonplace language seems, after the rhythms of Othello's spacious and noble misconception. It almost makes one weep to read prim critical reductions of this terrible error which we are never asked to approve, only *to understand in process.* The precise poetic quality of this tragic fantasy as it usurps the world is what we are asked to see—what we do see. Jealousy is what we call it before Shakespeare has brought us within it; afterwards we know how a violent "purity" of faith in Othello has been used by Shakespeare to raise an otherwise uncomprehended indignity of life to the level of tragedy. The tragedy is made out of the patient contemplation of one man's reactions to torment, his consequent re-editing of reality, and his subsequent conduct.

In Ford's hands the theme of misalliance is apparently abstracted, and the Duke is given a set speech or two early in the play to let us know that he dotes on his wife's beauty and that he realizes that he has gone against custom in marrying beneath his rank:

> Though my gray-headed senate . . .
> Would tie the limits of our free affects [affections]—
> Like superstitious Jews,—to match with none
> But in a tribe of princes like ourselves . . .
> But why should princes do so, that command
> The storehouse of the earth's rich minerals?

(I,i)

As superficially similar as this is to the standard plot-postulates of Fletcherian
tragicomedy, I think we would be wrong to follow the current fashion and
reduce the play to mechanical, problem-play exploration of the consequences
of the Duke's foolish disregard of custom in making this willful misalliance.
The truth seems to be rather that Ford is troubled by the Duke's presence
and can supply him with no real interior function. Now and then he is
recalled to the stage, to watch from a position of bemused detachment the
apish deformations of behavior visible, as usual, in Ford's minor characters.
Ford makes a gesture at the theme of "authority," which orders Shakespeare's
play, when he has the Duke exclaim,

> How we
> Who sway the manage of authority
> May be abused by smooth officious agents!
> (I, ii)

The critical significance of Ford's quandary is detectable right here. If one's
authority is to be abused with tragic (rather than comic or merely didactic)
consequences, then the authority must be *conveyed*, not merely assumed as
an artistic convenience. Ford's Duke appears on the stage only spasmodically,
and merely to be manipulated by his embittered sister and the purportedly
fiendish servant, D'Avolos, who together perform Iago's dark functions. The
effect is of a goodly catalogue of officious agents, of much intended malice
and much *cause* for suffering of which we see little convincing evidence. One
senses a deeply insufficient engagement of Ford's imagination. What he *really*
wanted to write about here, I think, is how the fineness of the lovers was a
product of the Duke's jealousy. The Duke's presence as a lens for conventionally evaluating their acts, however, is a technical embarrassment not to
be overcome. Either the Duke is right, in which case the lovers are morally
swamped; or he is as irrelevant as Soranzo in *'Tis Pity,* a person whose claims
are negligible and whose sufferings have no dramatic assertion whatsoever.
Ford, by borrowing the half-remembered authority of Othello's compelling
figure, has deepened his artistic predicament. It makes it harder to ignore
the Duke, a thing we must do if we are to feel the effect of what is viable
in the play. What he has yet to learn is that the noble lover and the jealous
lover must be one and the same. Ford, the student of misalliance, has
misallied themes in this play. As a result, the whole play has a dreamlike
quality, and an uninvited irony of tone playing over its surface.

There is much to interest us in the crisscross pattern of true and counterfeit loves, of true and counterfeit reports, of true honor and its deceptive
likeness, of false sacrifice as a self-relieving act and true sacrifice as giving

up what you want most for reasons of Conradian delicacy. There is a real dignity in the lovers' acceptance of the roles they wish to play and then act out to their logical and terrible conclusion. The Duchess, when accused by her husband before he sacrifices her, makes no excuses, asks no mercy, but rather, accepts her role gladly; she only demands the right to define it as it really is, not as it seems to be. She has no wish to be a real martyr for counterfeit reasons. Fernando's attraction was physical, a fact she faces without illusion. She will not falsify her own nature to buy life. The heroic self in Ford is one free of illusions about what one intends to be. Fordian heroes can read their own motives, however conventionally base.

The entire play, *Love's Sacrifice,* centers to one side of the issues that characterize a normal adultery-revenge play. Ford's interest is not in what people think happens, what is said to happen, or even in the possibilities for physical action, but in what happens to the sensibilities of the people involved—how those who are apparently wrong achieve dignity and how the one apparently right (the Duke), sacrifices everything, always too late and always without comprehension. The unmodulated descent into terrible self-knowledge, which makes *Othello* the most searing of Shakespeare's plays, is totally lacking here, not because the Duke does not repent of his error, but because he has no artistically achieved character, through empathy with which we can know the quality of this change. The Duke's only recourse at the end is a cold, self-destructive fury, whereby to make a meaningless sacrifice of himself. The Duke has never had the existentialist opportunity that confers privilege in Ford's world; he has had no chance to choose a role, to counterfeit a true self. Ford does not make the same mistake with Giovanni in *'Tis Pity.*

IV

'Tis Pity She's a Whore has all the assurance *Love's Sacrifice* lacks. The first act has such a neat economy of attack, such a rare directness, that it argues Ford's confident impatience to give body to a world he sees rising before him. The writing blooms with certitude. It is worth the trouble to state how Ford builds the telling structure of his first act. It has four parts: Giovanni's incestuous compulsion is presented through an argument, entered *in medias res,* between the Friar and Giovanni. This stands apart like Euripides' prologue to *Hippolytus,* where the causal agency is announced, so that we are free to concentrate on the human consequences.

Next we see Annabella beleaguered by suitors whose characteristics are venality, cowardice, and corrupt worldliness. By their defects of quality these

suitors create a predisposition in favor of the girl's need for love; we grow
sensitive to her isolation and learn to justify her despair of beauty and dignity
in her life. Ford's strategy throughout is here prefigured. The carefully
contrived world of the play is one in which marriage is debased, sacraments
are violated, vows are disregarded, churchly and secular sanctions are loosened
and enfeebled. Without being baroquely overdrawn, the world of the play
is made to act (in its negations of beauty) as a foil to the desperate choices
of Giovanni and his sister. This is not, of course, because Ford approves of
incest, but it is done to put the unthinkable within access of thought. Not
the least of the functions of tragedy is to enlarge our imaginative tolerance.

The necessary climate being indicated, Ford brings the lovers together.
They declare their loves, and, in a fashion obligatory in Ford's world, cement
a pact, a mutual vow. Vows are important in Ford's world where an aestheticism of morality prevails, with its accompanying distaste for an ignoble
and pointlessly frivolous existence distracted by too much meaningless privilege. By a solemn vow, one circumscribes his choices and hence gains a
predictable future. Vows are at once the expression of taste and the most
arbitrary and compelling form of self-definition—a vow can confer identity.
We should pay attention to vows in Ford's plays. The one exchanged between
Giovanni and Annabella is like a betrothal, and each repeats the same formula
on their "mother's dust":

> I charge you,
> Do not betray me to your mirth or hate:
> *Love me or kill me.*
>   (I,iii. *Italics mine*)

Contrary to conventional opinion, this is precisely what Giovanni does;
his love being corrupted, he kills his sister. Once we credit the literal and
sanctified binding force of this vow, much of Giovanni's frenetic behavior
in the latter part of the play, his "mirth or hate," become intelligible. More
of that later.

With great rapidity, Ford has shown us the isolation of both Giovanni
and Annabella and then brought them together with a resolution quiet and
fiercely pure. They now will have significance only in relation to this arbitrary
vow whereby they have separated themselves from any hope of conventional
felicity. This counterfeit marriage represents a radical misalliance which is
made narrowly sacred by an arbitrary vow. It is the perfect concentrate of
Ford. It is also typical of Ford that this scene should be counterpointed
immediately with Bergetto's fatuous trivialities, as his prejudicially cheerful
inanities are permitted to speak for the world the lovers are denying. But

Ford is not content, even with this marvellously compressed total, as his accomplishment in the first act. He makes one other point which invites careful reflection. The uncle of Bergetto, a straightforward sort of man without any illusions but still hopeful, watches the idiotic ineptitude of his nephew (whose suit to Annabella he is trying to forward) and factually observes, "Ah, Sirrah, then I see there is no changing of nature. Well, Bergetto, I fear though wilt be a very ass still" (I,iv). There are useful implications in this comical assertion of our fixed natures.

One of the commonest criticisms of Ford as an artist concerns the evident unsuccess of his comic subplots. This is possibly unjustified, since we are beginning to see how funny is the ardent status-seeking of the stupid and unqualified now that we are again socially swamped by it. But by the use of comic characters (required to express unchangeable qualities), Ford can slyly forestall any hesitation we might feel in accepting the inflexible, self-defeating commitments which are the hallmark of his tragic protagonists. Ford's world, in consequence, must often be solemn and pompous, lest its close alliance with the world of comedy—the arbitrary quality of his characters—be too distractingly apparent.

We are led directly from this to the special dilemma of dramatists like Ford (and Euripides, whom he resembles in many ways). Ford centers his dramatic world on fixed and irrevocable commitments which the characters themselves contract. Fernando, Giovanni, Penthea in *The Broken Heart,* Perkin Warbeck—all hold sacred their own declarations of purpose, and their tragedy relates to these openly stated dramatic vows and is displaced from any external agency which can operate only as a secondary cause. Ford's characters are self-defining and nonpolitical. They do not so much defy society as deny its relevance to their lives.

Observing this, we find in Ford's nondramatic prose the source of a moral contradiction which is latent in the stoical as it is in the extreme protestant ethic. In *A Line of Life* we find him saying, "where the actors of mischief are a nation, there and amongst them to live well is a crown of immortal commendation." The difficulty comes in determining what it means "to live well" when a community standard of intelligible virtue is lacking. One must be his own light. Elsewhere in the same work, Ford opines, "Let no man rely too much on his own judgment; the wisest are deceived." Without the guidance of a community whose approbation one seeks and by whose judgments one abides, how is one to avoid the deceptions which lurk even in the choices of the wisest? The Stoic notion of Reason is troublingly like this Humean consensus of the approbation of the best people. The unearned confidence of modern theologues aside, the difficulty in reconciling these two contradictions—that one can no more live by the lights of a corrupt community than he can be the sole sponsor of his own morality—creates the very area in which tragedy is to be found. Ford found it there and Giovanni gives expression to it; he is a martyr to the tragic limitations of the Stoic vision. It is priggish to suppose that, in times of extreme social dislocation, there is always a better vision than the stoical one available. If a little of this is conceded, then Giovanni is a legitimate tragic figure. Let me conclude my discussion of *'Tis Pity* by indicating precisely in what I think his tragedy consists.

While watching the play, one grows strangely tolerant of the unaccommodated Giovanni, to whom the mindless frivolity of a Bergetto, the casual immorality of a Soranzo, the slack conventional optimism of his father, and the angular traditional arguments of the Friar are alike irrelevant to the passionate central truth of his life—that his sister is good and beautiful. Since he has been educated to prefer the good and the beautiful, he prefers her with a kind of exclusive purity of vision which has at once the narrowness of madness and the cultivated clarity of a splendid sanity. But Ford knows that a vow, a reasoned choice made in the stillness of a moment of seeming truth, must then suffer the tests of a world which impinges on one's acts. A miscalculation of one's purposes, a misalliance of purpose and capacity, can spell corruption. Ford saw, and makes us see, that for Giovanni and for Annabella what has happened is a deeply working denial that others have a reality commensurate to the sense of their own being.

In their ignorance, they overrate themselves. They become coarsened by the necessity they are under to engage in pretenses to preserve the "utopia for two." From the moment Giovanni wants more to preserve his rights in his sister than her sense of her own dignity and freedom, he begins to deteriorate morally. We can mark the stages: an embarrassing, callow bravura when speaking of his sexual privileges which (solipsistically) he supposes even the Friar must envy (II,v); a possessive edginess (II,vi); an hysterical inflation of language which mounts as he grows less and less capable of crediting any other feelings but his own (V, ii). In the final murder we can see very clearly that Giovanni is no longer *with* his sister. He acts unilaterally. He no longer possesses the love to share even his plans for a *Liebestod* with her. His selfishness has grown perfect, his love become an abstract and self-oriented thing. He is true only to the negative sanction of their "marriage" vow,

> Do not betray me to your mirth or hate:
> Love me or kill me.
>
> (I,iii)

We watch the monomaniacal workings of his mind as he *does* betray her to "mirth and hate" and, having done so, having killed all but the gorgeous verbal residue of their love, he kills her.

Giovanni's tragedy is deep and it does provoke terror and pity, for like Othello's, it rests on the most terrible sacrifice of love—not of the object of love only, but of one's ability to give and receive love. 'Tis Pity is a tragedy of the attrition of dignity and humanity of a man in the possession of Átē. The tragic moral is not readily abstractable, and has nothing to do with incest as such. It is rooted in Ford's profound grasp of the psychological auto-intoxication which can result from too arbitrary a dedication of one's mysterious humanity. Like Othello, Giovanni is so obviously the dreadfully suffering victim of his own tragic infatuation with phantoms that we are moved closer to the core of our own humanity. The judgment is in the situation; we need not impose one.

Ford's choice of incest as a theme around which to build his greatest play was not itself arbitrary. From it he obtained an intensification of his grasp of the spiritual roots of jealousy that nothing else could have given *him*. A good complementary text for 'Tis Pity is D. H. Lawrence's study of Edgar Allan Poe, from which I quote two passages:

> The trouble with man is that he insists on being master of his own fate, and he insists on *oneness* . . . having discovered the ecstasy of spiritual love, he insists that he shall have this all the time . . . He does not want to return to his own isolation.

And

> It is easy to see why each man kills the thing he loves. To *know* a living thing is to kill. You have to kill a thing to know it satisfactorily. For this reason, the desirous consciousness, the spirit, is a vampire . . . Keep KNOWLEDGE for the world of matter, force, and function. It has got nothing to do with being.

Ford raised a conventional theme of stage jealousy to a level of comprehension at which I think he would have understood exactly these urgent words of Lawrence's, so instinct with our own aroused sense of the sanctity of being. In brilliantly literalizing the metaphor that the truth of love is written in the heart of the beloved, he has made Giovanni's desperate gouging-out of Annabella's heart more than a piece of sensationalism. It is an act exactly appropriate to Giovanni's austerely curious, intellectual, character; it is also the perfect correlative of the frenzied, higher jealousy to which Ford is giving tragic expression.

To speak one last time in conjunction with Lawrence,

> the love is between brother and sister. When the self is broken, and the mystery of the recognition of *otherness* fails, then the longing for identification becomes lust . . . it is this longing for identification, utter merging, which is at the base of the incest problem.

Listen to the triumphant words of Giovanni as he shows the heart of Annabella,

> 'tis a heart,
> A heart, my lords, in which is mine entombed.
>
> (V, vi)

Ford has traced this tragic confusion to its very source. He has answered for himself a question asked by Bianca, importuning Fernando to make love to her in *Love's Sacrifice,* "what's a vow? a vow? Can there be sin in unity?" This is the radical misalliance—this uncomprehended urge to a unity life does not permit. Aristophanes' comic parable to explain love in Plato's *Symposium* can here be seen as the deep source of human tragedy as well. Giovanni, like Othello, asks for a quality of certitude life does not afford, and hence he "violates the delicacy" of things. Incest is a model of this— the vehicle of his tragedy; the failure in mutual faith is at once its moral and its cause. After thus tracing Ford's patient exploration of the jealousy that tragically undermines essential faith, it is hard to see in him the purposeless and soulless opportunist of T.S. Eliot's caricature.

FREDSON BOWERS

The Decadence of Revenge Tragedy

*T*he *Cardinal* (1641), Shirley's greatest tragedy, completes the trend by presenting in a brilliant fashion, a clear-cut, coherent Kydian revenge tragedy, polished and simplified in his best manner. The play has been most often compared to *The Duchess of Malfi* because of consequences resulting when an interested person tries to enforce affection. This theme, however, implicit in Webster's tragedy, was not put forward with the vigor found in *The Cardinal,* and Ford's *Broken Heart* with its powerful lesson on freedom of choice seems more probable as the source for Shirley's special and conspicuous pleading.

    The Cardinal is not an especially derivative play, however. Shirley went chiefly to *The Spanish Tragedy* for the larger construction of his plot, and though various other dramas contributed characters and incidents, these were chiefly used to bring the old Kydian tragedy up to date. An outline of *The Cardinal* fits almost point for point into the outline of Kyd's play. In both there is much preliminary action leading up to the murder which is to be revenged. In both this murder is committed by a jealous lover to rid himself of his rival who has won the heroine's heart. Both murderers are backed by intriguing villains who are anxious for the marriage to raise the fortunes of their houses. The murder calls forth the counter-revenge, which is ordered with extreme deceit and dissimulation including a feigned reconciliation. While Rosaura, like Hieronimo, goes mad from excessive grief, the portrayal of her madness is more closely allied to *Hamlet,* since she resolves to pretend insanity in order to deceive her enemies but from time to time lapses into actual distraction. Like *Hamlet* is the emphasis put upon her melancholy. A

From *Elizabethan Revenge Tragedy: 1587–1642.* © 1940, 1968 by Princeton University Press.

masque is used to commit a murder, a body is exhibited, ingenious deaths are contrived with great irony. An effect somewhat similar to Bel-Imperia's self-immolation after her revenge is secured in Hernando's suicide.

Various other details are taken from the dramas which developed the Kydian form. The lust of the villain for the victim of his schemes is prominent in such plays as *Antonio's Revenge* and *The Atheist's Tragedy,* although the closest resemblance comes in *Alphonsus, Emperor of Germany, The Bloody Brother,* and *Sicily and Naples,* from which last, perhaps, the particular form of the cardinal's revenge may have been borrowed. Hernando, the accomplice, has been compared to Bosola. It is true that in the disinterested quality of their revenges they bear a certain resemblance, but Bosola's previous position as accomplice to the villains is a wide variant, and a closer approach to type may be found in Hamond in *The Bloody Brother* who has been himself directly injured. Stephanos in *The Roman Actor* has the same disinterested motives, but other suggested parallels to Baltazar in *The Noble Spanish Soldier* and Ziriff in *Aglaura* are wide of the mark, as are comparisons of Hernando as revenger to Sciarrha and to Vindici. Indeed, Hernando corresponds most closely in his position in the plot to Hermegild in the Albovine story.

These matters of influence aside, *The Cardinal* is an expert work of the theater. The situations are clear-cut, the action rapid, and the characters strongly drawn. Action, however, has taken the place of the Kydian emotion with its accompaniments of a hesitating, overwrought revenger, blood and thunder, and ghosts. Rosaura's madness does not come until late and is sparingly exhibited. One moment she is seen planning to pretend madness, and the next as insane in fact. Since this change from sanity to actual distraction is accomplished offstage, the audience is not permitted to see the slow disintegration of a mind as in *The Spanish Tragedy, Hamlet,* or *Antonio's Revenge.* Similarly, there is no hesitation, and much of the important planning of the intrigue is done offstage. Pursuing an entirely different course from that of Kyd, Shirley has his characters do their thinking behind the scenes. All the audience sees is the thinking which has turned into action. Such a method makes invariably for a brisker play but a more shallow one; the polish has rubbed up the surface at the expense of the inner glow.

Yet the brilliance of Shirley's achievement, particularly when viewed in the light of the sterile treatment of revenge in the dilettante plays of his contemporaries, must not be minimized. If in bringing the old revenge tragedy up to date he has lost much of the emotion and the high tragedy of a soul on the rack, if his characters are slightly too facile in conceiving and acting revenge, he has at the same time sloughed off the bathos and hysteria, the rant and bombast, which at times had made the Kydian form a butt for laughter. His characters are ordinary persons in an ordinary world, who set about righting their wrongs as best they can. Some remnants of the older tradition persist, as in Rosaura's real madness under the weight of her burden and in the constant references to the religious and expiatory nature of revenge for her dead lover Alvarez. Yet even if Rosaura's distraction does not fit too smoothly in the plot, the revenger's talk of sacrificing to the ghost of Alvarez is necessary to show the nobility of Hernando's character and the essential justice of the vengeance. Without it, Hernando would have been a malicious man exploiting Rosaura's grievance for his own small ends.

The plays of the fourth period, especially that group yet to be considered, show in general an extreme degeneration in the convention of revenge. Only perfunctory motivation and action are given to a serious Kydian blood-revenge; consequently, all the true Kydian ethical spirit, the moral approach to a vital problem of character, is entirely missing. Although his *Cardinal* is not entirely divorced from this fault, Shirley has created a true revenge tragedy in which the entire play centers upon blood-revenge for murder. Vengeance is not perfunctorily relegated to the background until it is time for the catastrophe, nor is it hidden in artificial obscurity of motive. He has achieved a nice balance of characters and situation; in pure construction and actability *The Cardinal* is one of the best of the Elizabethan revenge plays. Furthermore, there are evidences in his careful delineation of character that Shirley up to a certain point in the play intended a conception of life which would closely approach the ethical content of the best revenge tragedy.

The early, or Kydian, tragedy of revenge had presented a hero-revenger who, forced by his overwhelming duty and outraged passion into too bloody courses, had lost all ethical adjustment to normal life and was eventually forced to pay the penalty in death. The necessarily treacherous and evil course of his revenge soon produced the feeling that he could not have been a good man even at the start, and we have such bad revengers in a good cause as Hoffman, Vindici, Maximus, and Francisco. The natural transition was thereupon made to the convention that revenge was the prerogative of villains alone, as exemplified in the villain plays *The Turk* and *Women Beware Women*. The realization grew, however, that good men did revenge, and that there still remained dramatic material in showing the results of their departure from heavenly and earthly laws on a practical plane of morality. A form of problem play, such as *The Fatal Dowry*, was produced. This form in the best plays yielded to the broader artistic conception of life as a balanced whole in which people are neither all good nor all bad. The justice of revenge was occasionally recognized but also its harms and cruelties in a social as well as a personal sense. *The White Devil*, *The Changeling*, *The Roman Actor*, *The*

Cruel Brother, *The Broken Heart*, and *Love's Sacrifice* all in one way or another portray this feeling. Shirley himself in *The Maid's Revenge*, *Love's Cruelty*, and to some extent in the portrait of Sciarrha in *The Traitor* had written in this mood.

The Cardinal may roughly be placed in this genre although the conception is not so clear or consistent. The cardinal with his ambitious schemes is the real villain, and his murder is truly the catastrophe of the play. Columbo is not wholly an evil but more an overrough and cruel man who lacks entirely the finer sensibilities which would have released Rosaura from her painful contract. Shirley is forced to produce the conflict between Hernando and Columbo to provide sufficient motivation for Hernando's revenge, but even greater emphasis is laid on Hernando's generous espousal of Rosaura's wrongs so that he is in effect her champion. Hernando himself partakes a trifle too much of the overbloody nature of the misled revenger. His anger is rather too personal and pronounced, and he betrays himself when he fiercely desires the damnation of the cardinal's soul as well as the destruction of his body. Hernando, however, is definitely no hypocrite; and his expiatory death, while it does no more than forestall the certain justice of the king, places him in the ranks of those revengers who were willing to suffer death for a good cause. At any rate, the noble method of revenge by formal duel in which he engages Columbo should remove him from the category of a villain.

Rosaura, the duchess, is a more complex person. It is her misjudgment of Columbo's character which really produces the tragedy. Not strong enough to resist with frank integrity the combined pressure of king and cardinal, she has weakly allowed herself to give the impression of acquiescence to Columbo's courtship, and so have involuntarily deceived him in a serious matter which he cannot forgive. The feeble exercise of her wiles in the writing of the letter, the fatal misinterpretation which, owing to her past deceit, Columbo gives it, and finally the reckless and injudicious haste with which she accepts his playful release and rushes into marriage, form a pyramid of feminine error which, when dealing with a man of Columbo's nature, can lead only to tragic consequences. Moreover, feminine jealousy plays its part in her revenge. The last push is given to her resolution by Columbo's vengeful and ostentatious courting of one of her ladies-in-waiting. She plans to seek a bloody revenge on Columbo and the cardinal, who she firmly believes instigated the murder of her Alvarez, and then to die.

So far her portrait has been that of a humanly faulty but not a vicious woman, and her resolution not to outlive her revenge has greatly purified her motives. Almost immediately, however, and with no perceptible motivation, she forgets her resolution and promises to marry Hernando if he is successful in her revenge. In consequence Rosaura allies herself to the hated class of Elizabethan husband-poisoners who had made the same promise to their accomplices, and, on the stage, to such villainesses as Rhodolinda in *Albovine* who had offered the same conditions to Paradine. This incident causes the most grievously blurred morality in Shirley's play, and is the one loose thread in his plot. Rosaura never refers to it again except in a distorted form in her ravings, which Hernando misapplies. Furthermore, the plan is never put into execution. Hernando kills himself immediately after he has stabbed the cardinal, in spite of his expressed eagerness of a few moments before to live to enjoy Rosaura. The insertion of the incident is puzzling, because immediately afterwards Shirley reverts to his former conception of Rosaura and never pursues farther the red herring of her villainy.

In her vengeance Rosaura is single-minded to a fault. She persistently believes that the cardinal instigated the murder of her husband and, in fact, accuses him to his face. Yet Shirley has given no indication of such a fact, and the cardinal's comments during the masque which precedes the murder show distinctly that he has no connection with it. He answers Rosaura with an eloquent denial and a spirited defense of his championing the cause of his nephew Columbo which should convince any audience that he was innocent of any connection with the murder. Rosaura pretends to believe him, but her acceptance is pure dissimulation, for on his departure she disclaims her feigned reconciliation and starts her plans for his murder. The cardinal has admittedly been guilty of corrupting his sovereign, of forcing Rosaura's match with Columbo, and of securing the reinstatement of Columbo after the murder of Alvarez. His brilliant and sound defense to Rosaura, however, places him in the minds of the audience as an erring ambitious man but not a murderer, and so not deserving of a revenge for that murder. Some sympathy must inevitably have been taken away from Rosaura on her refusal to believe him and on her immediate plans to secure his death for an act of which he was innocent.

So far the interpretation has been only what is latent in Shirley's text, and has avoided as much as possible that facile error of reading into Elizabethan plays the nuances and conceptions which may be present only in the critic's own mind. Such a warning is necessary when we find that the ordering of the catastrophe destroys the whole of the more subtle distinctions in character which seem to have been built up in the evolution of the plot. According to what has gone before we should expect to find a clearly expressed or implied moral, not only on the faultiness of the characters but also on the inevitability of the result; or at least we should expect a suggestion that Rosaura, while grievously wronged, had in her turn mistaken justice and committed wrong.

On the contrary, the characters who have been gray throughout the drama suddenly part into black and white. The cardinal, from whom all Machiavellism had been missing, appears with an absurd villainous scheme of rape and poison to revenge Columbo. When Hernando's stab foils his plans, the person whose eloquent and sincere defense has shown him to be merely a man and so deserving of some meed of sympathy, suddenly turns black villain and with atheistical deceit, tricks Rosaura to her death. Rosaura, certainly a femininely faulty woman, by the metamorphosis of the cardinal is transformed into a guiltless heroine, whose cruel fate is universally mourned with not the slightest hint of censure. The change is too sudden and too sweeping to be caused by anything other than a weakening of conception, the result of Shirley's occasional theatricality. The collapse in characterization of the cardinal, the key figure in the drama, into a mere stage villain is peculiarly similar to the metamorphosis of Barabas, caused by whatever means, from a creation of humanly villainous grandeur to a bogey man to frighten children. With the collapse of the cardinal all ethical spirit in the characterization vanishes. The play fails to fulfil its brilliant promise. Fletcherian theatricality has destroyed the real potentialities of the last great tragedy of revenge.

Chronology

1553	John Lyly born in Kent.
1558	Thomas Kyd born in London.
ca. 1560	George Chapman born in Hitchin, Hertfordshire.
1564	William Shakespeare born. Christopher Marlowe born.
1565	Kyd attends Merchant Taylors school in London.
1569	Lyly enters Magdalen College, Oxford; receives BA in 1573 and MA in 1575.
ca. 1572	Thomas Dekker born in London.
ca. 1573	Ben Jonson born.
ca. 1574	Chapman attends Oxford, though he does not receive a degree.
1576	John Marston born.
1578	Lyly publishes *Euphues: The Anatomy of Wit*.
1579	John Fletcher born at Rye in Sussex.
1580	Lyly publishes *Euphues and his England*. Thomas Middleton baptized in London.
ca. 1580	John Webster born. Cyril Tourneur born.
1583	Philip Massinger baptized in Salisbury.

1584	Lyly publishes *Campaspe* and *Sappho and Phao*.
ca. 1584	Francis Beaumont born in Leicestershire.
ca. 1585	Kyd writes *The First Part of Hieronimo*.
1586	John Ford baptized at Ilsington, Devonshire.
ca. 1587	Kyd writes *The Spanish Tragedy*.
1591	Lyly publishes *Endimion*. Kyd and Marlowe reported together, living or writing in the same room.
1592	Lyly publishes *Gallathea* and *Midas*. Kyd arrested, under suspicion for public libel and heresy. Marston matriculates at Brasenose College, Oxford. Enters Middle Temple.
ca. 1593	Dekker begins writing for the Lord Admiral's Men.
1594	Kyd dies. Chapman publishes *The Shadow of Night*.
1595	Chapman publishes *Ovid's Banquet of Sense*.
1596	James Shirley born in London. Beaumont enters Pembroke College, Oxford.
1597	Lyly publishes *Woman in the Moon*.
1598	Chapman publishes *Achilles Shield* and *Seven Books of the Iliad*, both translations from the Greek. Dekker listed by Francis Mere as one of the Foremost English Tragedians. He is also arrested for debt in this year. Marston publishes *The Metamorphosis of Pygmalion's Image* and *The Scourge of Villainy*.
ca. 1598	Webster admitted to the Middle Temple.
ca. 1599	Marston writes *Histriomastix, Antonio and Mellida*, and *Jack Drum's Entertainment*.
1600	Chapman arrested for debt.
ca. 1600	Tourneur publishes *The Transformed Metamorphosis*.

1601	Lyly publishes *Love's Metamorphosis*. Marston writes *Antonio's Revenge*.
1602	Massinger enters St. Alban Hall, Oxford. Ford admitted to the Middle Temple.
1603	Dekker and Middleton collaborate on *The Magnificent Entertainment Given to King James*.
ca. 1603	*The Malcontent* written by Marston and performed.
1604	Middleton's *The Phoenix* performed.
ca. 1604	Chapman's *All Fools, Monsieur d'Olive*, and *Bussy D'Ambois* performed. Webster and Dekker collaborate on *Westward Ho!* and *Northward Ho!*
1605	Chapman collaborates with Jonson and Marston on *Eastward Ho!*
ca. 1605	Chapman's *The Widow's Tears* and *The Tragedy of Caesar and Pompey* performed. Fletcher writes *Woman's Prize*.
1606	Ford publishes an elegiac poem, *Fame's Memorial*, and a pamphlet, *Honour Triumphant*. John Lyly dies.
ca. 1606	Beaumont writes *The Woman Hater*. Tourneur writes *The Revenger's Tragedy*.
1607	*The Revenger's Tragedy* published. Middleton publishes *The Phoenix, Michaelmas Term, A Trick to Catch the Old One*, and *The Family of Love*. Dekker and Webster publish *The Famous Historie of Sir Thomas Wyatt*.
ca. 1607	Beaumont writes *The Knight of the Burning Pestle*.
1608	Shirley enters Merchant Taylors' school. Chapman's *The Conspiracy and Tragedy of Charles, Duke of Byron* published. Marston imprisoned on an undetermined charge.

ca. 1608   Fletcher writes *The Faithful Shepherdess*.
            Middleton and Dekker collaborate on *The Roaring Girl*.

    1609   Dekker publishes *Gull's Handbook*.
            Marston ordained priest in a parish church.
            Chapman publishes his *Twelve Books of the Iliad*.

ca. 1609   Beaumont and Fletcher write *Philaster* and *Coxcomb*.

ca. 1610   Tourneur writes *The Atheist's Tragedy*.

    1611   Beaumont and Fletcher's *A King and No King* performed.
            Tourneur's *The Atheist's Tragedy* published.

ca. 1611   Webster's *White Devil* written and performed.
            Chapman's *Revenge of Bussy D'Ambois* published.
            Tourneur's now lost tragicomedy *The Nobleman* is performed
            and published.

ca. 1612   Chapman arrested for debt.

    1613   Beaumont writes the *Inner Temple Masque*.
            Middleton's *A Chaste Maid at Cheapside* performed.

1613–19   Dekker imprisoned for debt.

ca. 1614   Middleton's *The Witch* performed.

    1615   Chapman publishes his complete translation of the *Odyssey*.

    1616   Beaumont and Fletcher's *The Scornful Lady* published.
            Beaumont dies.
            Shakespeare dies.

ca. 1616   Fletcher publishes *Mad Lover* and *Loyal Subject*.

    1617   Shirley receives BA from Cambridge.
            Tourneur arrested by order of the Privy Council and released
            on bond by Sir Edward Cecil.

ca. 1617   Middleton collaborates with Rowley on *A Fair Quarrel*.
            Massinger begins writing for the King's Men.
            Webster revises *The Duchess of Malfi* for a stage revival.

    1618   Massinger, Middleton, and Rowley write *The Old Law*.

    1619   Middleton's *The Inner Masque* performed.

ca. 1619   Webster's *The Devil's Law Case* written and performed.

ca. 1620   Dekker collaborates with Massinger, Ford, and Webster.

1621   Ford, Dekker, and Rowley's *The Witch of Edmonton* performed.

ca. 1621   Middleton's *Women Beware Women* performed.
Massinger writes *The Maid of Honor*, and *A New Way to Pay Old Debts*.

1622   Middleton and Rowley's *The Changeling* performed.

ca. 1623   Massinger writes *The Duke of Milan* and *The Bondman*.

1624   Middleton's *A Game at Chesse* performed.

1625   Tourneur, serving as secretary to Sir Edward Cecil, falls ill during the expedition against Cadiz and dies in Kinsale, Ireland February 18, 1626.
Fletcher dies.

1625–36   Shirley writes for Queen Henrietta's company.

1626   Massinger writes *The Roman Actor*.

1627   Middleton is buried on July 4 at Newington.

1628   Ford's *The Lover's Melancholy* performed.

1632   Dekker dies.

ca. 1632   Massinger writes *The City Madam*.
Shirley writes *Hyde Park*.

1633   Massinger writes *The Guardian*.
Ford publishes *'Tis Pity She's A Whore*, *Love's Sacrifice*, and *The Broken Heart*.

1634   Ford publishes *Perkin Warbeck*.
Chapman dies in London.
Marston dies in London.

ca. 1634   Webster dies.

1639   Last certain record of Ford, when he publishes a dedication to *The Lady's Trial*.

1640   Massinger dies in London.

1641   Shirley writes *The Cardinal*.

1666   Shirley dies in London.

Contributors

HAROLD BLOOM, Sterling Professor of the Humanities at Yale University, is the author of *The Anxiety of Influence, Poetry and Repression*, and many other volumes of literary criticism. His forthcoming study, *Freud: Transference and Authority*, attempts a full-scale reading of all of Freud's major writings. A MacArthur Prize Fellow, he is general editor of five series of literary criticism published by Chelsea House.

JOCELYN POWELL is the author of *Restoration Theatre Production*.

SCOTT McMILLIN is Professor of English at Cornell University and the editor of the Norton Edition, *Restoration and Eighteenth-Century Comedy*.

PETER SACKS is Associate Professor in the writing seminars at The Johns Hopkins University.

HAROLD E. TOLIVER is the author of *Animate Illusions: Explorations of Narrative Structure* and *The Past That Poets Make*.

ALVIN B. KERNAN, Andrew Mellon Professor of Humanities at Princeton University, is the author of *The Plot of Satire* and *The Playwright as Magician*.

G. WILSON KNIGHT was Professor of English Emeritus at Leeds University and the author of *The Wheel of Fire* and *The Burning Oracle*.

JACKSON I. COPE is the author of *The Metaphoric Structure of "Paradise Lost,"* as well as a book on Joyce. He teaches at the University of California, Los Angeles.

EDWIN MUIR was a poet and translator, and the author of *The Politics of King Lear* and *The Estate of Poetry*.

L. G. SALINGAR was Lecturer in English at Cambridge University and the author of *Shakespeare and the Traditions of Comedy*.

B. J. LAYMAN has written other articles on Elizabethan drama and currently teaches at the Lawrence Institute of Technology.

EUGENE M. WAITH is Professor of English Emeritus at Yale University and has written *The Herculean Hero* and *Ideas of Greatness*.

M. C. BRADBROOK is Professor of English Emeritus at Cambridge and the author of *Themes and Conventions of Elizabethan Tragedy* and *The Growth and Structure of Elizabethan Comedy*.

MICHAEL NEILL teaches English at the University of Auckland, New Zealand, and has written a number of articles on Elizabethan drama.

R. J. KAUFMANN is Professor of English at the University of Rochester.

FREDSON BOWERS, University Professor Emeritus at the University of Virginia, is the author of *Textual and Literary Criticism*.

Bibliography

Baker, Howard. *Induction to Tragedy*. Baton Rouge: Louisiana State University Press, 1939.

Bentley, G. E. *The Jacobean and Caroline Stage*. Oxford: Clarendon Press, 1941–56.

Bradbrook, M. C. *Themes and Conventions of Elizabethan Tragedy*. Cambridge: Cambridge University Press, 1935.

————. *The Growth and Structure of Elizabethan Comedy*. London: Chatto and Windus, 1955.

Champion, Larry S. *Tragic Patterns in Jacobean and Caroline Drama*. Knoxville: University of Tennessee Press, 1977.

Clemen, Wolfgang. *English Tragedy Before Shakespeare*. London: Methuen, 1961.

Doran, Madeleine. *Endeavours of Art: A Study of Form in Elizabethan Drama*. Madison: University of Wisconsin Press, 1954.

Eliot, T. S. *Essays on Elizabethan Drama*. New York: Harcourt, Brace, 1960.

Ellis-Fermor, Una M. *The Jacobean Drama*. London: Methuen, 1953.

Empson, William. *Some Versions of Pastoral*. London: Chatto and Windus, 1935.

Herndl, George C. *The High Design: English Renaissance Tragedy and the Natural Law*. Lexington: University Press of Kentucky, 1970.

Herrick, Marvin T. *Tragicomedy: Its Origin and Development in Italy, France and England*. Urbana: University of Illinois Press, 1955.

Huebert, Ronald. " 'An Artificial Way to Grieve': The Forsaken Women in Beaumont, Fletcher, Massinger, and Ford." *ELH* 44 (1977): 601–21.

Kirsch, Arthur C. *Jacobean Dramatic Perspectives*. Charlottesville: University of Virginia Press, 1972.

Knight, G. Wilson. *The Golden Labyrinth*. London: Phoenix House, 1962.

Knights, L. C. *Drama and Society in the Age of Ben Jonson*. London: Chatto and Windus, 1937.

Levin, Richard. *The Multiple Plot in English Renaissance Drama*. Chicago: University of Chicago Press, 1971.

McDonald, Charles Osborne. *The Rhetoric of Tragedy: Form in Stuart Drama*. Amherst: University of Massachusetts Press, 1966.

Ornstein, Robert. *The Moral Vision of Jacobean Tragedy*. Madison: University of Wisconsin Press, 1965.

Prior, Moody E. *The Language of Tragedy*. New York: Columbia University Press, 1947.

Ribner, Irving. *Jacobean Tragedy*. London: Methuen, 1967.

Stroup, Thomas B. *Microcosmos: The Shape of the Elizabethan Play*. Lexington: University Press of Kentucky, 1965.

Ure, Peter. *Elizabethan and Jacobean Drama*. New York: Harper and Row, 1974.

Weld, John. *Meaning in Comedy: Studies in Elizabethan Romantic Comedy*. Albany: State University of New York Press, 1975.

Wells, Henry W. *Elizabethan and Jacobean Playwrights*. New York: Columbia University Press, 1939.

JOHN LYLY

Barish, Jonas A. "The Prose Style of John Lyly." *ELH* 23 (1956): 14–36.

Berek, Peter. "Artifice and Realism in Lyly, Nashe and *Love's Labor's Lost*." *Studies in English Literature* 23 (1983): 207–21.

Bergeron, David M. "The Education of Rafe in Lyly's *Gallathea*." *Studies in English Literature* 23 (1983): 197–206.

Best, Michael R. "Lyly's Static Drama." *Renaissance Drama* 1 (1968): 75–86.

Bevington, David. *Tudor Drama and Politics*. Cambridge, Mass.: Harvard University Press, 1968.

Bond, Sallie. "John Lyly's *Endimion*." *Studies in English Literature* 14 (1974): 189–99.

Ettin, Andrew V. "Magic into Art: The Magician's Renunciation of Magic in English Renaissance Drama." *Texas Studies in Literature and Language* 19 (1977): 268–93.

Gannon, C. C. "Lyly's *Endimion*: From Myth to Allegory." *English Literary Renaissance* 6 (1976): 220–43.

Harbage, Alfred. *"Love's Labor's Lost* and the Early Shakespeare." *Philological Quarterly* 41 (1962): 18–36.

Helgerson, Richard. *The Elizabethan Prodigals*. Berkeley and Los Angeles: University of California Press, 1977.

Hilliard, Stephen S. "Lyly's *Midas* as an Allegory of Tyranny." *Studies in English Literature* 12 (1972): 243–58.

Huppe, Bernard F. "Allegory of Love in Lyly's Court Comedies." *ELH* 14 (1947): 93–113.

Knapp, Robert S. "The Monarchy of Love in Lyly's *Endimion*." *Modern Philology* 73 (1976): 353–67.

Lindheim, Nancy R. "Lyly's Golden Legacy: *Rosalynde* and *Pandoslo*." *Studies in English Literature* 15 (1975): 3–20.

Olson, Paul H. *"A Midsummer Night's Dream* and the Meaning of Court Marriage." *ELH* 24 (1957): 95–119.

Parnell, Paul E. "Moral Allegory in Lyly's *Loves Metamorphosis*." *Studies in Philology* 52 (1955): 1–16.

Saccio, Peter. *The Court Comedies of John Lyly: A Study in Allegorical Dramaturgy*. Princeton: Princeton University Press, 1969.

———. "The Oddity of Lyly's *Endimion*." In *Elizabethan Theatre V*. Hamden, Conn.: Archon Books, 1975.

Sandbank, Shimon. "Euphuistic Symmetry and the Image." *Studies in English Literature* 11 (1971): 1–13.

Scragg, Leah. "Shakespeare, Lyly and Ovid: The Influence of *Gallathea* on *A Midsummer Night's Dream*." *Shakespeare Survey* 30 (1977): 125–34.

Turner, Robert Y. "Some Dialogue of Love in Lyly's Comedies." *ELH* 29 (1962): 276–88.

Weltner, Peter. "The Antinomic Vision of Lyly's *Endimion*." *English Literary Renaissance* 3 (1973): 5–29.

Westlund, Joseph. "The Theme of Tact in *Campaspe*." *Studies in English Literature* 19 (1976): 213–21.

THOMAS KYD

Adams, Barry B. "The Audience of *The Spanish Tragedy*." *Journal of English and Germanic Philology* 68 (1969): 221–36.

Ardolino, Frank. " 'Sit We Down to See the Mystery': Detection and Allegory in *The Spanish Tragedy*." *Allegorica* 5 (1980): 168–76.

Ayres, Philip J. "Degrees of Heresy: Justified Revenge and Elizabethan Narratives." *Studies in Philology* 69 (1972): 461–74.

Baines, Barbara J. "Kyd's Silenus Box and the Limits of Perception." *Journal of Medieval and Renaissance Studies* 10 (1980): 41–51.

Baker, Howard. "Ghosts and Guides: Kyd's *Spanish Tragedy* and the Medieval Tragedy." *Modern Philology* 33 (1935): 27–35.

Barish, Jonas A. "*The Spanish Tragedy*, or The Pleasures and Perils of Rhetoric." In *Elizabethan Theatre.* Stratford-Upon-Avon Studies 9 (1966): 59–85.

Broude, Ronald. "Time, Truth, and Right in *The Spanish Tragedy*." *Studies in Philology* 68 (1971): 130–45.

Colley, John S. "*The Spanish Tragedy* and the Theatre of God's Judgements." *Papers on Language and Literature* 10 (1974): 241–53.

Coursen, Herbert R., Jr. "The Unity of *The Spanish Tragedy*." *Studies in Philology* 65 (1968): 768–82.

Craig, Hardin. "The Shackling of Accidents: A Study of Elizabethan Tragedy." *Philological Quarterly* 19 (1940): 1–19.

Empson, William. "*The Spanish Tragedy*." *Nimbus* 3 (1956): 16–29.

Freeman, Arthur. *Thomas Kyd: Facts and Problems.* Oxford: Clarendon Press, 1967.

Hallet, Charles A., and Elaine S. Hallet. *The Revenger's Madness: A Study of Revenge Tragedy Motifs.* Lincoln: University of Nebraska Press, 1980.

Hallet, Charles A. "Andrea, Andrugio and King Hamlet: The Ghost as Spirit of Revenge." *Philological Quarterly* 56 (1977): 43–64.

Hamilton, Donna B. "*The Spanish Tragedy*: A Speaking Picture." *English Literary Renaissance* 4 (1974): 203–17.

Harbage, Alfred. "Intrigue in Elizabethan Tragedy." In *Essays on Shakespeare and Elizabethan Drama in Honor of Hardin Craig*, edited by Richard Hosley. Columbia: University of Missouri Press, 1962.

Hunter, G. K. "Ironies of Justice in *The Spanish Tragedy*." *Renaissance Drama* 8 (1965): 89–104.

Jensen, E. J. "Kyd's *Spanish Tragedy*: The Play Explains Itself." *Journal of English and Germanic Philology* 64 (1965): 1–16.

Johnson, S. F. "*The Spanish Tragedy*, or Babylon Revisited." In *Essays on Shakespeare and Elizabethan Drama in Honor of Hardin Craig*, edited by Richard Hosley. Columbia: University of Missouri Press, 1962.

Kay, Carol McGinnis. "Deception Through Words: A Reading of *The Spanish Tragedy*." *Studies in Philology* 74 (1977): 20–38.

Lamb, Margaret. "Beyond Revenge: *The Spanish Tragedy*." *Mosaic* 9, no. 1 (1975): 33–40.

Levin, Michael H. " 'Vindicta Mihi!': Meaning, Morality and Motivation in *The Spanish Tragedy.*" *Studies in English Literature* 4 (1964): 307–24.

McMillin, Scott. "The Book of Seneca in *The Spanish Tragedy.*" *Studies in English Literature* 14 (1974): 201–8.

Racliffe, John D. "Hieronimo Explains Himself." *Studies in Philology* 54, no. 2 (1957): 112–18.

Roberts, Josephine A., and James F. Gaines. "Kyd and Garnier: The Art of Amendment." *Comparative Literature* 31 (1979): 124–33.

Rozett, Martha. "Aristotle, The Revenger and the Elizabethan Audience." *Studies in Philology* 76 (1979), 239–61.

THOMAS DEKKER

Bergeron, David M. "Thomas Dekker's Lord Mayor's Shows." *English Studies* 51 (1970): 2–15.

Burelbach, Frederick. "War and Peace in *The Shoemaker's Holiday.*" *Tennessee Studies in Language and Literature* 13 (1968): 99–108.

Champion, Larry S. "From Melodrama to Comedy: A Study of the Dramatic Perspective in Dekker's *The Honest Whore*, Parts I and II." *Studies in Philology* 69 (1972): 192–209.

———. "Westward-Northward: Structural Development of Dekker's *Ho* Plays." *Comparative Drama* 16 (1982): 251–66.

Cheney, Patrick. "Moll Cutpurse as Hermaphrodite in Dekker and Middleton's *The Roaring Girl.*" *Renaissance and Reformation* 7 (1983): 120–34.

Halstead, William L. "Dekker's *Cupid and Psyche* and Thomas Heywood." *ELH* 11 (1944): 182–91.

Kinney, Arthur F. "Thomas Dekker's *Twelfth Night.*" *University of Toronto Quarterly* 41 (1971): 63–73.

Manheim, Michael. "The Construction of *The Shoemaker's Holiday.*" *Studies in English Literature* 10 (1970): 315–23.

Mortenson, Peter. "The Economies of Joy in *The Shoemaker's Holiday.*" *Studies in English Literature* 16 (1976): 241–52.

Novarr, David. "Dekker's Gentle Craft and *The Lord Mayor of London.*" *Modern Philology* 57 (1960): 233–9.

Pendry, E. D. "Thomas Dekker in the Magistrate's Court." *English Literary Renaissance* 3 (1973): 53–9.

Reynolds, George F. "The Aims of a Popular Elizabethan Dramatist." *Philological Quarterly* 20 (1941): 340–44.

Ure, Peter. "Patient Madam and Honest Whore: The Middleton-Dekker Oxymoron." *Essays and Studies* 19 (1966): 18–40.

JOHN MARSTON

Aggeler, Geoffrey D. "Stoicism and Revenge in Marston." *English Studies* 51 (1970): 507–17.

Andrews, Michael C. "*Jack Drum's Entertainment* as Burlesque." *Renaissance Quarterly* 24 (1971): 226–31.

Ayres, Philip. "Marston's *Antonio's Revenge*: The Morality of the Revenging Hero." *Studies in English Literature* 12 (1972): 359–74.

Baines, Barbara. "*Antonio's Revenge*: Marston's Play on Revenge Plays." *Studies in English Literature* 23 (1983): 277–94.

Berland, Ellen. "The Function of Irony in Marston's *Antonio and Mellida*." *Studies in Philology* 66 (1969): 739–55.

Caputi, Anthony. *John Marston, Satirist*. Ithaca: Cornell University Press, 1961.

Cousins, A. D. "The Protean Nature of Man in Marston's Verse Satires." *Journal of English and Germanic Philology* 79 (1980): 517–29.

Finkelpearl, Philip J. *John Marston of the Middle Temple: An Elizabethan Dramatist in his Social Setting*. Cambridge: Harvard University Press, 1969.

Foakes, R. A. "John Marston's Fantastical Plays: *Antonio and Mellida* and *Antonio's Revenge*." *Philological Quarterly* 41 (1962): 222–39.

Hunter, G. K. "English Folly and Italian Vice: The Moral Landscape of John Marston." In *Jacobean Theatre*, edited by John Russell Brown and Bernard Harris. London: Edward Arnold, 1960.

Jensen, Ejner J. "Theme and Imagery in *The Malcontent*." *Studies in English Literature* 10 (1970): 367–84.

Kernan, Alvin B. "John Marston's Play *Histriomastix*." *Modern Language Quarterly* 19 (1958): 134–40.

Kiefer, Christian. "Music and Marston's *The Malcontent*." *Studies in Philology* 51 (1954): 163–71.

Peter, John. "John Marston's Plays." *Scrutiny* 17 (1950): 132–53.

Presson, Robert K. "Marston's *Dutch Courtezan*: The Study of an Attitude in Adaptation." *Journal of English and Germanic Philology* 55 (1956): 406–13.

Salomon, Brownell. "The Theological Basis of Imagery and Structure in *The Malcontent*." *Studies in English Literature* 14 (1974): 271–84.

Ure, Peter. "John Marston's *Sophonisba*: A Reconsideration." *Durham University Journal* 10 (1949): 81–90.

Wharton, T. F. "Old Marston or New Marston: The *Antonio* Plays." *Essays in Criticism* 25 (1975): 357–69.

Yearling, Elizabeth M. " 'Mount Tufty Tamburlaine': Marston and Linguistic Excess." *Studies in English Literature* 20 (1980): 257–69.

Zall, Paul M. "John Marston, Moralist." *ELH* 20 (1953): 186–93.

JOHN WEBSTER

Baker, Susan C. "The Static Protagonist in *The Duchess of Malfi.*" *Texas Studies in Literature and Language* 22 (1980): 343–57.

Bawcutt, N. W. " '*Don Quixote*,' Part I and '*The Duchess of Malfi.*'" *Modern Language Review* 66 (1971): 488–91.

Belsey, Catherine. "Emblem and Antithesis in *The Duchess of Malfi.*" *Renaissance Drama* 11 (1980): 115–34.

Bergeson, David. "The Wax Figures in *The Duchess of Malfi.*" *Studies in Engish Literature* 18 (1978): 331–39.

Berlin, Normand. "*The Duchess of Malfi*: Act V." *Genre* (1970): 351–63.

Berry, Ralph. *The Art of John Webster*. Oxford: Clarendon Press, 1972.

Bliss, Lee. *The World's Perspective: John Webster and the Jacobean Drama*. New Brunswick: Rutgers University Press, 1983.

Bogard, Travis. *The Tragic Satire of John Webster*. Berkeley: University of California Press, 1955.

Bradbrook, M. C. *John Webster: Citizen and Dramatist*. New York: Columbia University Press, 1980.

Calderwood, James L. "*The Duchess of Malfi*: Styles of Ceremony." *Essays in Criticism* 12 (1963): 133–47.

Ekeblad, Inga-Stina. "The 'Impure Art' of John Webster." *Review of English Studies* 9 (1958): 253–67.

———. "A Webster Villain: A Study of Character Imagery in *The Duchess of Malfi.*" *Orpheus* 3 (1956): 126–33.

Empson, William. " 'Mine Eyes Dazzle.' " *Essays in Criticism* 14 (1964): 80–86.

Forker, Charles R. "Love, Death and Fame: The Grotesque Tragedy of John Webster." *Anglia* 91 (1973): 194–218.

———. "The Love-Death Nexus in English Renaissance Tragedy." *Shakespeare Survey* 8 (1975): 211–30.

Gill, Roma. "A Reading of *The White Devil.*" *Essays and Studies* 19 (1966): 41–59.

Gunby, D. C. "*The Devil's Law Case*: An Interpretation." *Modern Language Review* 63 (1968): 545–58.

Hurt, J. R. "Inverted Rituals in Webster's *The White Devil.*" *Journal of English and Germanic Philology* 61 (1962): 42–47.

Jardine, Lisa. "*The Duchess of Malfi*: A Case Study in the Literary Representation of Women." In *Teaching the Text*, edited by Susanne Kappeler and Norman Bryson. London: Routledge and Kegan Paul, 1983.

Layman, B. J. "The Equilibrium of Opposites in *The White Devil*." *PMLA* 74 (1959): 336–47.

McElroy, John F. "*The White Devil, Women Beware Women* and the Limits of Rationalist Criticism." *Studies in English Literature* 19 (1979): 295–312.

McLeod, Susan H. "Duality in *The White Devil*." *Studies in English Literature* 20 (1980): 271–85.

Morris, Brian, ed. *John Webster*. London: Ernest Benn, 1970.

Neill, Michael. "Monuments and Ruins as Symbols in *The Duchess of Malfi*." In *Drama and Symbolism*, edited by James Redmond. Cambridge: Cambridge University Press, 1982.

Pearson, Jacqueline. *Tragedy and Tragicomedy in the Plays of John Webster*. Totowa, N.J.: Barnes and Noble Books, 1980.

Price, Hereward T. "The Function of Imagery in Webster." *PMLA* 70 (1955): 717–39.

Rabkin, Norman, ed. *Twentieth Century Interpretations of "The Duchess of Malfi."* Englewood Cliffs, N.J.: Prentice-Hall, 1968.

Schuman, Samuel "The Ring and the Jewel in Webster's Tragedies." *Texas Studies in Literature and Language* 14 (1972): 253–68.

Selzer, John L. "Merit and Degree in Webster's *The Duchess of Malfi*." *English Literary Renaissance* 11 (1981): 70–80.

Wadsworth, Frank W. "Webster's *Duchess of Malfi* in the Light of Some Contemporary Ideas on Marriage and Remarriage." *Philological Quarterly* 35 (1956): 394–407.

Whitman, Robert F. "The Moral Paradox of Webster's Tragedy." *PMLA* 90 (1975): 894–903.

Wilkinson, Charles. "Twin Structures in John Webster's *The Duchess of Malfi*." *Literature and Psychology* 31 (1981): 52–65.

GEORGE CHAPMAN

Adams, Robert P. "Critical Myths and Chapman's Original *Bussy D'Ambois*" *Renaissance Drama* 9 (1966): 141–61.

Ayres, Philip J. "Chapman and Revenge." In *Shakespeare and Some Others: Essays on Shakespeare and Some of His Contemporaries*, edited by Alan Brissenden. Adelaide, Australia: University of Adelaide Press, 1976.

Barber, C. L. "The Ambivalence of *Bussy D'Ambois*." *Review of English Literature* 2 (1961): 38–44.

Battenhouse, Roy. "Chapman and the Nature of Man." *ELH* 12 (1945): 87–105.

Bement, Peter. "The Imagery of Darkness and Light in Chapman's *Bussy D'Ambois*." *Studies in Philology* 64 (1967): 187–98.

Bergson, Allen. "The Ironic Tragedies of Marston and Chapman: Notes on Jacobean Tragic Form." *Journal of English and Germanic Philology* 69 (1970): 613–30.

———. "Stoicism Achieved: Cato in Chapman's Tragedy of *Caesar and Pompey*." *Studies in English Literature* 17 (1977): 295–302.

Bliss, Lee. "The Boys From Ephesus: Farce, Freedom and Limit in *The Widow's Tears*." *Renaissance Drama* 10 (1970): 159–67.

Cannon, Charles Kendrick. "Chapman on the Unity of Style and Meaning." *Journal of English and Germanic Philology* 68 (1969): 245–64.

Craig, Jane Melbourne. "Chapman's Two Byrons." *Studies in English Literature* 22 (1982): 271–83.

Crawley, Derek. "Decision and Character in Chapman's *The Tragedy of Caesar and Pompey*." *Studies in English Literature* 7 (1967): 277–97.

Grant, Thomas Mark. *The Comedies of George Chapman: A Study in Development.* Salzburg: Institut für Englische Sprache und Literatur, Universität Salzburg, 1972.

Hardin, Richard F. "Chapman and Webster on Matrimony: The Poets and the Reformation of Ritual." *Renaissance and Reformation* 4 (1980): 65–73.

Helgerson, Richard. "The Elizabethan Laureate: Self-Presentation and the Literary System." *ELH* 46 (1979): 193–220.

Hibbard, G. R. "George Chapman's Tragedies and the Providential View of History." *Shakespeare Survey* 20 (1967): 27–31.

Higgins, Michael. "Chapman's 'Senecal Man.'" *Review of English Studies* 21 (1945): 183–91.

———. "The Development of the 'Senecal Man.'" *Review of English Studies* 23 (1947): 24–33.

Hogan, A. P. "Thematic Unity in Chapman's *Monsieur d'Olive*." *Studies in English Literature* 11 (1971): 295–306.

Homan, Sidney R. "Chapman and Marlowe: The Paradoxical Hero and the Divided Response." *Journal of English and Germanic Philology* 68 (1969): 391–406.

Ide, Richard. *Posssessed with Greatness: The Heroic Tragedies of Chapman and Shakespeare.* Chapel Hill: University of North Carolina Press, 1980.

Kistler, Suzanne F. "The Significance of the Missing Hero in Chapman's *Caesar and Pompey*." *Modern Language Quarterly* 40 (1979): 339–57.

———. " 'Strange and Far Removed Shores': A Reconsideration of *The Revenge of Bussy D'Ambois*." *Studies in Philology* 77 (1980): 128–44.

Lever, J. W. "Chapman: The *Bussy* Plays." In *The Tragedy of State*. London: Methuen, 1971.

McCollom, William G. "The Tragic Hero and Chapman's *Bussy D'Ambois*." *University of Toronto Quarterly* 18 (1949): 227–33.

MacLure, Millar. *George Chapman*. Toronto: University of Toronto Press, 1966.

Presson, Robert K. "Wrestling with this World: A View of George Chapman." *PMLA* 84 (1969): 44–50.

Rees, Ennis. *The Tragedies of George Chapman: Renaissance Ethics in Action*. Cambridge, Mass.: Harvard University Press, 1954.

Schoenbaum, Samuel. "*The Widow's Tears* and the Other Chapman." *Huntington Library Quarterly* 23 (1960): 321–38.

Waddington, Raymond B. "Prometheus and Hercules: The Dialectic of *Bussy D'Ambois*." *ELH* 34 (1967): 21–48.

Waith, Eugene M. *The Herculean Hero in Marlowe, Chapman, Shakespeare and Dryden*. New York: Columbia University Press, 1962.

Weidner, Henry M. "The Dramatic Uses of Homeric Idealism: The Significance of Theme and Design in George Chapman's *The Gentleman Usher*." *ELH* 28 (1961): 121–36.

———. "Homer and the Fallen World: Focus of Satire in George Chapman's *The Widow's Tears*." *Journal of English and Germanic Philology* 62 (1963): 518–32.

CYRIL TOURNEUR

Adams, Henry H. "Cyril Tourneur on Revenge." *Journal of English and Germanic Philology* 48 (1949): 72–78.

Ayres, Philip J. *Tourneur: "The Revenger's Tragedy."* London: Edward Arnold, 1977.

Barish, Jonas A. "The True and False Families of *The Revenger's Tragedy*." In *English Renaissance Drama: Essays in Honor of Madeleine Doran and Mark Eccles*, edited by Standish Henning, et al. Carbondale: Southern Illinois University Press, 1976.

Bowers, Fredson. *Elizabethan Revenge Tragedy, 1587–1642*. Princeton: Princeton University Press, 1940.

Dollimore, Jonathan. "Two Concepts of Mimesis: Renaissance Literary Theory and *The Revenger's Tragedy.*" In *Drama and Mimesis*, edited by James Redmond. Cambridge: Cambridge University Press, 1980.

Ekeblad, Inga-Stina. "An Approach to Tourneur Imagery." *Modern Language Review* 54 (1959): 489–98.

Eliot, T. S. "Cyril Tourneur." In *Elizabethan Dramatists*. New York: Harcourt, Brace, 1960.

Higgins, Michael H. "The Influence of Calvinistic Thought in Tourneur's *Atheist's Tragedy.*" *Review of English Studies* 19 (1943): 255–62.

Huebert, Ronald. "*The Revenger's Tragedy* and the Fallacy of The Excluded Middle." *University of Toronto Quarterly* 48 (1978): 10–22.

Huston, Diehl. " 'Reduce thy Understanding to Thine Eye': Seeing and Interpreting in *The Atheist's Tragedy.*" *Studies in Philology* 78 (1981), 47–60.

Jacobson, Daniel Jonathan. *The Language of "The Revenger's Tragedy.*" Salzburg: Institut für Englische Sprache und Literatur, Universität Salzburg, 1974.

Kaufmann, R. J. "Theodicy, Tragedy and the Psalmist: Tourneur's *Atheist's Tragedy.*" *Comparative Drama* 3 (1969): 241–62.

Kistner, Arthur L. "Morality and Inevitability in *The Revenger's Tragedy.*" *Journal of English and Germanic Philology* 71 (1972): 36–46.

Lisca, Peter. "*The Revenger's Tragedy*: A Study in Irony." *Philological Quarterly* 38 (1959): 242–51.

Murray, Peter B. *A Study of Cyril Tourneur*. Philadelphia: University of Pennsylvania Press, 1965.

Oates, J. C. "The Comedy of Metamorphosis in *The Revenger's Tragedy.*" *Bucknell Review* 11 (1962): 38–52.

Pearce, Howard. "*Virtu* and *Poesis* in *The Revenger's Tragedy.*" *ELH* 43 (1976): 19–37.

Schoenbaum, Samuel "*The Revenger's Tragedy*: Jacobean Dance of Death." *Modern Language Quarterly* 15 (1954): 201–7.

Simmons, J. L. "The Tongue and Its Office in *The Revenger's Tragedy.*" *PMLA* 92 (1977): 56–68.

Stull, William L. " 'This Metamorphosed Tragoedie': Thomas Kyd, Cyril Tourneur, and the Jacobean Theatre of Cruelty." *Ariel: A Review of English Literature* 14 (1983): 35–49.

Walz, Eugene P. "Synechdoche and Cyril Tourneur: Language in *The Revenger's Tragedy.*" *Massachusetts Studies in English* 2 (1970): 103–6.

Wigler, Stephen. "If Looks Could Kill: Fathers and Sons in *The Revenger's Tragedy.*" *Comparative Drama* 9 (1975): 206–25.

Wilds, Nancy G. " 'Of Rare Fire Compact': Image and Rhetoric in *The*

Revenger's Tragedy." Texas Studies in Literature and Language 17 (1975): 61–74.

FRANCIS BEAUMONT AND JOHN FLETCHER

Appleton, William W. *Beaumont and Fletcher: A Critical Study*. London: Allen & Unwin, 1956.

Astington, John H. "The Popularity of *Cupid's Revenge*." *Studies in English Literature* 19 (1979): 215–27.

Bliss, Lee. "Defending Fletcher's Shepherds." *Studies in English Literature* 23 (1983): 295–310.

Danby, Francis. *Poets on Fortune's Hill: Studies in Sidney, Shakespeare, Beaumont and Fletcher*. London: Faber & Faber, 1952.

Davies, H. Neville. "Beaumont and Fletcher's *Hamlet*." In *Shakespeare: Man of the Theatre*, edited by Kenneth Muir, et al. Newark: University of Delaware Press, 1983.

Davison, Peter. "The Serious Concerns of *Philaster*." *ELH* 30 (1963): 1–15.

Finkelpearl, Philip J. "Beaumont, Fletcher and 'Beaumont and Fletcher': Some Distinctions." *English Literary Renaissance* 1 (1971): 144–64.

Gosset, Suzanne. "Masque Influence on the Dramaturgy of Beaumont and Fletcher." *Modern Philology* 69 (1972): 199–208.

———. "The Term 'Masque' in Shakespeare and Fletcher and *The Coxcomb*." *Studies in English Literature* 14 (1974): 285–95.

Green, Paul D. "Theme and Structure in Fletcher's *Bonduca*." *Studies in English Literature* 22 (1982): 305–16.

Leech, Clifford. *The John Fletcher Plays*. Cambridge: Harvard University Press, 1962.

Miller, Ronald F. "Dramatic Form and Dramatic Imagination in Beaumont's *The Knight of the Burning Pestle*." *English Literary Renaissance* 8 (1978): 67–84.

Mincoff, Marco. "Fletcher's Early Tragedies." *Renaissance Drama* 7 (1964): 70–94.

Neill, Michael. " 'The Simetry Which Gives a Poem Grace': Masque, Imagery and the Fancy of the *Maid's Tragedy*." *Renaissance Drama* 3 (1970): 111–135.

———. "The Defence of Contraries: Skeptical Paradox in *A King and No King*." *Studies in English Literature* 21 (1981): 319–32.

Pearse, Nancy C. *John Fletcher's Chastity Plays: Mirrors of Modesty*. Lewisburg, Penn.: Bucknell University Press, 1973.

Samuelson, David A. "The Order in Beaumont's *The Knight of the Burning Pestle.*" *English Literary Renaissance* 9 (1979): 302–18.

Savage, James E. "Beaumont and Fletcher's *Philaster* and Sidney's *Arcadia.*" *ELH* 14 (1947): 194–206.

Wilson, Harold S. "*Philaster* and *Cymbeline.*" *English Institute Essays, 1951.* New York: Columbia University Press, 1952.

Woodson, William C. "The Casuistry of Innocence in *A King and No King* and Its Implications for Tragicomedy." *English Literary Renaissance* 8 (1978): 312–28.

THOMAS MIDDLETON

Bartier, R. H. *Thomas Middleton.* New York: Columbia University Press, 1958.

Bryant, J. A., Jr. "Middleton as a Modern Instance." *Sewanee Review* 84 (1976): 572–94.

Champion, Larry S. "Tragic Vision in Middleton's *Women Beware Women.*" *English Studies* 57 (1976): 410–24.

Charney, Maurice B. "Webster vs. Middleton, or the Shakespearean Yardstick in Jacobean Tragedy." In *English Renaissance Drama: Essays in Honor of Madeleine Doran and Mark Eccles,* edited by Standish Henning, et al. Carbondale: Southern Illinois University Press, 1976.

Cope, Jackson I. "The Date of Middleton's *Women Beware Women.*" *MLN* 76 (1961): 295–300.

Core, George. "The Canker and the Muse: Imagery in *Women Beware Women.*" *Renaissance Papers* (1968): 65–78.

Covatta, Anthony. *Thomas Middleton's City Comedies.* Lewisburg, Penn.: Bucknell University Press, 1973.

Davies, Richard A., and Alan R. Young. " 'Strange Cunning' in Thomas Middleton's *A Game At Chess.*" *University of Toronto Quarterly* 45 (1976): 236–45.

Doob, Penelope B. R. "A Reading of *The Changeling.*" *English Literary Renaissance* 3 (1973): 188–206.

Duffy, Joseph M. "Madhouse Optics: *The Changeling.*" *Comparative Drama* 8 (1974): 184–98.

Farr, Dorothy M. *Thomas Middleton and the Drama of Realism.* Edinburgh: Oliver and Boyd, 1973.

Foster, Verna Ann. "The Deed's Creature: The Tragedy of Bianca in *Women Beware Women.*" *Journal of English and Germanic Philology* 78 (1979): 508–21.

Heinemann, Margot. *Puritanism and Theatre: Thomas Middleton and the Op-

position Drama Under the Early Stuarts. Cambridge: Cambridge University Press, 1980.

Holmes, David M. *The Art of Thomas Middleton*. Oxford: Clarendon Press, 1970.

Holzknecht, Karl L. "The Dramatic Structure of *The Changeling*." In *Renaissance Papers*, edited by Allan H. Gilbert. Orangeburg: University of South Carolina Press, 1954.

Jacobs, Henry E. "The Constancy of Change: Character and Perspective in *The Changeling*." *Texas Studies in Literature and Language* 16 (1975): 651–74.

Johnson, Paula. "Dissimulation Anatomized: *The Changeling*." *Philological Quarterly* 56 (1977): 329–38.

Jordan, Robert. "Myth and Psychology in *The Changeling*." *Renaissance Drama* 3 (1970): 157–65.

Kaplan, Joel H. "Middleton's Tamburlaine," *English Language Notes* 13 (1976): 258–60.

Krook, Dorothea. *Elements of Tragedy*. New Haven: Yale University Press, 1969.

Lake, David J. *The Canon of Thomas Middleton's Plays*. London: Cambridge University Press, 1975.

Marottia, Arthur F. "The Purgations of Middleton's *The Family of Love*." *Papers on Language and Literature* 7 (1971): 80–84.

Mooney, Michael E. " 'Framing' as Collaborative Technique: Two Middleton-Rowley Plays." *Comparative Drama* 13 (1979): 127–41.

Muir, Kenneth. "The Role of Livia in *Women Beware Women*." In *Poetry and Drama, 1570–1700: Essays in Honor of Harold F. Brooks*, edited by Antony Coleman et al. London: Methuen, 1981.

Potter, John. " 'In Time of Sports': Masques and Masking in Middleton's *Women Beware Women*." *Papers on Language and Literature* 18 (1982): 368–83.

Ricks, Christopher. "Word Play in *Women Beware Women*." *Review of English Studies* 12 (1961): 237–50.

———. "The Moral and Poetic Structure of *The Changeling*." *Essays in Criticism* 10 (1960): 290–306.

Rowe, George E., Jr. *Thomas Middleton and the New Comedy Tradition*. Lincoln: University of Nebraska Press, 1979.

Schoenbaum, Samuel. *Middleton's Tragedies*. New York: Columbia University Press, 1955.

Sherman, Jane. "The Pawn's Allegory in Middleton's *A Game At Chess*." *Review of English Studies* 29 (1978): 147–59.

PHILIP MASSINGER

Bennet, A. L. "The Moral Tone of Massinger's Dramas." *Papers on Language and Literature* 2 (1966): 207–16.

Bliss, Michael D. "Massinger's *City Madam* and the Lost *City Honest Man*." *English Literary Renaissance* 7 (1977): 368–81.

Butler, Martin. "Massinger's *City Madam* and Caroline Tradition." *Renaissance Drama* 13 (1982): 157–87.

Dunn, T. A. *Philip Massinger: The Man and the Playwright*. London: T. Nelson and Sons, 1957.

Edwards, Philip. "Massinger the Censor." In *Essays on Shakespeare and Elizabethan Drama in Honor of Hardin Craig*, edited by Richard Hosley. Columbia: University of Missouri Press, 1962.

———. "The Royal Pretenders in Massinger and Ford." *Essays and Studies* 27 (1974): 18–36.

Eliot, T. S. "Philip Massinger." In *Essays on Elizabethan Drama* New York: Harcourt, Brace, 1960.

Evenhuis, Francis D. *Massinger's Imagery*. Salzburg: Institut für Englische Sprache und Literatur, Universität Salzburg, 1973.

Fothergill, Robert A. "The Dramatic Experience of Massinger's *The City Madam* and *A New Way to Pay Old Debts*." *University of Toronto Quarterly* 43 (1973): 68–86.

Gross, Alan G. "Contemporary Politics in Massinger." *Studies in English Literature* 6 (1966): 279–90.

———. "Social Change and Philip Massinger." *Studies in English Literature* 7 (1967): 329–42.

Hogan, A. P. "Imagery of Acting in *The Roman Actor*." *Modern Language Review* 66 (1971): 273–81.

Hoy, Cyrus. "Verbal Formulae in the Plays of Philip Massinger." *Studies in Philology* 56 (1959): 600–18.

Knights, L. C. "The Significance of Massinger's Social Comedies with a Note on 'Decadence'." In *Drama and Society in the Age of Ben Jonson*. London: Chatto and Windus, 1937.

Lyons, John O. "Massinger's Imagery." *Renaissance Papers* (1955): 47–54.

Neill, Michael. "Massinger's Patriarchy: The Social Vision of *A New Way to Pay Old Debts*." *Renaissance Drama* 10 (1979): 185–213.

Thomson, Patricia. "The Old Way and the New Way in Dekker and Massinger." *Modern Language Review* 51 (1956): 168–78.

Thorssen, M. J. "Massinger's Use of *Othello* in *The Duke of Milan*." *Studies in English Literature* 19 (1979): 313–26.

JOHN FORD

Anderson, Donald. "The Heart and the Banquet: Imagery in Ford's *'Tis Pity* and *The Broken Heart*." *PMLA* 87 (1972): 397–405.

Barton, Anne. "He that Plays the King: Ford's *Perkin Warbeck* and the Stuart History Play." In *English Drama: Essays in Honor of Muriel Clara Bradbrook*, edited by Marie Axton and Raymond Williams. Cambridge: Cambridge University Press, 1977.

Blayney, Glenn. "Convention, Plot and Structure in *The Broken Heart*." *Modern Philology* 56 (1958): 1–19.

Brissenden, Alan. "Impediments to Love: A Theme in John Ford." *Renaissance Drama* 7 (1964): 95–102.

Bueler, Lois E. "Role Splitting and Reintegration: The Tested Women Plot in Ford." *Studies in English Literature* 20 (1980): 325–44.

Candido, Joseph. "The 'Strange Truth' of *Perkin Warbeck*." *Philological Quarterly* 59 (1980): 300–316.

Champion, Larry S. "Ford's *'Tis Pity She's A Whore* and the Jacobean Tragic Perspective." *PMLA* 90 (1975): 78–87.

Farr, Dorothy M. *John Ford and the Caroline Theatre*. New York: Barnes and Noble, 1978.

Greenfield, Thelma N. "The Language of Process in Ford's *The Broken Heart*." *PMLA* 87 (1972): 397–405.

Hamilton, Sharon. "Huntly as Tragic Chorus in Ford's *Perkin Warbeck*." *Papers on Language and Literature* 16 (1980): 250–59.

Hogan, A. P. "*'Tis Pity She's A Whore*: The Overall Design." *Studies in English Literature* 17 (1977): 303–16.

Homan, Sidney R. "Shakespeare and Dekker as Keys to Ford's *'Tis Pity She's A Whore*" *Studies in English Literature* 7 (1967): 269–76.

Hoy, Cyrus. "'Ignorance in Knowledge': Marlowe's Faustus and Ford's Giovanni." *Modern Philology* 67 (1960): 147–54.

Kaufmann, R. J. "Ford's 'Waste Land': *The Broken Heart*." *Renaissance Drama* 3 (1970): 167–87.

Kelly, Michael J. "The Values of Action and Chronicle in *The Broken Heart*." *Papers on Language and Literature* 7 (1971): 150–58.

Kistner, Arthur L. and M. K. Kistner. "The Dramatic Functions of Love in the Tragedies of John Ford." *Studies in Philology* 70 (1973): 62–76.

McDonald, Charles O. "The Design of John Ford's *The Broken Heart*: A Study in the Development of Caroline Sensibility." *Studies in Philology* 59 (1962): 141–61.

Monsarrat, G. D. "The Unity of John Ford: *'Tis Pity She'a A Whore* and *Christ's Bloody Sweat.*" *Studies in Philology* 77 (1980): 247–70.

Muir, Kenneth. "The Case of John Ford" *Sewanee Review* 84 (1976): 614–29.

Neill, Michael. " 'Anticke Pageantrie': The Mannerist Art of *Perkin Warbeck.*" *Renaissance Drama* 7 (1976): 117–50.

———. "The Moral Artifice of *The Lover's Melancholy.*" *Engish Literary Renaissance* 8 (1978): 85–106.

———. "Ford's Unbroken Art: The Moral Design of *The Broken Heart.*" *Modern Language Review* 75 (1980): 249–68.

Requa, Kenneth A. "Music in the Ear: Giovanni as Tragic Hero in Ford's *'Tis Pity She's A Whore.*" *Papers on Language and Literature* 7 (1971): 13–25.

Sensabaugh, G. F. *The Tragic Muse of John Ford.* Stanford: Stanford University Press, 1944.

———. "John Ford Revisited." *Studies in English Literature* 4 (1964): 195–216.

Stavig, Mark. *John Ford and the Traditional Moral Order.* Madison: University of Wisconsin Press, 1968.

Ure, Peter. "Cult and Initiates in Ford's *Love's Sacrifice.*" *Modern Language Quarterly* 11 (1950): 298–306.

———. "Marriage and the Domestic Drama in Heywood and Ford." *English Studies* 32 (1951): 200–216.

Waith, Eugene M. "Struggle for Calm: The Dramatic Structure of *The Broken Heart.*" In *English Renaissance Drama: Essays in Honor of Madeleine Doran and Mark Eccles*, edited by Standish Henning, et al. Carbondale and Edwardsville: Southern Illinois University Press, 1976.

JAMES SHIRLEY

Belsey, Catherine. "Tragedy, Justice and the Subject." In *1642: Literature and Power in the Seventeenth Century*, edited by Francis Barker et al. Colchester: Department of Literature, University of Essex, 1981.

Cogan, Nathan. "James Shirley's *The Example*: Some Reconsiderations." *Studies in English Literature* 17 (1977): 317–31.

Forsythe, Robert. *The Relations of Shirley's Plays to the Elizabethan Drama.* New York: Columbia University Press, 1914.

Harbage, Alfred. *Cavalier Drama.* New York: Modern Language Association of America; London: Oxford University Press, 1936.

Levin, Richard. "The Triple Plot of *Hyde Park*." *Modern Language Review* 62 (1967): 17–27.

McGrath, Juliet. "James Shirley's Use of Language." *Studies in English Literature* 6 (1966): 323–39.

Underwood, Dale. *Etherege and the Seventeenth Century Comedy of Manners*. New Haven: Yale University Press, 1957.

Acknowledgments

"John Lyly and the Language of Play" by Jocelyn Powell from *Elizabethan Theatre*, Stratford-Upon-Avon Studies no. 9 (1966), © 1966 by Edward Arnold (Publishers) Ltd. Reprinted by permission.

"The Figure of Silence in *The Spanish Tragedy*" by Scott McMillin from *ELH* 39 (1972), © 1972 by The Johns Hopkins University Press. Reprinted by permission.

"Where Words Prevail Not: Grief, Revenge, and Language in Kyd and Shakespeare" by Peter Sacks from *ELH* 49 (1982), © 1982 by The Johns Hopkins University Press. Reprinted by permission.

"*The Shoemaker's Holiday*: Theme and Image" by Harold E. Toliver from *Boston University Studies in English* 5, no. 4 (Winter 1961), © 1961 by The Trustees of Boston University. Reprinted by permission.

"Tragical Satire in *The Malcontent*" and "Tragical Satire in *The Duchess of Malfi*" (originally entitled "Tragical Satire") by Alvin B. Kernan from *The Cankered Muse* by Alvin B. Kernan, © 1959 by Yale University Press. Reprinted by permission.

"*The Duchess of Malfi*" by G. Wilson Knight from *The Malahat Review* 4 (October 1967), © 1967 by *The Malahat Review*. Reprinted by permission.

"George Chapman: Myth as Mask and Magic" by Jackson I. Cope from *The Theatre and the Dream* by Jackson I. Cope, © 1973 by The Johns Hopkins University Press. Reprinted by permission.

" 'Royal Man': Notes on the Tragedies of George Chapman" by Edwin Muir from *Essays on Literature and Society* by Edwin Muir, © 1949 by Edwin Muir, 1965 by The Hogarth Press, Ltd. Reprinted by permission of Harvard University Press.

"*The Revenger's Tragedy* and the Morality Tradition" by L. G. Salingar from *Scrutiny* 6, no. 4 (March 1938), © 1961 by Cambridge University Press. Reprinted by permission of Cambridge University Press and Deighton Bell & Co. Ltd.

"Tourneur's Artificial Noon: The Design of *The Revenger's Tragedy*" by B. J. Layman from *Modern Language Quarterly* 34, no. 1 (March 1973), © 1973 by University of Washington Press. Reprinted by permission.

"The Rhetoric of Tragicomedy: The Poet as Orator" by Eugene M. Waith from *The Pattern of Tragicomedy in Beaumont and Fletcher* by Eugene M. Waith, © 1952 by Yale University Press. Reprinted by permission.

"Thomas Middleton" by M. C. Bradbrook from *Themes and Conventions of Elizabethan Tragedy* by M. C. Bradbrook, © 1935 by Cambridge University Press. Reprinted by permission.

"Massinger's Patriarchy: The Social Vision of *A New Way to Pay Old Debts*" by Michael Neill from *Renaissance Drama*, edited by Leonard Barkan, © 1979 by Northwestern University Press. Reprinted by permission.

"Ford's Tragic Perspective" by R. J. Kaufmann from *Texas Studies in Literature and Language* 1, no. 4 (Winter 1960), © 1960 by University of Texas Press. Reprinted by permission.

"The Decadence of Revenge Tragedy" by Fredson Bowers from *Elizabethan Revenge Tragedy: 1587–1642*, © 1940, renewed 1968 by Princeton University Press. Reprinted by permission.

Index